access to history

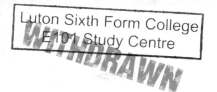

Civ
Rac
the
for

09

VIVIENNE

In order to ensure that this resource offers high-quality support for the associated Pearson qualification, it has been through a review process by the awarding body. This process confirms that this resource fully covers the teaching and learning content of the specification or part of a specification at which it is aimed. It also confirms that it demonstrates an appropriate balance between the development of subject skills, knowledge and understanding, in addition to preparation for assessment.

Endorsement does not cover any guidance on assessment activities or processes (e.g. practice questions or advice on how to answer assessment questions), included in the resource nor does it prescribe any particular approach to the teaching or delivery of a related course.

While the publishers have made every attempt to ensure that advice on the qualification and its assessment is accurate, the official specification and associated assessment guidance materials are the only authoritative source of information and should always be referred to for definitive guidance.

Pearson examiners have not contributed to any sections in this resource relevant to examination papers for which they have responsibility. Examiners will not use endorsed resources as a source of material for any assessment set by Pearson.

Endorsement of a resource does not mean that the resource is required to achieve this Pearson qualification, nor does it mean that it is the only suitable material available to support the qualification, and any resource lists produced by the awarding body shall include this and other appropriate resources.

Caution: several of the historical extracts and quotations in this book contain words that are vulgar and offensive.

Acknowledgements are listed on page 252.

Every effort has been made to trace all copyright holders, but if any have been inadvertently overlooked the Publishers will be pleased to make the necessary arrangements at the first opportunity.

Although every effort has been made to ensure that website addresses are correct at time of going to press, Hodder Education cannot be held responsible for the content of any website mentioned in this book. It is sometimes possible to find a relocated web page by typing in the address of the home page for a website in the URL window of your browser.

Hachette UK's policy is to use papers that are natural, renewable and recyclable products and made from wood grown in sustainable forests. The logging and manufacturing processes are expected to conform to the environmental regulations of the country of origin.

Orders: please contact Bookpoint Ltd, 130 Milton Park, Abingdon, Oxon OX14 4SB. Telephone: +44 (0)1235 827720. Fax: +44 (0)1235 400454. Lines are open 9.00a.m.–5.00p.m., Monday to Saturday, with a 24-hour message answering service. Visit our website at www.hoddereducation.co.uk

First published in 2016 by
Hodder Education
An Hachette UK Company
Carmelite House, 50 Victoria Embankment
London EC4Y 0DZ

Impression number	10	9	8	7	6	5	4	3	2	1
Year		2019	2018	2017	2016	2015				

Cover photo © Bettmann/CORBIS
Produced, illustrated and typeset in Palatino LT Std by Gray Publishing, Tunbridge Wells
Printed and bound by CPI Group (UK) Ltd, Croydon CR0 4YY

A catalogue record for this title is available from the British Library

ISBN 978 1471838255

Contents

Dedication

Keith Randell (1943–2002)

The *Access to History* series was conceived and developed by Keith, who created a series to 'cater for students as they are, not as we might wish them to be'. He leaves a living legacy of a series that for over 20 years has provided a trusted, stimulating and well-loved accompaniment to post-16 study. Our aim with these new editions is to continue to offer students the best possible support for their studies.

CHAPTER 1

Introduction: black Americans to 1865

Prior to the American Civil War (1861–5), most black Americans lived in the South as slaves. Disagreements over the expansion of slavery led to the Civil War between the Northern states and the Southern states. Although President Abraham Lincoln had not gone to war to end slavery, the North's victory led to its abolition. These developments are traced in sections on:

★ White perceptions of black Americans to 1850

★ Slavery and the Civil War

Key dates

1600s	White immigrants to North America imported and enslaved black Africans	**1861–5**		Civil War between Southern slave states and Northern states
1776	The Declaration of Independence	**1862**	**Sept.**	Emancipation Proclamation announced
1787	Constitution of the new United States of America	**1863**	**Jan.**	Emancipation Proclamation issued
		1865		13th Amendment abolished slavery

 ## White perceptions of black Americans to 1850

▶ *How did white perceptions of black Americans and slavery vary in the period before 1850?*

In the seventeenth century, white Europeans were engaged upon the conquest of the North American continent. They imported and enslaved black Africans, and considered it justified because

● Africans had a different, non-Christian culture and whites perceived them as uncivilised heathens and inferior.

● European technological superiority seemed to prove black cultural and racial inferiority.

● Africans did not look like Europeans, so whites considered it appropriate to treat them differently.

- As there was work that needed to be done and too few white men to do it, slaves were deemed essential for cheap and plentiful labour.

In 1776, when the white American colonists demanded freedom from British rule in their Declaration of Independence, there were 2.5 million people in British North America and 500,000 of them were black slaves. Few slave owners were willing to acknowledge the contradiction between their ideas of freedom and the existence of slavery. The Declaration's ringing phrases about equality were not considered applicable to black Americans.

? Which words in Source A could be used to argue against slavery?

SOURCE A

From the American colonists' Declaration of Independence from British rule, 4 July 1776.

We hold these truths to be self-evident, that all men are created equal; that they are endowed by their Creator with certain inalienable rights; that among these are life, liberty, and the pursuit of happiness. That, to secure these rights, governments are instituted among men, deriving their just powers from the consent of the governed; that, whenever any form of government becomes destructive of these ends, it is the right of the people to alter or to abolish it, and to institute a new government, laying its foundations on such principles …

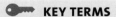

KEY TERMS

Constitution The rules and system by which a country's government works. The USA has a written constitution.

Federal government The USA, as a federation of many separate states (such as South Carolina and New York), has a federal government. The federal government consists of the President, Congress and the Supreme Court (see Figure 1.1).

The American Constitution and race relations

In 1783, the British government recognised American independence. The Americans needed to establish their own form of government for the 13 former colonies, which they now called states. The states sent 55 delegates to discuss a new **constitution**, and 19 of them owned slaves.

The new American Constitution would have a great and long-lasting impact upon black Americans. First, it treated slavery as acceptable and appropriate, and thus confirmed black inequality. Second, it reserved considerable powers to state governments, which opened the way to future clashes between states and the **federal government** over the conditions under which black Americans lived. Third, it guaranteed certain rights to American citizens, which enabled black American campaigners in future years to take the moral high ground when demanding those rights.

KEY FIGURE

Thomas Jefferson (1743–1826)

Principal author of the Declaration of Independence and one of the Founding Fathers of the United States. He was President of the United States 1801–9.

Differing perceptions of slavery

The white colonists who had eloquently demanded freedom from British tyranny frequently overlooked the unequal treatment of non-whites. For example, although **Thomas Jefferson** probably wrote 'all men are created equal', he was ambivalent about enslavement. He never publicly admitted his affection for his long-standing slave-mistress or acknowledged their children (he finally freed them in his will). He said he despised slavery, but although he once spoke of freeing all his slaves, he never did. He said he found it difficult to decide

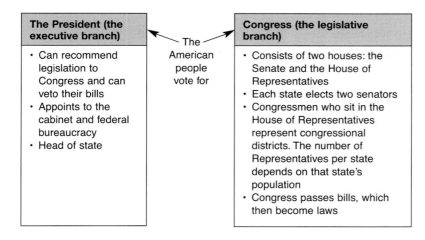

Figure 1.1 Federal government in the USA.

whether blacks were inferior to whites or simply made so by what Southerners called the 'peculiar institution' of slavery. He claimed that freeing those brought up in slavery would be like abandoning children.

Unlike Jefferson, most white people were decisively pro- or anti-slavery. By the early nineteenth century, slavery had been abolished in most Northern states and some Northerners (**abolitionists**) advocated the abolition of slavery throughout the United States. However, most white Southerners were pro-slavery:

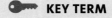 **KEY TERM**

Abolitionists Those who wanted to end slavery.

- Plantation owners believed the profitability of their plantations depended upon slave labour.
- The 75 per cent of white Southerners who did not own slaves thought freed slaves would be competition for wage-paying jobs.
- They feared freed black slaves might prove hostile.
- As over 90 per cent of black Americans lived in the South (slaves outnumbered whites in states such as South Carolina and Mississippi), many felt that freed slaves would threaten white supremacy and racial purity.

When Northern abolitionists increasingly criticised slavery, resentful Southerners sought new justification with the 'positive good' argument, which claimed that slavery was necessary because black people were happy-go-lucky, lazy, ignorant and inferior to whites, and would not be able to survive unless fed and clothed by caring white slave owners. Southerners also emphasised that past great civilisations such as that of Rome were based upon slavery and that Jesus Christ never condemned it.

Northern perceptions of black Americans

Although Northern abolitionists criticised slavery, **free blacks** in the North lacked political, economic and social equality prior to the American Civil War.

In 1860, there were roughly a quarter of a million free blacks in the North, but only around 7 per cent were able to vote. One opponent of black suffrage described black Americans as 'peculiar' people, 'incapable' of exercising the vote 'with any sort of discretion, prudence or independence'. Many Northerners disliked and discriminated against black people. For example, between 1851 and 1853, Indiana, Iowa and Illinois each passed laws to block black immigration into the state. Black workers were the first to lose their jobs during economic recessions and white mobs frequently attacked black workers for accepting lower wages. Racial antagonism was evident. 'It is certainly the wish of every patriot', said a leading member of the **Republican Party**, that 'our union should be homogeneous in race and of our own blood.' In Northern towns, black Americans were excluded from white institutions and public facilities, and were unofficially segregated in schools, churches and housing. When a white **Quaker** teacher admitted a black girl to her Connecticut school, white patrons boycotted it and had the teacher arrested on trumped-up charges. The Quakers of Pennsylvania welcomed black people to their religious services but maintained segregated burial places.

Only a minority of Northern whites favoured **integration** and the abolition of slavery, and even some of the Northern abolitionists looked down on black people. Indeed, the French visitor Alexis de Tocqueville considered racism stronger in the North than the South in the 1830s.

Many black Americans preferred **segregation**. Life in segregated areas enabled them to maintain their cultural identity in their own churches and to avoid white authority. Proximity seemed to exacerbate racial tension: a high proportion of race riots occurred in areas containing a large black minority.

KEY TERMS

Free blacks In the North in particular, many blacks had been freed from slavery by their owners.

Republican Party Emerged in the 1850s. It was against slavery.

Quakers A Christian group notable for its pacifism and democratic religious meetings.

Integration The social mixing of people of different colours and cultures.

Segregation The separation of people because of race (for example, separate housing, schools and transport).

Summary diagram: White perceptions of black Americans to 1850

Northerners	Mid-19th century	Southerners
• Abolitionists increasingly critical of South and slavery – immoral • Most Northerners still discriminated against black Americans – considered them inferior		• Plantation agriculture required ample cheap labour • Southerners increasingly resentful and anxious about Northern criticism • Justified slavery as 'positive good' – cannot look after themselves; acceptable in ancient times

> **Black people in America**
>
> Prior to the 1960s, black Americans were referred to by both black and white people as 'Negroes'. From the 1970s, the terms 'black Americans' and 'African Americans' replaced Negro. The three terms are used interchangeably in this book.

 # Slavery and the Civil War

▶ *How did the Civil War affect black Americans?*

In the years 1861–5, the Northern states fought against and eventually defeated the Southern states in the American Civil War.

The outbreak of the Civil War

When white Americans moved westwards across the continent during the early nineteenth century, new land was acquired and new states were created. Many Northerners were opposed to the extension of slavery to the new states. Some

- had been turned against slavery by abolitionists
- objected to the presence of non-whites in new territories to which Northerners might want to migrate
- feared cheap slave labour would make it harder for whites to gain employment in the new states
- opposed the addition of more slave states, because that would mean more members of **Congress** in favour of slavery, which would increase the political power of the South.

Continued clashes between Northerners and Southerners over whether new territories should become slave states created bitterness. The Republican Party opposed the extension of slavery, so Southerners feared for the future of slavery when the Republican Abraham Lincoln was elected President of the United States. This prompted the Southern states to form a new nation, the Confederate States of America (the **Confederacy**) (see Figure 1.2, page 6). When President Lincoln raised Northern armies to bring the South back into the United States, the Civil War began. After four years of bitter fighting, the North won.

Was the Civil War a war to end slavery?

As far as Lincoln was concerned, slavery constituted 'the greatest wrong inflicted on any people' and he had opposed its extension to any new states. However, he had been willing to accept its continued existence in the South and he was convinced of black inferiority. He told a black audience that, unalterably and undeniably, 'not a single man of your race is made the equal of a single man of ours.' 'It is', he said, 'better for us to be separated.'

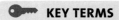 **KEY TERMS**

Congress The American equivalent to Britain's parliament, consisting of the Senate and the House of Representatives. Voters in each American state elect two senators to sit in the Senate and several congressmen (the number depends on the size of the state's population) to sit in the House of Representatives.

Confederacy When the Southern states left the Union of the United States, they became the Confederate States of America, known as the Confederacy for short. Supporters of the Confederacy were called Confederates.

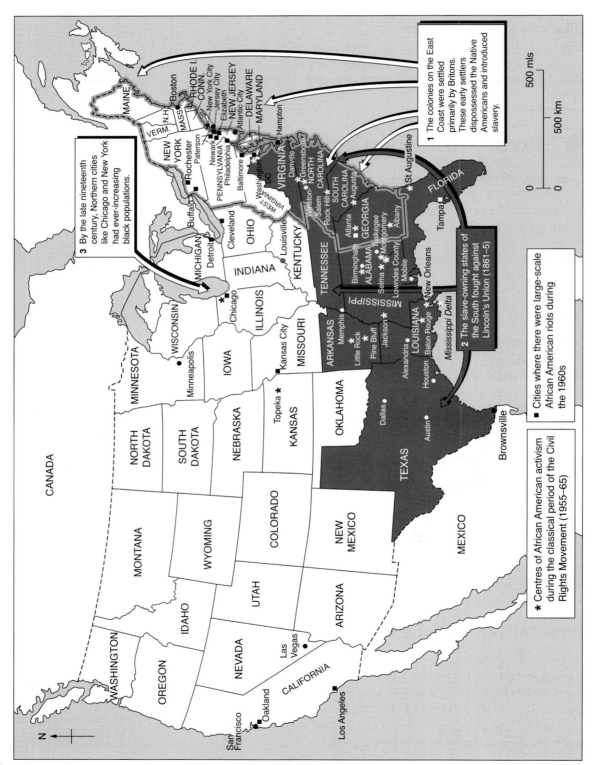

1 The colonies on the East Coast were settled primarily by Britons. These early settlers dispossessed the Native Americans and introduced slavery.

3 By the late nineteenth century, Northern cities like Chicago and New York had ever-increasing black populations.

2 The slave-owning states of the South fought against Lincoln's Union (1861–5)

■ Cities where there were large-scale African American riots during the 1960s

★ Centres of African American activism during the classical period of the Civil Rights Movement (1955–65)

Figure 1.2 A map illustrating black American history.

Abraham Lincoln

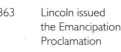

1809	Born in a log cabin in Kentucky
1831	Moved to Illinois; worked as store clerk, postmaster, surveyor
1834	Elected to Illinois state legislature
1837	Became a lawyer
1842	Married Mary Todd, whose Kentucky family owned slaves
1846	Elected to the House of Representatives
1856	Joined the new Republican Party. Increasingly focused on the slavery issue
1860	Elected President in November
	In December, the first Southern state seceded (withdrew) from the Union of the United States
1861	The Confederate States of America established in February
	Confederate forces fired on a federal fort in April; Lincoln raised forces to defeat the South
1862	Lincoln announced the Emancipation Proclamation
1863	Lincoln issued the Emancipation Proclamation
1864	Re-elected President
1865	Confederacy surrendered; Lincoln assassinated by actor and Confederate sympathiser John Wilkes Booth

Lincoln is important in any history of American race relations because he began freeing the slaves with his Emancipation Proclamation of 1862. Subsequent generations of blacks revered him as the 'Great Emancipator', but historians disagree over the relative importance of political calculation and genuine idealism in his actions, and over the extent of his racism. He was certainly vital to the defeat of the pro-slavery Confederacy, after which the South and race relations would never be the same again.

SOURCE B

From Abraham Lincoln's speeches during his debate with Stephen Douglas, his rival candidate in the race to represent Illinois in the US Senate, 1858 (available at: http://quod.lib.umich.edu/l/lincoln/lincoln3/1:20.1?rgn=div2;view=fulltext).

I am not, nor ever have been in favor of bringing about in any way the social and political equality of the white and black races ... I am not nor ever have been in favor of making voters or jurors of negroes, nor of qualifying them to hold office, nor to intermarry with white people; and I will say in addition to this that there is a physical difference between the white and black races which I believe will for ever forbid the two races living together on terms of social and political equality. And in as much as they cannot so live, while they do remain together there must be the position of superior and inferior, and I as much as any other man, am in favor of having the superior position assigned to the white man ... The real issue in this controversy ... is the sentiment on the part of one class that looks upon the institution of slavery as a wrong, and another class that does not look upon it as a wrong ... The Republican Party ... look upon it as being a moral, social and political wrong ...

Judging from Source B, how did Abraham Lincoln view black Americans and slavery in 1858?

❓ What arguments does Source C give against emancipation?

Lincoln did not go to war to end slavery but to preserve the **Union** of the United States:

> *If I could save the Union without freeing any slave I would do so and if I could save it by freeing all the slaves I would do it; and if I could save it by freeing some and leaving others alone I would also do that.*

As President, he remained willing to protect slavery where it already existed, especially as he sought to avoid alienating his supporters in the slave states that fought on the side of the North (Kentucky, Maryland, Missouri and Delaware). 'We did not go to war to put down slavery', Lincoln told Congress in December 1861. One infuriated abolitionist said Lincoln was 'a wet rag' on the slavery issue, 'halting, prevaricating, irresolute, weak'. However, in September 1862, only a few days after telling a Chicago audience (see Source C) that the **emancipation** of the slaves would be unwise, Lincoln announced his Emancipation Proclamation, which would come into force in January 1863.

SOURCE C

Arguments given by Abraham Lincoln to some Chicago Christian ministers in September 1862 (available at: http://quod.lib.umich.edu/l/lincoln/ lincoln5/1:933.1?hi=0;rgn=div2;view=fulltext;q1=Strength).

I admit that slavery is the root of the rebellion ... I would also concede that emancipation would help us in Europe, and convince them that we are incited by something more than ambition. I grant further that it would help somewhat at the North, though not so much, I fear, as you and those you represent imagine ... And then unquestionably it would weaken the rebels by drawing off their laborers, which is of great importance. But I am not sure we could do much with the blacks. If we were to arm them, I fear that in a few weeks the arms would be in the hands of the rebels ... I will mention another thing, though it meet only your scorn and contempt. There are fifty thousand bayonets in the Union armies from the Border Slave States. It would be a serious matter if, in consequence of a proclamation such as you desire, they should go over to the rebels ...

Lincoln's Emancipation Proclamation

Generations of black Americans felt grateful to the President who issued the Emancipation Proclamation. Lincoln's proclamation said slaves in Confederate states conquered by Union forces in the future would be free, 'as an act of justice, warranted by the Constitution, upon military necessity'. However, the proclamation allowed slavery to continue in the slave-owning Union states and in any other state occupied by Union armies or returning to the Union before January 1863. In practice, the proclamation did not liberate a single slave. So why had Lincoln issued the Emancipation Proclamation?

- Some **Radical Republicans** believed slavery was immoral and made a mockery of the Declaration of Independence. Lincoln agreed.
- Most Republicans blamed slave owners for the Civil War, and many believed that if slavery continued, North/South divisions could not be resolved and the bloody Civil War would have been pointless.
- It was thought that once Lincoln committed the North to emancipation, foreign nations such as Britain would be reluctant to continue helping the Confederacy.
- Army commanders did not know what to do with the 500,000 refugee slaves who came to Northern army camps situated in Southern states. Under the Fugitive Slave Act (1850), the slaves were property and should have been returned to their masters, but that seemed inhumane, because their masters would punish them. One Union soldier said in early 1862, 'I don't care a damn for the darkies but I'm blamed if I could … send a runaway back.' More importantly, returning the slaves was unintelligent. Slaves were vital to the Confederacy's camps as useful labourers. During 1861–2, Lincoln, Union generals and Congress tried evading this issue by calling slaves 'contraband of war', but Radical Republicans preferred outright condemnation of the institution of slavery because that would give the North the moral high ground in the war.
- Military necessity was probably Lincoln's main motive. The North's forces were struggling in 1862 and the proclamation aimed to hamper the South's war effort. In 1863, Lincoln wrote that black soldiers were 'a resource which, if vigorously applied now, will soon close the contest. It works doubly, weakening the enemy and strengthening us.' Nearly 250,000 black Americans served in the Northern army, entering it just when the North's forces were becoming dangerously depleted.

The Confederacy fought on after the Emancipation Proclamation, prompting Lincoln to assert in January 1863 that the freedom of slaves in rebellious states was now a Union war aim, 'an act of justice', not just 'military necessity'. After Lincoln's death in 1865, the 13th **Amendment** abolished slavery throughout the United States.

Changing Northern perceptions of black Americans during the Civil War

Although the extension of slavery was probably the major cause of the Civil War (1861–5), that war was not fought to end slavery. Most Northerners thought they were fighting to save the Union, not to free Southern slaves whom they considered likely to migrate to the North, flood the labour market and cause racial tension.

There was considerable antagonism towards black Americans in the North before and during the Civil War. In the summer of 1862, there were anti-black

KEY TERMS

Radical Republicans Members of the Republican Party who were most enthusiastic about ending slavery.

Amendment Under the Constitution, Congress could add 'amendments' (changes or new points) to the Constitution. Amendments needed ratification (approval) by 75 per cent of states.

riots in several American cities, and Lincoln told a group of black visitors to the White House, 'There is an unwillingness on the part of our people, harsh as it may be, for you free colored people to remain among us.' He urged them to emigrate to Africa. Some hostile newspapers claimed that Lincoln had got America into a Civil War to help undeserving black people, and in the 1864 presidential election, **Democrat** accusations that Lincoln was a 'Negro lover' plotting **miscegenation** appealed to many Northern white voters.

The first Southern slaves who rushed to join Union forces were not welcomed. Northern white conservatives disliked the idea of arming black Northerners because they considered them inferior and unreliable. Although black troops were invariably brave and enthusiastic, they were given the worst and most dangerous tasks and were usually paid less than whites.

However, perceptions changed during the war, especially after the heroism of the all-black 54th Massachusetts Infantry (the theme of the 1989 movie *Glory*). Initially, Lincoln had not wanted black soldiers in the Union army, but he changed his mind. He was impressed by their performance and he considered giving the vote to 'the very intelligent' and most gallant. By 1865, 10 per cent of Union troops were black and they made an important contribution to victory. In 1863, an Irish mob had attacked black soldiers in New York, but when New Yorkers gave black soldiers an affectionate farewell parade in 1865, the *New York Times* thought it signalled 'a new epoch'. That proved over-optimistic. The change of viewpoint on black soldiers did not mean that Northern prejudice against black Americans had ended.

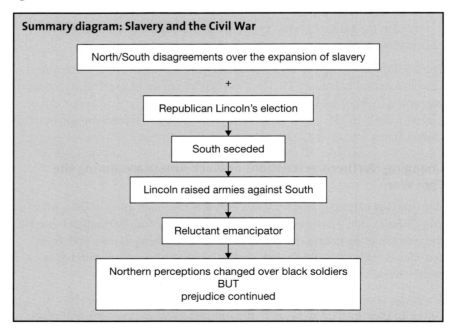

Summary diagram: Slavery and the Civil War

North/South disagreements over the expansion of slavery

+

Republican Lincoln's election

South seceded

Lincoln raised armies against South

Reluctant emancipator

Northern perceptions changed over black soldiers
BUT
prejudice continued

Chapter summary

Africans were imported into North America as slaves from the seventeenth century onwards. Although the white colonists were keen to be free from British rule, they allowed slavery to continue. Some were aware of the irony of their contradictory position. By the mid-nineteenth century, slavery had ended in the Northern states. Some Northern abolitionists criticised the South's retention of the 'peculiar institution', but many Northerners disliked and discriminated against free blacks.

Northerners and Southerners disagreed over the extension of slavery to newly acquired Western territories. The Republican Party opposed the expansion of slavery, and the election of the Republican Abraham Lincoln to the presidency in 1860 prompted the South to secede from the Union. Lincoln raised Union armies to defeat the South, and accomplished this in the Civil War years of 1861–5. However, Northern racism flourished throughout the war and Lincoln's emancipation of the slaves was controversial. The black military contribution to the Union war effort impressed some Northerners, but white fears of and hostility toward black Americans continued.

 # Refresher questions

1 Why could the Declaration of Independence be considered a hypocritical document?

2 In what ways did the American Constitution have a great and long-lasting impact upon black Americans?

3 How did contemporaries justify slavery?

4 How were free black Americans treated in the North before the Civil War?

5 Why did the Civil War break out in 1861?

6 Why did many free black Americans in the North prefer to live in segregated areas?

7 Was the Civil War a war to end slavery?

8 Why did Lincoln issue the Emancipation Proclamation?

9 To what extent did Northern perceptions of black Americans change in the Civil War?

10 Was Lincoln really the 'Great Emancipator'?

CHAPTER 2

'Free at last', 1865–77

After the North's victory in the American Civil War, the defeated South had to be reincorporated into the Union. This presented many problems: the South's economy had suffered great wartime damage, the Confederate political system was now obsolete, and there were great disagreements in both the North and the South over the social position and political and economic rights of former slaves. These problems and disagreements are covered in this chapter in sections on

★ The 13th Amendment (1865)

★ Radical Reconstruction (1867–77)

★ The white backlash

Key dates

1864	April	Senate approved 13th Amendment (slavery unconstitutional)	1867	Military Reconstruction Act: Congressional Reconstruction began
	Nov.	Lincoln re-elected	1868	Ratification of 14th Amendment (black Americans granted citizenship)
1865	Jan.	House of Representatives approved 13th Amendment	1870	Ratification of 15th Amendment (black American males enfranchised)
	April	Civil War ended; President Lincoln assassinated		Force Acts gave President Grant powers to crush the Klan
	April–Dec.	Presidential Reconstruction/ Reconstruction Confederate style	1872	Amnesty Act helped restore political power to ex-Confederates
	Dec.	New Congress blocked restoration of Confederate elite; 13th Amendment ratified	1875	Civil Rights Act tried to prevent discrimination in public places
1866	April	Civil Rights Act Ku Klux Klan established	1877	Withdrawal of federal troops from the South ended Reconstruction

The 13th Amendment (1865)

▶ *Why and with what results was the 13th Amendment passed?*

When President Lincoln's Emancipation Proclamation came into effect in January 1863, it did not end slavery in the United States. Throughout the remainder of 1863, abolitionists appealed to the federal government for a constitutional amendment to end slavery: for example, the abolitionist Women's National Loyal League's petition for a 13th Amendment that would end slavery acquired an unprecedented 500,000 signatures.

In 1864, President Lincoln stood for re-election. In June, he insisted that the Republican **platform** should contain a call for a constitutional amendment to end slavery, but when that proved unpopular with white voters, he and the Republicans went quiet on the issue. Meanwhile, supporters of the amendment sustained their pressure. For example, in 1864, the National Convention of Colored Men met in Syracuse, New York. The Convention endorsed Lincoln's candidacy, and demanded citizenship, the vote, and land for freed slaves.

The Senate had passed the 13th Amendment ending slavery in April 1864. After Lincoln's re-election in November 1864, his administration had to work incredibly hard to get the House of Representatives to approve it. The House finally did so on 31 January 1865. Radical Republican Thaddeus Stevens subsequently claimed that 'the greatest measure of the nineteenth century was passed by corruption, aided and abetted by the purest man in America'. Lincoln had told his Cabinet colleagues and congressional allies to do whatever it took to get the 13th Amendment through the House of Representatives. That included government posts and financial bribes for Democrats. By December 1865, months after Lincoln's death, the requisite number of states had ratified the 13th Amendment.

 KEY TERM

Platform The policies of a political party during, for example, the presidential election.

> ## The text of the 13th Amendment
>
> Section 1. Neither slavery nor involuntary servitude, except as a punishment for crime whereof the party shall have been duly convicted, shall exist within the United States, or any place subject to their jurisdiction.
>
> Section 2. Congress shall have power to enforce this article by appropriate legislation.

Reasons for the 13th Amendment

There were several reasons why the 13th Amendment was passed. The end of slavery was a moral issue for some Americans, especially abolitionists such as the Women's National Loyal League. More importantly, events during the Civil War had ensured that there was no turning the clock back. So many black

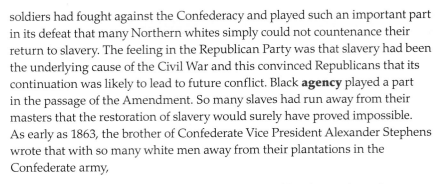

KEY TERM

Agency In this context, when black Americans took control of their own destiny, as opposed to having their fate determined by white Americans.

soldiers had fought against the Confederacy and played such an important part in its defeat that many Northern whites simply could not countenance their return to slavery. The feeling in the Republican Party was that slavery had been the underlying cause of the Civil War and this convinced Republicans that its continuation was likely to lead to future conflict. Black **agency** played a part in the passage of the Amendment. So many slaves had run away from their masters that the restoration of slavery would surely have proved impossible. As early as 1863, the brother of Confederate Vice President Alexander Stephens wrote that with so many white men away from their plantations in the Confederate army,

> *Our Negro population are going to give us great trouble. They are becoming extensively corrupted … slavery is already so undermined and demoralized as never to be of much use to us, even if we had peace and independence today. The institution has received a terrible shock which is tending to its disintegration and ruin.*

Finally, Lincoln worried about the constitutional status of slavery. The Emancipation Proclamation was a war measure that would be of dubious validity once the war had ended. As the original Constitution of 1787 had recognised the existence of slavery and in effect approved it, Lincoln felt that a constitutional amendment was the best and indeed the only proper way to abolish slavery (some members of Congress felt that a law would have done just as well).

The importance of the 13th Amendment

Lincoln said that the 13th Amendment was 'a king's cure for all the evils. It winds the whole thing up.' However, as the leading black activist **Frederick Douglass** said, 'The work does not end with the abolition of slavery, but only begins.' Abolition was the essential first step toward equality for former slaves: after the 13th Amendment, each black American had freedom of movement and control of his or her own fate. However, the struggle to get the 13th Amendment through Congress and to obtain the necessary ratification by three-quarters of the states had demonstrated widespread white anxiety about the implications of the release of several million black slaves. As Douglass well knew, there were many limitations on future black progress, amongst which were the economic, social and political realities of life in the post-war South and the attitude of Congress and the President toward black equality.

 **KEY FIGURE**

Frederick Douglass (1818–95)

After his escape from slavery, he became the most famous and effective black abolitionist. During and after the Civil War, he campaigned for black equality.

Economic position of ex-slaves and the development of sharecropping

The 13th Amendment was important because when it confirmed the end of slavery, it transformed the economy of the South. The pre-war Southern economy had depended heavily upon slave labour. Now plantation owners would have to reward workers for their labour. When Union General William

Sherman marched through Georgia during the Civil War, he heard former slaves crying for '40 acres and a mule', because they considered it unfair that plantations built upon their unpaid labour should remain in the hands of their previous owners. However, the pleas of the vast majority of freed slaves went unanswered.

Freed black slaves had acquired freedom of movement but they lacked land or money and over 90 per cent of them were illiterate. As a result, most had little choice but to remain in the South and trapped in poverty. When plantation owners and the Freedmen's Bureau encouraged former slaves to return to the plantations where they had once been enslaved, many did so. They worked as tenant farmers (**sharecroppers**) for the white elite. The white landowners provided the land, seed and tools, while the black tenants supplied the labour. The resulting crop was usually shared equally between them. For some, sharecropping meant freedom from white supervision and a greater incentive to work; for others, tenant farming seemed no better than slavery. One black veteran complained, 'If you call this freedom, what do you call slavery?' The work and the master remained the same and some of the security had gone. One Louisiana planter found a positive in this new world: 'When I owned niggers, I used to pay medical bills and take care of them – I do not think I shall trouble so much now.'

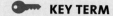 **KEY TERM**

Sharecropper A white landowner provided the land, seed, tools and orders, while a black worker (the sharecropper) provided the labour. The crop produced was usually divided between the two men.

The Freedmen's Bureau

In March 1865, Congress established the Freedmen's Bureau. It was designed to help freed slaves through the provision of food, clothes, fuel and medical care. It also gave assistance to poor white Southerners. Congress passed an act re-authorising the Freedmen's Bureau in spring 1866. Some contemporaries (and historians) attacked it as a corrupt and inefficient Republican tool that encouraged a dependency culture. However, it did some good work in helping the poor with healthcare, education and employment, and bureau agents monitored state and local law courts on behalf of black litigants. The Freedmen's Bureau stopped work in June 1872, not because it was no longer needed but because Northerners were beginning to lose interest in the South.

Social tensions

The 13th Amendment was important in that it generated great social tension in the South. Most Southern whites resented the new social order because of racism, fear, and bitterness over the losses suffered during the Civil War.

The majority of Southern whites were unwilling to accept black people as their equals. They were embittered and resentful because the war and the Union armies had destroyed the South's economy and around half of white Southern males of military age had died or been seriously wounded. Freed black slaves were a galling reminder that it had all been in vain. Southern whites resented new-found black self-confidence and were fearful that newly freed slaves might resort to violence: a Mr Powell of Arkansas asked, 'How long before my ass will be kicked by every Negro that meets me?'

Many former slaves had fought in the Union army and had learned to read and write in army schools. In summer 1865, they took the lead in organising mass meetings and petitions for civil equality. Black demands and white resentment led to widespread violence in the South during 1865–6. In summer 1866, particularly serious race riots occurred in Memphis, Tennessee, and New Orleans, Louisiana. In Memphis, fights between black veterans and white police encouraged the formation of white mobs: at least 40 black males were murdered, black females were raped, and black churches and schools were destroyed. There were many white attacks upon black people across the South: Texas courts indicted 500 white men for the murder of black Americans during 1865–6, but not one of them was convicted. Freed slave George King summed it up: 'The Master he says we are all free, but it don't mean we is white. And it don't mean we is equal.'

The need for a political settlement

The 13th Amendment was important in that it exacerbated tensions over the reincorporation of the South into the Union. There were differing visions over the role of the freed slaves in the political settlement. Radical Republicans were keen to see freed slaves have the vote and they resisted the re-establishment of the political domination of the old white elite. However, not everyone agreed. One South Carolina Unionist opined, 'We don't believe that because the nigger is freed he ought to be saucy.' When South Carolina ratified the Amendment in November 1865, it declared that 'any attempt by Congress towards legislating upon the political status of former slaves would be contrary to the Constitution of the United States.' Other Southern states added their own interpretive declarations to their ratification of the 13th Amendment.

The President who had to deal with the issue of a new political settlement was not Abraham Lincoln. It was Andrew Johnson.

A new President

Within days of the surrender of the Confederate army at Appomattox in April 1865, President Lincoln was assassinated by a disgruntled Confederate sympathiser. In an ominous reminder that this had not been a war against racism, and to the great embarrassment of Mrs Lincoln, the New York City Council voted to exclude black mourners from Lincoln's funeral procession.

Vice President Andrew Johnson became President. Johnson faced the problem of what to do with the defeated Southern states. The war had destroyed the South's political system, ruined its economy, and transformed its society through the collapse of slavery. The Southern states had to be reincorporated into the Union and the process of introducing and managing this change was known as **Reconstruction**.

 **KEY TERM**

Reconstruction
The process of rebuilding and reforming the 11 ex-Confederate states and restoring them to the Union.

Andrew Johnson

1808	Born in poverty in Raleigh, North Carolina
1843–53	Congressman
1853–7	Governor of Tennessee
1857–62	Senator
1865	Lincoln's Vice President from January to April
1865–9	President of the United States
1865	Implemented Presidential Reconstruction
1866	Clashed with Congress over Reconstruction
1868	Narrowly avoided impeachment
1875	Died within days of his election to the US Senate

Background

Born and raised in the South, Johnson came from a poor family. After a successful career as a tailor ('My work never ripped or gave way'), he rose to political prominence through his election to state and national offices. When the Civil War broke out, he remained loyal to the Union, despite having been a vociferous supporter of slavery. As a Unionist, Southerner and Democrat, he was the obvious choice to be Lincoln's **running mate** in the 1864 campaign, in which Lincoln sought to present himself as a unifier (Lincoln and Johnson ran on a National Union Party **ticket**). Within six weeks of their victory in the presidential election, Vice President Johnson was President.

Significance

Johnson's presidency was noted for his unsuccessful Presidential Reconstruction and then for his unsuccessful opposition to Radical Reconstruction. As a firm believer in **states' rights**, he was content to see the re-establishment of the Southern white Confederate elite and white supremacy in 1865. As a result, Johnson clashed with Congress over the continuation of the Freedmen's Bureau and the passage of the 1866 **civil rights** bill, which guaranteed citizenship for black Americans. Congress overrode his vetoes of those bills, their relationship was irreparably damaged, and Johnson only narrowly avoided **impeachment**.

KEY TERMS

Running mate When a political party chooses a presidential candidate to represent that party, the candidate chooses someone to run with him, who would then become Vice President in the event of their electoral victory.

Ticket The platform (policies) of a party's presidential candidate and his running mate.

States' rights Under the American Constitution, the states retained many rights (for example over voting and education) and resented federal government interference in their exercise of those rights.

Civil rights These include having the vote in free elections, equal treatment under the law, equal opportunities in areas such as in education and work, and freedom of speech, religion and movement.

Impeachment Under the American Constitution, Congress has the power to bring an errant President to trial, to impeach him.

President Andrew Johnson's response

Many of those present at President Lincoln's inauguration had observed Andrew Johnson in an obviously drunken state (he had been trying to calm his nerves) and were horrified at the thought of his ever becoming President. However, Radical Republicans had been impressed by the former slave owner's consistently tough wartime stance on the future of leading Confederates: for example, in 1864, Johnson had said, 'Traitors must be punished and impoverished.'

🔑 KEY TERMS

Presidential Reconstruction President Johnson's policies toward the South during 1865 allowed the Southern white Confederate elite to re-establish their power. This period is also known as Reconstruction Confederate style.

Black Codes Laws passed by the Southern states in 1865–6 in order to control the freed slaves, especially economically.

Reconstruction Confederate style President Johnson's policies toward the South during 1865 allowed the Southern white Confederate elite to re-establish their power. This period is also known as Presidential Reconstruction.

However, the Radical Republicans were to be disappointed. President Johnson hoped to restore the South to the Union on his terms before Congress met in December 1865 and he moved to conciliate the traditional white Southern elite because he believed:

- the loyalty of white Southerners needed to be restored as the South was to be part of the Union again
- federal intervention in the political, economic and social systems of individual states was against states' rights
- black Americans were not the equals of white Americans and should not be given the vote ('Mr Jefferson meant the white race … [when he said] all men are created equal')
- conciliatory policies toward the South were the best way to ensure his own re-election in 1868.

Under Johnson's **Presidential Reconstruction**, any Southern state that accepted the end of slavery and rejected the Confederacy was readmitted into the Union. Unsurprisingly, Southern whites speedily reasserted their supremacy. White officials who had served the Confederacy were now elected to govern the Southern states, and they introduced '**Black Codes**' to ensure that blacks did not gain economic, social, political or legal equality. This was '**Reconstruction Confederate style**'.

Black Codes

Black Codes varied from state to state, but they invariably supported economic, social and political inequality. Many codes made it impossible for black Americans to purchase or rent land, to obtain an education, to vote, or to receive any meaningful protection from the law (juries were all-white).

❓ Judging from Source A, what views did different groups of Americans hold on black enfranchisement?

SOURCE A

From a June 1865 letter written by President Andrew Johnson to Governor William Sharkey of Mississippi. Quoted in Craig Smith, *Silencing the Opposition*, State University of New York Press, 2011, pp. 60–1.

If you could extend the elective franchise to all persons of color who can read the Constitution of the United States in English and write their names and to all persons of color who own real estate valued at not less than two hundred and fifty dollars and pay taxes thereon, you would completely disarm the adversary and set an example the other States would follow. This you can do with perfect safety and you thus place the Southern States, in reference to free persons of color, upon the same basis with the free States. I hope and trust your convention will do this, and as a consequence, the radicals, who are wild upon negro franchise, will be completely foiled in their attempts to keep the Southern States from renewing their relations to the Union by not accepting their senators and representatives.

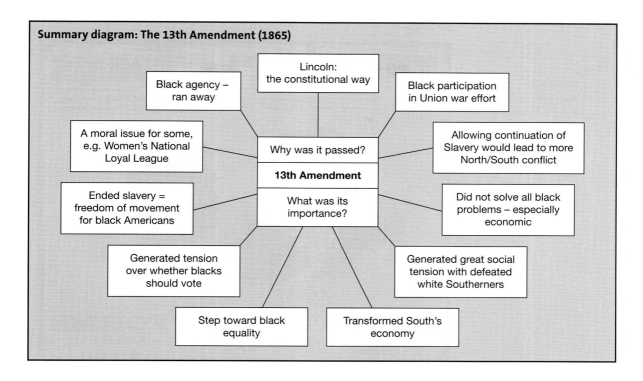

Summary diagram: The 13th Amendment (1865)

2 Radical Reconstruction (1867–77)

▶ *How did Reconstruction affect black and white Southerners?*

When Congress met in December 1865, there were great North/South tensions. Northern members were dissatisfied with 'Reconstruction Confederate style'. Many Northerners still felt bitterness toward the South and the reports from the Freedmen's Bureau officials, army officers and former slaves all suggested that the supremacy of the traditional white elite had been restored under Presidential Reconstruction. Southern white supremacist violence disgusted Northern white opinion, and Congress feared a violent black backlash. Most Northern Republicans believed that freed slaves should have some rights, and some were keen for the Southern black population to have the vote, knowing that they would opt for the party of Abraham Lincoln. The Republicans were dismayed that the Democrats remained the dominant party in the 1865 elections in the South, and that amongst the newly elected Southern congressmen were the Vice President of the Confederacy, 58 Confederate congressmen, and four Confederate generals. This was too much for the Republican majority in Congress, who refused to let these members of the Confederate elite take their seats. The Republican Congress also refused to recognise the new state governments in the South, because they were dominated by the old Confederate elite.

SOURCE B

An advertising poster published by the Democrat Party in Pennsylvania in 1866.

In what ways is Source B designed to encourage people in the Northern state of Pennsylvania to vote for the Democratic Party?

KEY TERMS

Bill If a member of Congress or the President wants a law to be made, he introduces a bill into Congress. If the bill is passed by Congress and accepted by the President, it becomes an Act or law.

Veto The American Constitution gave the President the right to reject bills, but, with a sufficiently large number of votes, Congress can override the presidential veto.

Act A bill passed by Congress and accepted by the President becomes an Act or law.

Two **bills** caused particularly bitter clashes between congressional Republicans on the one hand, and the Republican President Johnson and the Democrats on the other. The first bill aimed to extend the life of the Freedmen's Bureau, set up by Congress in 1865 to help ex-slaves. The second aimed to give blacks civil rights. Johnson exercised his **veto** on both bills, but Congress overrode him and both bills became **Acts** in 1866. Under the 1866 Civil Rights Act, all people born in the United States automatically acquired citizenship (with the exception of Native Americans) and recognition was given to the federal government's right to intervene in state affairs to protect citizens' rights.

The 14th Amendment

In June 1866, the Republican-controlled Congress attempted to reinforce the 1866 Civil Rights Act by incorporating its provisions within the 14th Amendment, which

- struck down the Black Codes and guaranteed all citizens equality before the law
- confirmed that the federal government could intervene if a state tried to deny citizenship rights to any citizen
- banned most of the old Confederate elite from holding office.

SOURCE C

From the 14th Amendment.

Section 1.
All persons born or naturalized in the United States, and subject to the jurisdiction thereof, are citizens of the United States and of the state wherein they reside. No state shall make or enforce any law which shall abridge the privileges or immunities of citizens of the United States; nor shall any state deprive any person of life, liberty, or property, without due process of law; nor deny to any person within its jurisdiction the equal protection of the laws.

The passage of a constitutional amendment required the approval of 75 per cent of the states, but not surprisingly, all the old Confederate states (apart from Tennessee) rejected the 14th Amendment. Northerners were now totally exasperated by the South because:

- The rejection of the 14th Amendment seemed to confirm that the Southern states did not recognise that they had been defeated.
- Northern public opinion was alienated when white groups attacked black people during race riots in Southern cities such as Memphis and New Orleans in summer 1866.
- Secret organisations such as the Ku Klux Klan (see page 26) had been set up to terrorise black people.

As a result, Congress decided it had to enforce its own version of Reconstruction on the South. This began with the **Military Reconstruction Act**.

SOURCE D

From a speech in support of Congressional Radical Reconstruction by Radical Republican leader Thaddeus Stevens in Congress, 3 January 1867. Quoted in Beverly Wilson Palmer and Holly Byers Ochoa, *The Selected Papers of Thaddeus Stevens, Volume 2: April 1865–August 1868*, University of Pittsburgh Press, 1998, pp. 213, 220.

Since the surrender of the armies of the confederate States of America a little has been done toward establishing this Government upon the true principles of liberty and justice; and but a little if we stop here. We have broken the material shackles of four million slaves. We have unchained them from the stake so as to allow them locomotion, provided they do not walk in paths which are trod by white men. We have allowed them the unwonted privilege of attending church, if they can do so without offending the sight of their former masters. We have even given them that highest and most agreeable evidence of liberty as defined by the 'great plebeian' the 'right to work.' But in what have we enlarged their liberty of thought? In what have we taught them the science and granted them the privilege of self-government? We have imposed upon them the privilege of fighting our battles, of dying in defense of freedom, and of bearing their equal portion of taxes; but where have we given them the privilege of ever participating in the formation of the laws for the government of their native

A radical minority interpreted Section 1 to mean that black Americans would become fully equal with white Americans, but most whites were convinced it would not create black equality through black enfranchisement, black jurors and integrated schools. How do you suppose these two differing interpretations of Source C could have been made?

 KEY TERM

Military Reconstruction Act The several Reconstruction Acts passed by Congress during 1867–8 are variously referred to as 'First Reconstruction Act', 'Second Reconstruction Act' and so on, or the Reconstruction Act(s) or the Military Reconstruction Acts.

What positives and negatives has the Civil War brought to black Americans, according to Source D?

land? By what civil weapon have we enabled them to defend themselves against oppression and injustice? Call you this liberty? Call you this a free Republic where four millions are subjects but not citizens? … Twenty years ago … twenty million white men enchained four million black men. I pronounce it no nearer to a true Republic now when twenty-five million of a privileged class exclude five million from all participation in the rights of government …

No Government can be free that does not allow all its citizens to participate in the formation and execution of her laws. … Every man, no matter what his race or color; every earthly being who has an immortal soul, has an equal right to justice, honesty, and fair play with every other man; and the law should secure him those rights. The same law which condemns or acquits an African should condemn or acquit a white man … This doctrine does not mean that a negro shall sit on the same seat or eat at the same table as a white man.

The impact of military rule in the South

After the congressional mid-term elections of 1866, the Republican-dominated Congress passed the Military Reconstruction Act (1867) over President Johnson's veto. The Act said:

- Apart from Tennessee, no Southern state had a legal government.
- The South could not send representatives to Congress unless Congress agreed.
- The ex-Confederate states should be governed by military commanders.
- In order to return to the Union, Southern states had to draw up new constitutions that would allow black males to vote, ratify the 14th Amendment, and disqualify Confederate office holders from political participation.

The Act gave the federal government tools to impose **Congressional Reconstruction** (or **Radical Reconstruction**) in the South, where it aroused great white hostility. President Johnson thought it gave the Southern black population too much power and feared it would 'Africanise' the South. Although there were important things that the Act did not do (it did not create any federal agencies to protect black rights, give economic aid to the freed slaves, or **disfranchise** Southern whites), generations of Southerners and even many Northerners were adamant that the Reconstruction era was a disaster for white people.

The 15th Amendment

In the 1868 presidential election, the Republican Party candidate General **Ulysses S. Grant** won a narrow victory that owed much to Southern black voters. Grant supported Radical Reconstruction.

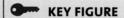 **KEY TERMS**

Congressional Reconstruction
See 'Radical Reconstruction'.

Radical Reconstruction
Also known as Congressional Reconstruction or Black Reconstruction. Post-Civil War policies imposed by Congress upon the South, which decreased the power of the old Confederate elite and increased the power of freed slaves.

Disfranchise Deprive someone of their vote.

KEY FIGURE

Ulysses S. Grant (1822–85)
A career soldier, General Grant was vital to the Union defeat of the Confederate armies in the Civil War. As commander of the US Army, he supervised Radical Reconstruction. As President of the United States (1869–77), he opposed white supremacists.

The Republicans sought to ensure the black vote in the South, so in 1869 they introduced the 15th Amendment. This said the 'right to vote should not be denied on account of race, color or previous conditions of servitude'. Given that only eight of the Northern states allowed black voting, this was revolutionary. However, once again, important things were left unsaid. The 15th Amendment did not:

- Guarantee men's right to vote.
- Forbid states to introduce literacy, property and educational tests for would-be voters.

The 14th and 15th Amendments were ratified in 1868 and 1870, respectively, and by the next year all the Southern states had been readmitted to the Union. Southern Republicans dominated the new state governments during Radical Reconstruction.

The significance of the presence of black representatives in federal and state legislatures

After the Civil War, 700,000 black males were registered to vote in the South, compared to 600,000 eligible whites. Black voters were Republicans because

- Radical Republicans had long advocated equal voting rights for black people
- the Republican President Abraham Lincoln was the 'Great Emancipator'
- Southern whites invariably voted Democrat.

In many ways, the results of black voting were positive. Between 1869 and 1877, 16 black congressmen and two black senators were elected to the US Congress. Over 700 black men served in state legislatures (see Figure 2.1, page 24). Most were former slaves. In Republican-controlled legislatures, black legislators contributed to the passage of laws that increased funding for public education and that required equal access to transportation and public facilities. Around 1000 black Americans were elected to local posts that gave them considerable power. Several black sheriffs were elected in rural Mississippi, while Republican city governments appointed black police and provided poor relief.

However, the proportion of black officials was far short of the proportion of black voters. White Republicans were outnumbered by black Republicans, but nevertheless dominated the Southern states during Reconstruction. No black state governor was elected and no state senate had a black majority. Only South Carolina (65 per cent black) had a black majority in the lower house. Senator Charles Caldwell, one of the two black US senators from Mississippi (over 50 per cent black), was shot by whites in a tavern. When he begged them to let him die out in the fresh air, they took him out to the street and shot him an extra 30 times.

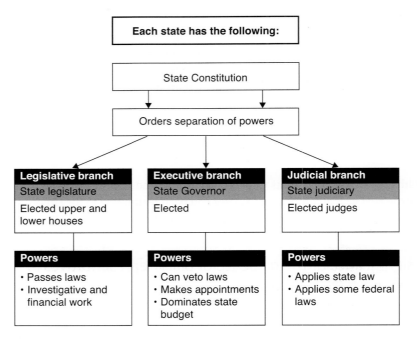

Figure 2.1 The structure of state government in the United States.

Black representation was highly significant in that it reflected a political revolution, but black people proved unable to dominate political life in the South because:

- They lacked education, organisation and experience.
- They were accustomed to white leadership and domination.
- They were in the minority in most states.
- There were divisions within the black community, especially between ex-slaves and the free-born blacks who saw themselves as superior.
- Sure of the black vote, the Republican Party usually put forward white candidates in the hope of attracting more white votes.
- Most white Republicans considered black people less able to govern than whites.
- Southern black leaders were usually moderates who had no desire to exclude ex-Confederates from office.

Southern Democrats and some early twentieth-century historians criticised Republican rule in the South as dominated by corrupt black politicians, but black politicians were neither more nor less corrupt than the white contemporaries who still dominated national politics.

The Civil Rights Act (1875)

In 1875, the outgoing Republican-controlled Congress passed a Civil Rights Act that aimed to prevent discrimination in public places such as railroads, hotels and theatres, although not in schools, cemeteries and churches. This Act had little effect on the South. The burden of enforcement was placed upon black litigants, and when in 1883 the **Supreme Court** (see page 3) ruled it unconstitutional, on the grounds that civil rights within a state were the responsibility of the state government, it was a clear sign that the white backlash had triumphed.

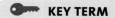

KEY TERM

Supreme Court
The judicial branch of the US federal government. The highest court in the land, it rules (adjuges) whether actions are in line with the American Constitution and the law.

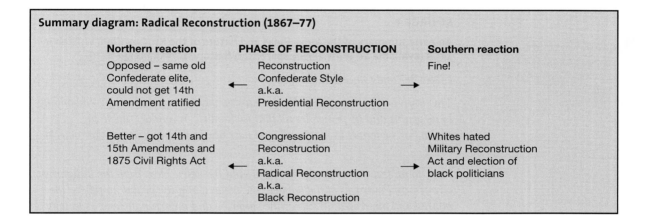

Summary diagram: Radical Reconstruction (1867–77)

Northern reaction	PHASE OF RECONSTRUCTION	Southern reaction
Opposed – same old Confederate elite, could not get 14th Amendment ratified	Reconstruction Confederate Style a.k.a. Presidential Reconstruction	Fine!
Better – got 14th and 15th Amendments and 1875 Civil Rights Act	Congressional Reconstruction a.k.a. Radical Reconstruction a.k.a. Black Reconstruction	Whites hated Military Reconstruction Act and election of black politicians

3 The white backlash

▶ *How did white Southerners begin to regain their supremacy?*

The historian Joel Williamson (1984) wrote that 'one of the great ironies of American history' was the way in which emancipation freed the slaves but also 'freed racism'. Under slavery, many Southern whites had a paternalistic attitude toward black people as child-like dependants. When slavery ended, they perceived black males as dangerous.

Although slavery had been abolished, white Southerners continued to believe in the arguments that had justified it. Frightened and resentful of the 'inferior' black race, Southern whites claimed that black people were immature, irrational, open to corruption, and therefore unfit to possess voting rights. One Mississippi man said that even an educated black American such as Booker T. Washington (see page 45) was no more fit to vote than 'the coconut-headed, chocolate-colored, typical little coon' who 'blacks my shoes' and was not 'fit to perform the supreme function of citizenship'. Many white Southerners depicted Reconstruction as an era of black rule, rape, murder and arson, and called for black disfranchisement. White supremacist groups went further and used violence to stop black voting. The best known of these groups was the Ku Klux Klan.

The Ku Klux Klan, the White League and the incidence of lynching

In 1866, armed white racist groups were established in most states of the old Confederacy. The Ku Klux Klan was a secret order established in Tennessee by war hero General Nathan Bedford Forrest. It aimed to restore white supremacy.

SOURCE E

? In what ways might Source E have appealed to a white Southerner in 1868?

An early summary of the aims, ideas and nature of the Ku Klux Klan, written in 1868 (available at: www.albany.edu/history/history316/kkk.html).

Character and Objects of the Order

This is an institution of chivalry, humanity, mercy, and patriotism; embodying in its genius and its principles all that is chivalric in conduct, noble in sentiment, generous in manhood, and patriotic in purpose; its peculiar objects being:

First, to protect the weak, the innocent, and the defenseless from the indignities, wrongs, and outrages of the lawless, the violent, and the brutal; to relieve the injured and oppressed; to succor the suffering and unfortunate, and especially the widows and orphans of Confederate soldiers.

Second, to protect and defend the Constitution of the United States, and all laws passed in conformity thereto, and to protect the states and the people thereof from all invasion from any source whatever.

Third, to aid and assist in the execution of all constitutional laws, and to protect the people from unlawful seizure and from trial, except by their peers in conformity to the laws of the land.

Titles

Section 1. The officers of this Order shall consist of a Grand Wizard of the Empire and his ten Genii; a Grand Dragon of the Realm and his eight Hydras; a Grand Titan of the Dominion and his six Furies; a Grand Giant of the Province and his four Goblins; a Grand Cyclops of the Den and his two Night Hawks; a Grand Magi, a Grand Monk, a Grand Scribe, a Grand Exchequer, a Grand Turk, and a Grand Sentinel.

Section 2. The body politic of this Order shall be known and designated as 'Ghouls.'

Territory and Its Divisions

… The territory embraced within the jurisdiction of this Order shall be coterminous with the states of Maryland, Virginia, North Carolina, South Carolina, Georgia, Florida, Alabama, Mississippi, Louisiana, Texas, Arkansas, Missouri, Kentucky, and Tennessee; all combined constituting the Empire …

Questions To Be Asked Candidates

… 5. Are you opposed to Negro equality both social and political?

6. Are you in favor of a white man's government in this country?

7. Are you in favor of constitutional liberty, and a government of equitable laws instead of a government of violence and oppression?

8. Are you in favor of maintaining the constitutional rights of the South?

9. Are you in favor of the reenfranchisement and emancipation of the white men of the South, and the restitution of the Southern people to all their rights, alike proprietary, civil, and political?

10. Do you believe in the inalienable right of self-preservation of the people against the exercise of arbitrary and unlicensed power?

The Klan grew rapidly between 1868 and 1871. Forrest estimated 40,000 members in Tennessee alone, and roughly half a million across the South. Southern Democrats encouraged and colluded in Klan terrorism, which targeted black officials, schools and churches.

White supremacists recognised the threat from black schools, churches and officials. Black literacy doubled during Reconstruction and literacy, along with office-holding and the vote, empowered black people. The black schools and black churches provided over 25 per cent of black officials, and church ministers provided political education and encouraged voting. Teachers too encouraged voting because political power led to increased funds for education. Fearful of the threat posed by an educated black population, the Ku Klux Klan destroyed 25 schools and killed 50 black teachers in Mississippi, in response to the state legislature's passage of a public school law in 1870.

When Republican state governments introduced laws to try to stop the Ku Klux Klan, they proved hard to enforce. Klansmen gave each other alibis, were frequently represented on juries, and when Governor Holden of North Carolina used the state militia against the Klan, the state legislature condemned him for 'subverting [the] personal liberty' of the Klansmen. In black majority areas, black militias fought back against the Klan, but in majority white areas, thousands of black Americans were killed.

KEY TERM

Lynching The unlawful killing of an individual by a mob.

The incidence of lynching, 1865–77

In the years 1865–77, thousands of black Americans in the South were unlawfully killed by white mobs. Historians do not know exactly how many were **lynched**, although there are statistics for many individual incidents. For example, in January 1871, 500 Klansmen attacked the Union County jail in South Carolina and lynched eight black prisoners. The lynchings were usually carried out at night-time and in rural areas, which is why it is difficult to know how many occurred. However, it is certain that the practice was widespread: this is attested by the indictment of several thousand Klansmen after the Ku Klux Klan Act was passed in 1871. There were so many indictments that the federal court system could not cope, so only a few leaders were actually tried. Most were released by 1875.

The federal government response to the Klan

In 1870–1, Congress responded to appeals for help from several state Governors by the passage of three Enforcement Acts. These Acts, also known as the Force Acts, protected the rights of black Americans to vote, hold office, serve on juries and receive equal protection under the law. The third of these Acts, also known as the Ku Klux Klan Act, gave President Grant the legal and military power to crush the Klan and it ended most of the Klan violence. After Grant imposed martial law in several areas of the South, hundreds of suspected Klansmen were imprisoned. However, ex-Confederate soldiers continued to use violence and intimidation against Republicans and black Republicans in particular, and other white supremacist groups sprang up. Amongst these were the White Leagues. The historian Stephen Tuck (2010) described the armed White Leagues as 'basically the Klan without the white sheets'. The first White League was set up in Louisiana after a disputed election in 1873 led to the establishment of a black militia that held the town of Colfax for a fortnight. Over 100 black Americans were killed in the 'Colfax Massacre'. In 1874, the White League assassinated several Republican officials in Louisiana, and White Leagues were soon established in other Southern states.

SOURCE F

? What can you infer from Source F about the relationship between black Americans and the law in North Carolina in the years after the Civil War?

The recollections of Ben Johnson, born a slave c.1848, were recorded by the Federal Writers' Project in 1936–8 (see page 82). Here, Johnson recalled what he remembered of the Ku Klux Klan in the years after the Civil War. Quoted in Federal Writers' Project, *North Carolina Slave Narratives*, Applewood Press, 2006, p. 10.

De most dat I can tell yo' 'bout is the Ku Klux. I neber will fergit when dey hung Cy Guy. Dey hung him fer a scandelous insult ter a white 'oman an' dey comed atter him a hundert strong. Dey tries him dar in de woods, an' dey scratches Cy's arm ter git some blood, an' wid dat blood dey writes dat he shall hang 'tween de heavens an' de yearth till he am daid, daid, daid, an' dat any nigger what takes down de body shall be hunged too. Well sar, de nex' mornin' dar he hung, right ober de road an' de sentence hangin' over his head.

Nobody'ud bother with dat body fer four days an' dar hit hung, swingin' in the wind, but de fou'th day de sheriff comes an' takes hit down.

Dar was Ed an' Cindy, who 'fore de war belonged ter Mr Lynch an' atter de war he told 'em to move. He gives 'em a month an' dey ain't gone, so de Ku Kluxes gits them.

The restoration of Democrat control in the South and the end of Reconstruction (1877)

Reconstruction brought some gains for black people, including

- political experience as voters and as elected officials
- freedom of movement, which enabled those who so desired to move to Southern cities (between 1865 and 1870 the black population of the South's ten largest cities doubled) or to the North or West (see Chapter 4)
- the confidence and opportunity to build and benefit from their own institutions. Black churches and the federal Freedmen's Bureau (1865–72) (see page 15) facilitated black access to education, so that black political leaders, businessmen, teachers, lawyers and doctors began to emerge. Black illiteracy rates fell from 90 per cent in 1860 to 70 per cent in 1880. Some of the educational institutions founded during Reconstruction, including colleges such as **Howard** (Washington DC), Fisk (Tennessee) and Atlanta University (Georgia), helped produce subsequent generations of civil rights leaders. Black churches became immensely popular and similarly influential.

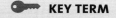 **KEY TERM**

Howard Prestigious black university in Washington DC.

However, Reconstruction came to an end in the late 1870s because:

- Although President Grant had opposed Ku Klux Klan violence in 1870, in 1875 he declared the 'whole public' to be 'tired out with these annual, autumnal outbreaks' of racial violence during elections. He was keen to end the North's concentration upon the South and to effect a reconciliation with white Southerners. For example, his 1872 Amnesty Act returned voting and office-holding rights to 150,000 ex-Confederates.
- Northerners had lost interest in the Southern black problem, as evidenced by the collapse of the Freedmen's Bureau in 1872. Indeed, Northern public opinion had grown tired of freedmen's problems and of black Americans in general.
- Radical Reconstruction had alienated most white Republicans in the South, even though it had not greatly increased black power and influence.
- From 1873, the United States suffered a severe economic depression. Voters blamed the Republicans, and as a result the Democrats gained control of the US Congress.

When Republican President Rutherford B. Hayes withdrew all federal troops from the Southern states in 1877, it was clear that the Republican Party and the North were uninterested in the South and willing to allow the restoration of white political supremacy.

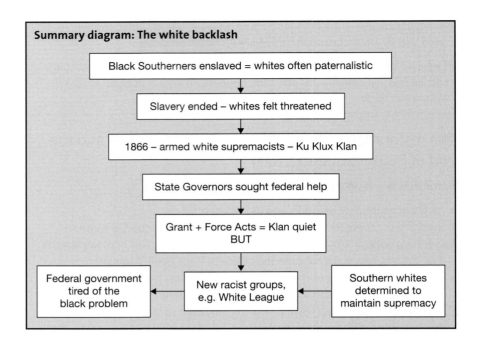

Summary diagram: The white backlash

Black Southerners enslaved = whites often paternalistic

↓

Slavery ended – whites felt threatened

↓

1866 – armed white supremacists – Ku Klux Klan

↓

State Governors sought federal help

↓

Grant + Force Acts = Klan quiet
BUT

↓

Federal government tired of the black problem ← New racist groups, e.g. White League ← Southern whites determined to maintain supremacy

Chapter summary

In 1865, moral and practical pressures led to the 13th Amendment to the American Constitution. It prohibited slavery and was a first step toward black equality in the South.

Lincoln's successor Andrew Johnson thought ending slavery was sufficient. During 1865 his 'Presidential Reconstruction' (or Reconstruction Confederate style) helped restore the old white Confederate elite to power in the South, where there was inevitable tension between freed black slaves and their former masters.

The Republican-dominated Congress that met in December 1865 considered the restoration of the old Confederate elite unacceptable – especially as that elite was invariably Democrat. Congressional or Radical Reconstruction was introduced and sustained in the South through the Military Reconstruction Act (1867). By virtue of that legislation and the 14th and 15th Amendments,

Congress ensured that black Americans became citizens and were able to vote. The power of the old Southern white elite was apparently eclipsed.

Black Southerners did not gain equality during Reconstruction. Although free to sell their labour, many struggled as sharecroppers. Whites still regarded them as inferior in every way, and although many black Republicans were elected to office, white Republicans dominated Southern politics. The development of a white backlash further limited black advances.

The white backlash took several forms. First, white supremacist groups such as the Ku Klux Klan used violence and intimidation against black people. Although President Grant crushed the Ku Klux Klan, others continued the violence and intimidation. Second, Northerners grew tired of the South and black problems: the Freedmen's Bureau was allowed to collapse, and in 1877 federal troops were withdrawn from the South. With the end of Northern Republican interest in the South, white supremacy was restored there.

Refresher questions

1 Why was the 13th Amendment passed?

2 In what ways was the 13th Amendment important?

3 How did sharecropping work?

4 In what ways did Southern whites attempt to reassert their supremacy in the years 1865–77?

5 Why was the 14th Amendment important?

6 What did the Military Reconstruction Act of 1867 say?

7 Why did the Republican Party support the 15th Amendment?

8 What impact did black voting have on the South in the years 1869–77?

9 Why were black Southerners unable to dominate political life in the South in the decade after the Civil War?

10 How important was the 1875 Civil Rights Act?

11 What sort of actions did Klansmen engage in?

12 Why did Reconstruction end in the late 1870s?

 Question practice

ESSAY QUESTIONS

1 To what extent was the Republican Party responsible for the end of Radical Reconstruction?

2 'The abolition of slavery and Radical Reconstruction failed to bring about black American equality.' With reference to the years 1865–77, how far do you agree with the assessment?

SOURCE ANALYSIS QUESTIONS

1 Study Source D (page 21). Assess the value of the source for revealing Radical Republican Representative Thaddeus Stevens' views on equality and the attitudes of white Americans toward freed black slaves in the late 1860s. Explain your answer, using the source, the information given about its origins and your own knowledge about the historical context.

2 Study Source E (page 26). Assess the value of the source for revealing the approach of the Ku Klux Klan to race problems and the attitudes of Southern whites toward black Americans in the late 1860s. Explain your answer, using the source, the information given about its origins and your own knowledge about the historical context.

CHAPTER 3

The triumph of Jim Crow, 1883–*c*.1900

Southern whites resented Reconstruction and sought new forms of race control to replace slavery. Northerners lost interest in the South in the later 1870s, which enabled white Southerners to reassert their racial supremacy. Jim Crow laws made segregation legal and black voters were disfranchised through a variety of methods. When all else failed, violence and intimidation were used, and perpetrators went unpunished because whites dominated law enforcement. This chapter covers these issues in sections on

★ The spread of the Jim Crow laws

★ Excluding black voters

★ The response of the Supreme Court

★ Black resistance

Key dates

1883	Civil Rights Cases	**1895**	Booker T. Washington's 'Atlanta Compromise' speech
1887	Florida rail travel change		
		1896	*Plessy v. Ferguson*
1890	Mississippi introduced income and literacy qualifications to stop black voting	**1898**	*Williams v. Mississippi* Louisiana's grandfather clause
1892	Anti-lynching campaigner Ida B. Wells fled the South	**1899**	*Cumming v. Board of Education*
		1909	NAACP established

1 The spread of the Jim Crow laws

▶ *When and why were the Jim Crow laws introduced?*

Although black Americans had not attained full social, political and economic equality after the Civil War, Southern whites remained fearful and hostile. The solutions to the race problem suggested by white politicians included the deportation of black Americans, mass black castration, and even 'utter extermination' (the suggestion of a Georgia congressman). However, white Southerners were for the most part reasonably content with the spread of laws that enforced segregation.

The reassertion of white supremacy in the South was facilitated by the federal government's loss of interest in protecting the black population of the South (see page 29) and by the powers given to individual states under the Constitution. With those powers, which included control of voting, education, transportation and law enforcement, Southern states introduced and sustained discriminatory **Jim Crow** laws that enshrined social divisions in law.

Prior to the Civil War, slavery enabled white Southerners to control the movements of most of the local black population. When slavery was abolished, whites quickly moved to continue such control through the ***de facto* segregation** of schools, housing and public facilities. At the same time as it passed the 14th Amendment (which did not plainly proscribe segregation), Congress had authorised segregated schooling in the nation's capital, demonstrating that it did not interpret that Amendment as anti-segregationist. Segregation spread quickly and was soon reinforced by law. Historians have disagreed over why ***de jure* segregation** was suddenly so consistently applied by the 1890s. Amongst their suggestions are:

- the support of the Supreme Court (see page 37)
- white anxiety over the rising proportion of black farm owners in the Deep South between 1880 (3.8 per cent) and 1900 (25 per cent). Black success necessitated segregation, which would reaffirm white supremacy
- the **railroad** expansion in the South in the 1870s, which forced railroad companies to consider the significance of the black and white races sitting in close proximity.

Railroad expansion was certainly significant. The legalisation of a 'color line' was first implemented in public transport. The history of the Florida railroad provides an early example of *de jure* segregation.

Changes to rail travel in Florida

Segregation by race on railroad **cars** was nothing new in the South (or North). The post-Civil War Black Codes (see page 18) frequently mandated railroad segregation: a Florida state law of 1865 punished blacks or whites who entered a railroad car reserved for the other race. The Black Codes did not survive Radical Reconstruction, but by 1883, black activist and journalist T. Thomas Fortune noted that the situation was deteriorating:

> *The Georgia and Florida railroads have become infamously notorious for 'bouncing' colored travellers, and for taking decent fare and giving miserable accommodations to such – accommodations in smoking cars, where the vilest impudent white scum resort to swear, to exhale rotten smoke and to expectorate pools of sickening excrementations of tobacco.*

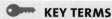

KEY TERMS

Jim Crow An early 1830s' comic, black-faced, minstrel character developed by a white performing artist that proved to be very popular with white audiences. When, after Reconstruction, the Southern states introduced laws that legalised segregation, these were known as 'Jim Crow laws'.

***De facto* segregation** Separation of the races in fact if not in law.

***De jure* segregation** Separation of the races imposed and supported by law.

Railroad Railway.

Cars Carriages.

SOURCE A

? Looking at the caption, date and place of publication of Source A, what is it possible to infer about railroad travel for black Americans in the nineteenth-century United States?

NEGRO EXPULSION FROM RAILWAY CAR, PHILADELPHIA.

An 1856 illustration from the *Illustrated London News*.

In 1887, the Florida state legislature passed a law mandating segregation in the first-class cars on Florida's railroads. The law said that 'all respectable Negro persons' were to be sold first-class tickets at the same rate as white passengers, and given a separate car 'equally as good and provided with the same facilities for comfort as for white persons'. Black ministers in Jacksonville urged their congregations to boycott lines that did not provide equal accommodation for all passengers, suggesting that separation was acceptable to the black community so long as provision was equal. The Florida state legislature suggested that black or white persons who entered railroad cars reserved for the other race could be sentenced to the pillory or whipped 39 times – or both. Other states followed Florida's example.

The extension of segregation

From 1881, *de jure* segregation was introduced in all areas of life in the South. At varying speeds and with varying degrees of consistency, Southern states and cities passed laws that insisted upon the separation of the races in trains, **streetcars**, stations, theatres, churches, parks, schools, restaurants and cemeteries. All aspects of life were legislated upon: whites were not to use black prostitutes; textbooks for use in white schools were not to be stored in the same place as those for black schools; black and white people were forbidden to play checkers (draughts) together.

Segregation was a daily reminder of black inequality. In 1892, black writer Anna Julia Cooper wrote about one of her train journeys. She was evicted from the first-class railroad car and then, at the railway station, 'I see two dingy little rooms with FOR LADIES swinging over one and FOR COLORED PEOPLE over the other, while wondering under which head I should come.'

KEY TERM

Streetcar Tram, bus.

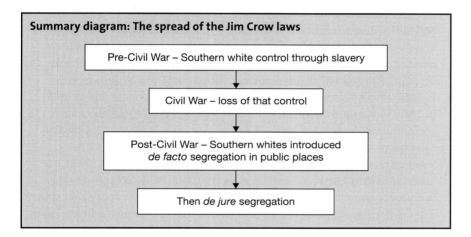

Summary diagram: The spread of the Jim Crow laws

Pre-Civil War – Southern white control through slavery

Civil War – loss of that control

Post-Civil War – Southern whites introduced *de facto* segregation in public places

Then *de jure* segregation

 2

Excluding black voters

▶ *How were black Southerners disfranchised?*

Although slavery had been abolished, Southern whites still believed in the arguments that had justified it. They produced a variety of old and new arguments to combat black voting. Their depiction of Radical Reconstruction as an era of black rule, rape, murder and arson was used as an argument for black disfranchisement. Some asserted that black males were immature, irrational, open to corruption, and consequently unfit to vote.

Apes and humans

The late nineteenth century saw the emergence of pseudo-scientific race theories. For example, Charles Carroll's *The Negro a Beast* (1900) placed black Americans nearer to apes than to human beings. In the early twentieth century, Harvard University's evolution display cabinet showed a monkey, then a black man, then a white man.

Southern white methods for the exclusion of black voters

Southern whites used a variety of methods to exclude black voters:

- White supremacist groups used violence to stop black voting (see page 28).
- In 1880, the South Carolina legislature decreased black representation by redrawing congressional districts. They put black voters in a single black-majority district, nicknamed the 'shoestring district', because the redrawing of the constituency boundaries had given it a long narrow shape.
- Fraud was frequent. For example, white Mississippi voting officials maintained that mules ate ballot papers from black-majority counties.
- During Reconstruction, the Southern states began introducing a **poll tax**. Georgia introduced one as early as 1871. Would-be voters had to pay the poll tax in order to register to exercise the franchise. Although this deprived impoverished whites of the vote, the disfranchisement disproportionately affected black Americans. In Arkansas, 71 per cent of the black electorate voted in 1890, but only 9 per cent voted after a poll tax was introduced.
- In 1882, South Carolina introduced a literacy qualification for voting, and in 1890, Mississippi became the first former Confederate state to call a constitutional convention for the sole purpose of excluding black voters. Mississippi introduced both literacy and income qualifications. Other Southern state legislatures followed, including South Carolina (1895), Louisiana (1898), Alabama and Virginia (1902). In 1908, Georgia was the last state to complete the process. White Southern registrars connived at the disqualification of literate black Americans by manipulating the literacy test. For example, they gave tests requiring impossibly detailed answers on state constitutions: late twentieth-century Harvard students tried and failed these tests.
- In 1898, the state of Louisiana sought to assist poor white voters who could not pay the poll tax or pass the literacy test. Louisiana did this through the introduction of '**grandfather clauses**': a man could vote if it were proved that an ancestor had voted before Reconstruction. Other states followed suit. As the vast majority of the South's black population had been enslaved, grandfather clauses ensured the exclusion of most black voters.

The impact on voter numbers in the South in the 1890s was great (see Table 3.1). By 1900, only 3 per cent of black Southern males could vote.

KEY TERMS

Poll tax Tax levied on would-be voters that made it harder for blacks (who were usually poor) to vote.

Grandfather clause Southern state laws allowed the illiterate to vote if they could prove an ancestor had voted before Reconstruction, which no African American could do.

Table 3.1 In 1898, Louisiana introduced a new state constitution which made black voting difficult

Year	Number of black voters
1896	130,334
1904	1,400
1910	730

The white primary

When the South became a one-party region after Reconstruction, the only choice available to voters was from one of several Democrats. Democrats introduced the white primary, in which white voters chose one of the Democrats seeking to represent the party. As a result, no black person had the opportunity to choose from amongst the Democrat candidates.

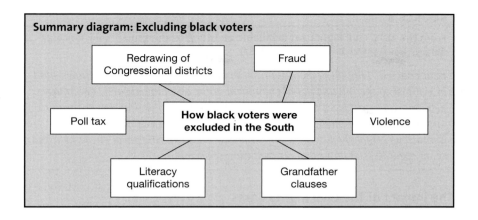

Summary diagram: Excluding black voters

3 The response of the Supreme Court

▶ *To what extent was the Supreme Court responsible for Jim Crow?*

Black American litigation over segregation and disfranchisement met unfavourable responses as the cases worked their way up the courts to the nation's highest court, the Supreme Court. The process began with the Slaughter-House Cases (1873), in which the Supreme Court ruled that the 14th Amendment (see page 20) was not intended to 'transfer the security and protection' of civil rights 'from the states to the federal government'.

The Supreme Court and the Civil Rights Cases (1883)

In 1883, the Supreme Court reviewed five similar civil rights cases in which black Americans had sued transportation companies, hotels and theatres that had refused them admittance or excluded them from 'white only' facilities.

The court gave consideration to the provisions of the Civil Rights Act of 1875, which had said that people of all races should have access to public facilities (see Source B, see page 38). After consideration, the court ruled that those provisions in the 1875 legislation, along with federal government intervention over racial discrimination on the part of private individuals and organisations, were unconstitutional. It declared that freed slaves were no longer to be 'a special favourite of the laws'.

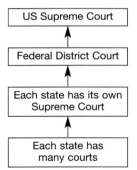

US Court Hierarchy

Figure 3.1 US court hierarchy.

To what did Source B refer when it spoke of 'previous condition of servitude'?

SOURCE B

From the 1875 Civil Rights Act (available at: http://teachingamericanhistory.org/library/document/civil-rights-act-of-1875/).

Be it enacted, That all persons within the jurisdiction of the United States shall be entitled to the full and equal enjoyment of the accommodations, advantages, facilities, and privileges of inns, public conveyances on land or water, theaters, and other places of public amusement; subject only to the conditions and limitations established by law, and applicable alike to citizens of every race and color, regardless of any previous condition of servitude.

The impact of the Civil Rights Cases

Only one of the nine Supreme Court justices, former slaveholder Justice John Marshall Harlan, dissented in the Supreme Court's ruling on the Civil Rights Cases in 1883. He recognised that the ruling was highly significant in that it would contribute to the loss of black civil rights through segregation (see Source C).

What does Source C see as the role of Congress in relation to racial equality?

SOURCE C

From Justice John Marshall Harlan's dissent to the 1883 Supreme Court ruling on the Civil Rights Cases. Born in Kentucky, Harlan (1883–1911) supported the Union in the Civil War but also supported slavery and opposed the Emancipation Proclamation. He changed his mind in the late 1860s, and became a strong supporter of civil rights. He was known as 'The Great Dissenter' because he dissented from the majority opinion in the Civil Rights Cases (1883) and *Plessy v. Ferguson* (1896) (available at: https://en.wikisource.org/wiki/Civil_Rights_Cases/Dissent_Harlan).

… I cannot resist the conclusion that the substance and spirit of the recent amendments of the Constitution have been sacrificed by a subtle and ingenious verbal criticism.

It is not the words of the law, but the internal sense of it that makes the law; the letter of the law is the body; the sense and reason of the law is the soul.

… I mean only, in this form, to express an earnest conviction that the court has departed from the familiar rule requiring, in the interpretation of constitutional provisions, that full effect be given to the intent with which they were adopted.

The purpose of the first section of the act of Congress of March 1, 1875, was to prevent race discrimination in respect of the accommodations and facilities of inns, public conveyances, and places of public amusement. It does not assume to define the general conditions and limitations under which inns, public conveyances, and places of public amusement may be conducted, but only declares that such conditions and limitations, whatever they may be, shall not be applied so as to work a discrimination solely because of race, color, or previous condition of servitude. The second section provides a penalty against anyone denying, or aiding or inciting the denial, of any citizen, of that equality of right given by the first section except for reasons by law applicable to citizens of every race or color and regardless of any previous condition of servitude …

Congress has not, in these matters, entered the domain of State control and supervision. It does not, as I have said, assume to prescribe the general conditions and limitations under which inns, public conveyances, and places of public amusement shall be conducted or managed. It simply declares, in effect, that, since the nation has established universal freedom in this country for all time, there shall be no discrimination, based merely upon race or color, in respect of the accommodations and advantages of public conveyances, inns, and places of public amusement …

I am of the opinion that such discrimination practised by corporations and individuals in the exercise of their public or quasi-public functions is a badge of servitude the imposition of which Congress may prevent under its power, by appropriate legislation, to enforce the Thirteenth Amendment; and consequently, without reference to its enlarged power under the Fourteenth Amendment, the act of March 1, 1875, is not, in my judgment, repugnant to the Constitution.

The Nation, a weekly magazine sympathetic to black Americans, recorded 'the calm with which the country receives the word that the leading section of the celebrated Civil Rights Act of 1875 has been pronounced unconstitutional'. That 'calm' was for the most part confined to the white population, although Source D suggests that not all white Southerners remained 'calm'. The Supreme Court's ruling led to black American outrage and protests across the United States. However, the protests were fruitless. The ruling encouraged the states of the South in the systematic imposition of Jim Crow laws that legitimised *de jure* segregation.

SOURCE D

From George Washington Cable's *The Silent South* (1885). Cable (1844–1925) was the son of slaveholders, a veteran of the Confederate army, the author of acclaimed fiction, and a passionate civil rights activist. The book's analysis of race relations outraged Cable's fellow white Southerners and forced him to go to live in the North. Quoted in Jonathan Bean, editor, *Race & Liberty in America: The Essential Reader*, University Press of Kentucky, 2009, pp. 98–103.

How does Source D see the situation of black Americans as having developed during the years 1865–85?

The late Southern slave has within two decades risen from slavery to freedom, from freedom to citizenship, passed on into political ascendancy, and fallen again from that eminence. The amended Constitution holds him up in his new political rights as well as a mere constitution can. On the other hand, certain enactments of Congress, trying to reach further, have lately been made void by the highest court of the nation. And another thing has happened. The popular mind in the old free States, weary of strife at arm's length, bewildered by its complications, vexed by many a blunder, eager to return to the cure of other evils, and even tinctured by that race feeling whose grosser excesses it would so gladly see suppressed, has retreated from its uncomfortable dictational attitude and thrown the whole matter over to the States of the South.

First, then, what are these sentiments [hostile to the black American]? Foremost among them stands the idea that he is of necessity an alien. He was brought to our shores a naked, brutish, unclean, captive, pagan savage, to be and remain a kind of connecting link between man and the beasts of burden … He accepted our dress, language, religion, all the fundamentals of our civilisation, and became forever expatriated from his own land; still he remained, to us, an alien …

Are the freedman's liberties suffering any real abridgement? The answer is easy. The letter of the laws, with a few exceptions, recognises him as entitled to every right of an American citizen; and to some it may seem unimportant that there is scarcely one public relation of life in the South where he is not arbitrarily and unlawfully compelled to hold toward the white man the attitude of an alien, a menial, and a probable reprobate, by reason of his race and color. One of the marvels of future history will be that it was counted a small matter …

there are thousands of Southern-born white men and women, in the minority in all these places in churches, courts, schools, libraries, theatres, concert-halls, and on steamers and railway carriages, who see the wrong and folly of these things, silently blush for them, and withhold their open protests only because their belief is unfortunately stronger in the futility of their counsel than in the power of a just cause …

Case v. Alabama

In 1883, in *Case v. Alabama*, the Supreme Court upheld an Alabama statute that imposed harsher penalties on fornication when the participants were of different races. It maintained that so long as both fornicators were subject to the same penalty, the races were being treated equally. This was an early case of 'separate but equal'.

The impact of *Plessy v. Ferguson* (1896)

The Supreme Court did not rule against the so-called Jim Crow laws that legalised segregation. In *Plessy v. Ferguson* (1896), it ruled that 'separate but equal' facilities for blacks and whites on public transportation did not contravene the 14th Amendment or American law. The court asserted that 'legislation is powerless to eradicate racial instincts'. The sole dissenter in *Plessy* was John Harlan, who vainly asserted, 'our Constitution is color-blind' and scolded the other eight justices for their relegation of black Americans to a 'condition of legal inferiority'.

> ## Who was Homer Plessy?
>
> Born in the unusually racially tolerant city of New Orleans, shoemaker and carpenter Homer Plessy (*c.*1862–1925) looked white, but one of his great grandparents was black. That made him 'Negro' in the state of Louisiana. In 1892, Plessy volunteered to be a 'guinea pig' for a group of New Orleans black activists who wanted to test the constitutionality of the 1890 Louisiana Separate Car Act. Plessy bought a first-class railroad ticket and boarded a 'white' carriage. The activists had told the conductor Plessy was legally black, so the conductor asked Plessy to obey the law and get out of the carriage. Plessy refused and the conductor handed him over to the authorities. Plessy was jailed for violating a state racial ordinance. Plessy's lawyers argued that his arrest violated the 13th and 14th Amendments, but the judge ruled in favour of states' rights. The Louisiana Supreme Court upheld the decision approving separate carriages, as did the Supreme Court in *Plessy v. Ferguson* (1896). The remainder of Plessy's life was relatively incident free.

Although provisions were 'separate' in the South, they were never 'equal' and the Supreme Court did not seek to ensure that they were. For example, Southern states spent ten times as much on white schools as on black. There was but one Supreme Court case involving racial equality in education in the *Plessy* era, and this was *Cumming v. Richmond County* [Georgia] *Board of Education* (1899).

Cumming v. Board of Education

Given the obstacles, it is surprising that black litigation against the Jim Crow laws happened as often as it did. J.W. Cumming and his black co-litigants found it very difficult to obtain a lawyer willing to argue their case in the Supreme Court, and other litigants were disheartened by their poverty, the lack of black success in the law courts, and the likelihood of white violence and intimidation. Bravely, Cumming and the other black litigants objected to the fact that a Georgia county had continued to fund a white high school but stopped funding a black one (there were only four black high schools in the whole of the South). The county argued that it was better to concentrate the limited funds available for black education on primary schools, where more black students could be aided. The Supreme Court unanimously rejected a 14th Amendment challenge to this county's activity as promoting separate and unequal, because the justices deemed inequality reasonable under the circumstances. The court thereby approved segregated schools. As always in the *Plessy* era, much depended upon the justices' personal views, and their views reflected white attitudes. Northern whites agreed with Southern whites that the Southern black population needed only a limited education. At the all-black Tuskegee Institute (see page 45), the curriculum focused upon industrial education and avoided academic subjects. President McKinley visited Tuskegee and praised that focus and the school administrators who 'evidently do not believe in attempting the unattainable'.

Cumming was yet another demonstration that the South, with the collusion of a Supreme Court that gave federal sanction to the Jim Crow laws, was able to ignore the Reconstruction era civil rights legislation and constitutional amendments. The *Williams* case would show the Supreme Court giving an unfavourable interpretation to the 15th Amendment.

> ## Who was 'black'?
>
> Each state's definition of how much 'Negro' blood made a person 'black' varied. In 1910, Virginia switched from the 'single-grandparent' definition that had made Homer Plessy 'black' in Louisiana during the 1890s, and declared that a black great-great-great grandparent made a person black. In 1930, Virginia said anyone with 'any Negro blood at all' was black – the so-called 'one-drop' measure. Louisiana had become more moderate by then: it was only those who *looked* black who *were* black. In 1887, Ida B. Wells (see page 47) wrote about a Tennessee white man who could not get a licence to marry a black woman, so he cut her finger and sucked her blood so he could say he had 'Negro blood'.

The Supreme Court and black disfranchisement

The Supreme Court did nothing to uphold the 15th Amendment, which had said that black males should have the vote. This was not surprising: even Northerners had long been reluctant to accept black voting. The Republican platform of 1868 had supported the vote for Southern blacks but insisted that 'the question of suffrage in the loyal States properly belongs to the people of those States'. During the 1880s and the 1890s, the Southern states adopted complex registration laws and literacy tests that made it difficult for black voters (see page 36) and decreased the number of elected black officials. Such ruses were not specifically prohibited in the 15th Amendment. Disfranchisement was done carefully: for example, during the 1901–2 Virginia disfranchising convention, one official said his mission was 'to discriminate to the very extremity of permissible action under the limitations of the Federal Constitution, with a view to the elimination of every negro voter who can be gotten rid of, legally'.

Williams v. Mississippi (1898)

In *Williams v. Mississippi*, a black defendant challenged his indictment for murder on the ground that Mississippi unconstitutionally excluded black Americans from grand juries. Under Mississippi law, jurors had to be qualified voters, and Williams challenged the suffrage qualifications in Mississippi's 1890 constitution, claiming that they had been adopted for purposes of discrimination and that they conferred excessive discretion on registrars. The Supreme Court ruled that the 1890 Mississippi state constitution was not discriminatory when it required voters to pass a literacy test and to pay the poll tax.

Supreme Court rulings such as *Williams* did not initiate or even promote discrimination against black Americans. Rather, the rulings played a confirmatory role. Even if the Supreme Court had ruled other than it did in *Williams*, there was no way that the federal government could have protected black voters. Northern whites had lost interest in black Americans and even if they had not, the federal government as yet lacked the necessary national bureaucratic apparatus to monitor and enforce any voting rights legislation.

Why Southern whites were able to restore white supremacy

White Southerners found it relatively easy to erode black freedoms after 1877 because:

- The Republican Party had been the main support and refuge for black Americans, but Republican voters were predominantly Northerners and Northerners were tired of the South's 'black question'. Indeed, an influx of black migrants into the North made Northerners far more sympathetic to Southern white sensibilities, while Southern white Republicans had grown increasingly unsympathetic toward black Republicans.
- The Southern black vote grew less important to the Republican Party when it gained more votes in Northern states.
- As bitter memories of the Civil War receded, Northern whites grew more anxious to effect a reconciliation with the white Southerners, who shared their common ancestry, history and religion. In 1876, Rutherford B. Hayes won the presidency on a platform of sectional reconciliation.
- The acquisition of an American empire furthered sectional reconciliation. Southerners fought alongside Northerners in the Spanish–American War of 1898. In that war, the United States gained Spanish territories with non-white populations to whom few Americans wished to grant equality.
- The federal government wanted to concentrate on the North rather than racial problems in the South, and neither presidents, Congress nor the Supreme Court sought to ensure black rights under the 14th and 15th Amendments.
- Supreme Court rulings generally reflected popular opinion, and even if the Supreme Court had sought to oppose the rise of Jim Crow, it lacked any power of enforcement. In *Giles v. Harris* (1903), the Court admitted that even if disfranchisement devices were unconstitutional, it was powerless to provide remedies. Furthermore, the *Plessy*-era race decisions were, according to the historian Michael Klarman (2004), 'not blatant nullifications of post-Civil War constitutional amendments designed to secure racial equality. On the contrary, *Plessy*-era race decisions were plausible interpretations of conventional legal sources: text, original intent, precedent, and custom.'
- After the Republicans concentrated on the North, the Democratic Party dominated the South and found it easy to assert white supremacy because black subordination and separation were increasingly viewed as the norm

in the rest of the United States. In 1896, a Boston newspaper covered the exclusion of a black bishop from a white hotel, saying that social equality between the races 'appears more unthinkable today than ever'. Northern schools were increasingly segregated in the early 1900s, for example, in Alton, Illinois, East Orange, New Jersey, Wichita, Kansas, and Oxford, Pennsylvania.

- Southern whites used violence and intimidation against the black population. For example, when black sugarcane workers in Louisiana went on strike for fair wages in 1887, over 30 of them were shot dead by white strikebreakers and private police forces. Lynchings were common (see page 28).
- The Constitution gave the Southern states power over voting, education, transport and law enforcement, which enabled segregation to spread and continue.
- The end of slavery had left former slaves with freedom of movement, but black activism was circumscribed by material and educational considerations. First, litigation was costly and most black Americans were poor. Second, relatively few black Americans possessed the level of education that inspired the confidence and ability to combat racism, whether through litigation or mass campaigns. Third, black schools and colleges depended upon Northern white fundraising, and some black leaders feared militancy might alienate donors.

Summary diagram: The response of the Supreme Court

Ruling	Support for Jim Crow
Slaughter-House Cases 1873	States have authority over civil rights
Civil Rights Cases 1883	1875 Civil Rights Act unconstitutional
Plessy v. Ferguson 1896	Separate but equal was not against the 14th Amendment
Williams v. Mississippi 1896	Literacy tests and poll tax acceptable
Cumming v. Richmond County Board of Education 1899	De jure school segregation acceptable

Black resistance

▶ *How and with what results did black Americans resist Jim Crow?*

The black response to the deterioration of their condition in the South varied. Most just accepted the situation; others were more proactive and left the South (see Chapter 4) or engaged in some other form of protest.

Protest versus accommodationism

In the late nineteenth century, some black leaders thought it better to quietly accommodate oneself to segregation in the South. **Accommodationists** believed that the best way forward was to accept segregation and make the most of economic opportunities through the development of black educational and vocational skills. The most famous accommodationist was **Booker T. Washington**. His stance was considered demeaning by members of the black elite, especially in the North, but given the situation in the South, Washington and the accommodationists had little choice. As it was, Southern white supremacists thought he sought too much.

In contrast, other black Americans held 'indignation meetings', formed equal rights leagues, filed lawsuits to combat discrimination, and boycotted newly segregated public transport in 25 states. One of the most vociferous and active of protesters was Ida B. Wells, who gained fame through her opposition to lynching.

Black reactions to lynching

Most historians believe the number of lynchings increased after the end of Reconstruction. Between 1880 and 1900, there were 1678 known lynchings of black Americans, mostly in the South. Lynchings revealed a great deal about race relations. Law enforcement officials, politicians, editors and jurors colluded and/or participated in lynchings and those responsible for the crime were never brought to justice. This suggests widespread support for the act of lynching and demonstrates how black Americans had no legal protection. Those who were lynched were usually accused of rape. Southern whites contended that the end of slavery had allowed the reversion of black males to savagery and made them desirous to demonstrate their social equality through sexual relations with white women. While Southern whites defended lynching as a necessary defence of Southern white women against black rapists (that 'black rapist' myth was also used to justify segregation and economic discrimination), lynching was also another means of race control.

Many black organisations hesitated to campaign against lynching in the 1880s. First, they were already on the defensive against accusations of the high black crime rate (the judicial system treated white criminals more leniently so statistics suggested that black criminality was greater than white). Second, such

 KEY TERM

Accommodationists
Those who favoured initial black concentration upon economic improvement rather than upon social, political and legal equality.

 KEY FIGURE

Booker T. Washington (1856–1915)
Born into slavery in Virginia, he emphasised that black economic advancement rather than confrontation was the key to progress. He established the Tuskegee Institute in Alabama. Its curriculum focused upon practical skills. He was recognised as America's premier black spokesman and several presidents consulted him, although other black leaders such as W.E.B. Du Bois opposed his accommodationism and advocated protest.

a campaign could get black males killed in the South. However, those black activists who chose to protest against lynching in the late nineteenth and early twentieth century represent, according to the historian Adam Fairclough (2001), 'the starting point of the modern civil rights struggle – the beginning of the fightback against white supremacy'.

> ## Urban lynching
>
> Lynchings usually occurred in rural areas and small towns. The preferred mode of murderous race control in urban areas was the race riot, as in 1906 when black males in Atlanta were reported in the press as being 'uppity', which inspired thousands of whites to enter Atlanta's black district and kill around 30 black Americans.

Ida B. Wells

Born into slavery in Mississippi, Ida B. Wells was one of the most famous black activists of the late nineteenth century. When in 1883 a white train conductor tried to drag her out of the first-class carriage for which she had paid, she bit his hand, left the train, sued the railroad company and won $200. Following another eviction in 1884 she sued again, winning $500. However, in 1887 the Tennessee Supreme Court decided in favour of the railroad company's appeal. 'Oh God', asked Wells, 'is there no justice in this land for us?'

The anti-lynching articles that Wells wrote for black publications from 1889 earned her the nickname 'Princess of the Press'. 'Nobody in this section of the country believes the old threadbare lie that Negro men rape white women', she raged in the *Memphis Free Speech*, which she co-owned. Wells considered the motive of lynching to be to 'get rid of Negroes who were acquiring wealth and property and thus keep the race terrorized'.

Wells' writing and speeches were highly effective. She did not hold back when talking about the horrors of lynching. She described one in Paris, Texas, where the accused rapist was poked with red-hot irons for 50 minutes, doused with kerosene and set on fire. The accused then tried to get away from the fire and was twice put back in. Wells recounted how the 10,000-strong audience fought for his bones, buttons and teeth as souvenirs. Souvenir-seeking audiences were not unusual. Sometimes, crowds of spectators arrived by a special train to watch a lynching. Occasionally, schoolchildren were given the day off to observe the spectacle. In her writing, Wells played effectively upon basic human emotions, including sympathy and self-interest. When Wells' condemnation of lynching aroused hostility, she moved North to Chicago, although she noted that 'lynching mania has spread throughout the North and Middle West' as a result of black migration from the South (see Chapter 4).

Ida B. Wells

1862	Born into a slave family in Mississippi
1884–7	Litigated against railroad car segregation in Tennessee
1891	Fired after several years' teaching because of criticism of inadequate segregated schools
1892	Forced to leave Tennessee and move North after publishing an anti-lynching article
1895	Married black Chicago lawyer Ferdinand Barnett
1908	Called for a national black organisation after riots and lynchings in Springfield, Illinois
1909	Founding member of NAACP (see page 48)
1913	Helped found Chicago's first black women's suffrage club, which assisted the election of Chicago's first black Alderman, Oscar de Priest (1915)
1917	Nominated delegate of Marcus Garvey's UNIA (see page 61) to the Paris Peace Conference but her passport was withdrawn after she protested the hanging of 12 black soldiers for participating in a riot in Houston, Texas
1918–19	Publicised post-war race riots, causing federal agencies to label her 'subversive'
1920s	Helped establish Chicago branch of A. Philip Randolph's Brotherhood of Sleeping Car Porters and Maids (see page 63)
1931	Died

Wells was important because of her lifelong, wide-ranging activism, particularly her publicising of the evils of lynching. She helped to establish community institutions and local and national organisations that helped both poor and middle-class blacks. She helped to empower black women by encouraging them to join organisations. Her favourite strategies of litigation, journalism and organisation were adopted by subsequent activists.

SOURCE E

From an 1893 Boston lecture by Ida B. Wells. Quoted in Shirley Wilson Logan, *With Pen and Voice*, Southern Illinois University Press, 1995, p. 85.

Repeated attacks on the life, liberty and happiness of any citizen … are attacks on distinctive American institutions … imperilling the foundation of government, law and order … The baby daughter of Tom Moss, too young to express how she misses her father, toddles to the wardrobe, seizes the legs of [his] trousers … hugs and kisses them with evident delight and stretches up her little hands to be taken up into the arms which will never more clasp his daughter. His wife holds Tom Moss, Jr., in arms, upon whose unconscious baby face the tears fall thick and fast when she is thinking of the sad fate of the father he will never see, and of the two helpless children who cling to her for the support she cannot give … [Tom Moss had been a] peaceable, law-abiding citizen …

What techniques are used in Source E in order to persuade a majority-white audience that lynching should be stopped?

Wells considered her black contemporaries a 'disorganized mass' who shared the blame for the post-Reconstruction deterioration in the black situation because of their passivity. She considered organisations the way forward and played an important part in the establishment of several of them, including the National Association for the Advancement of Colored People (NAACP).

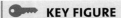 According to Source F, what is the situation of black Americans in the South, how can it be explained, and how could it be remedied?

SOURCE F

From an 1891 Ida B. Wells article in the *Memphis Free Speech*, describing the leaders of the National Afro-American League at the meeting in Knoxville, Tennessee. Quoted in Linda McMurray, *The Life of Ida B. Wells*, Oxford University Press, 1999, p. 121.

A handful of men, with no report of work accomplished, no one in the field to spread it, no plan of work laid out – no intelligent direction – meet and by their child's play illustrate in their own doings the truth of the saying that Negroes have no capacity for organization. Meanwhile a whole race is lynched, proscribed, intimidated, deprived of its political and civil rights, herded into boxes (by courtesy called separate cars) … and we sit tamely by without using the only means – that of thorough organisation and earnest work to prevent it. No wonder the world at large spits upon us with impunity.

KEY FIGURE

W.E.B. Du Bois (1868–1963)

A Massachusetts-born academic who published many criticisms of discrimination and helped establish the NAACP in order to combat it. He increasingly despaired of the USA, sympathised with the Soviet Union in the Cold War, and in 1961 emigrated to Africa and advocated international black unity.

After Wells' death in 1931, the black academic **W.E.B. Du Bois** credited her with beginning 'the awakening of the conscience of the nation', saying her 'work has easily been forgotten because it was taken up on a much larger scale by the NAACP and carried to greater success'. Although Wells failed to get the federal government to legislate against lynching, she put the issue in the public eye. For many years after her death, Wells was virtually forgotten outside Chicago, until greater black militancy and feminism revived interest in her life and career.

The National Association for the Advancement of Colored People (NAACP)

Established in 1909, the National Association for the Advancement of Colored People (NAACP) said it aimed to make America's 11 million black population economically, intellectually, politically and socially free and equal. The NAACP was a long-lasting and effective organisation.

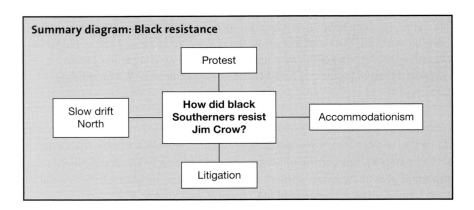
Summary diagram: Black resistance

Chapter summary

The Southern white backlash against Reconstruction led Southern state legislatures to promote black inequality through laws that segregated public places such as railroads (as in Florida in 1887) and made it difficult for blacks to vote through devices such as poll taxes, literacy and income qualifications, and grandfather clauses.

The spread of segregation was supported by the Supreme Court in a series of decisions that began with the ruling in the Civil Rights Cases (1883) that the 1875 Civil Rights Act was unconstitutional. Further condoning of segregation came with the *Plessy v. Ferguson* (1896) ruling, which declared the 'separate but equal' doctrine. In *Williams v. Mississippi* (1898), the court ruled that literacy tests and the poll tax were not unconstitutional, and in *Cumming v. Board of Education* (1899), it approved segregated schools.

Whites were able to restore white supremacy in the South because of white racism and/or apathy across the nation, the powers reserved to the states in the American Constitution, and the poverty and poor education of the majority of black Americans. Some black Southerners sought a better life outside the region, some were content to accept segregation, some railed against it. None of these black solutions proved particularly successful.

Refresher questions

1 What methods did white Southerners use to control black Americans in the late nineteenth century?

2 Was the 1887 Florida law on railroads revolutionary?

3 In what public places were blacks and whites segregated in the late nineteenth century?

4 What race theories were popular by 1900?

5 What arguments did white Southerners use against black voting?

6 How did Southern whites stop black people voting?

7 What was the significance of the Supreme Court's 1883 ruling on the Civil Rights Cases?

8 Upon what grounds did Justice Harlan oppose that ruling?

9 What was the significance of *Plessy v. Ferguson*?

10 What did the Supreme Court rule in *Williams v. Mississippi*?

11 Why did Southern whites find it relatively easy to erode black freedoms after 1877?

12 In what ways did black Americans resist the imposition of Jim Crow?

13 Why was Ida B. Wells significant?

Question practice

ESSAY QUESTIONS

1 How accurate is it to say that the Supreme Court played the crucial role in the spread of the Jim Crow laws in the last two decades of the nineteenth century?

2 'The Jim Crow laws did not introduce any totally new system of Southern race control.' How far do you agree with this statement?

SOURCE ANALYSIS QUESTIONS

1 Study Source C (page 38). Assess the value of Source C for revealing Justice Harlan's view of race and the attitude of the federal government to the deteriorating position of black Southerners in the last two decades of the nineteenth century. Explain your answer, using the source, the information given about its origin and your own knowledge about the historical context.

2 Study Source D (page 39). Assess the value of Source D for revealing the situation of black Americans in the South in the years 1865–85, and the attitude of white Southerners to that situation. Explain your answer, using the source, the information given about its origin and your own knowledge about the historical context.

CHAPTER 4

The changing geographical distribution of black Americans, c.1850–c.1930

Prior to the American Civil War, the vast majority of black Americans lived in the South as slaves. After the Civil War, freed slaves began to migrate North and West. In the early twentieth century, the slow drift North turned into a flood. The result was the development of large black communities in Northern cities such as New York, Chicago and Detroit, and Western cities such as Los Angeles. This large-scale population movement was known as the Great Migration. It was an improvement upon life in the South for many black Americans, but their presence in Northern cities alienated white residents.

The changing geographical distribution of black Americans before 1930 is covered in this chapter in sections on:

★ Black geographical distribution in the nineteenth century

★ The Great Migration

★ Case study: Harlem

Key dates

1865	13th Amendment abolished slavery	1919	Race riots in Chicago and 24 other American cities
1877	Radical Reconstruction ended, Jim Crow era began	1920s	Harlem Renaissance
1879	20,000 black 'Exodusters' migrated to Kansas	1920	Cotton prices slumped
		1921	Black community destroyed in Tulsa, Oklahoma
1892	Ida B. Wells forced to migrate North	1925	A. Philip Randolph established labour union for railroad porters
1900	Serious race riots in New York City		
1905	Mass migration into Harlem started		UNIA membership peaked
1908	Serious race riot in Springfield, Illinois	1935	Great race riot in Harlem

1 Black geographical distribution in the nineteenth century

▶ *Why and with what results did black Southerners migrate before 1900?*

In 1850, the total population of the United States was around 23 million people. A few black Americans were free: some of them lived in the South, more lived in the North. However, most of the 4 million black Americans lived in the South and were enslaved. Slave mobility was restricted because of superior white force and the high visibility and limited or non-existent education of escaped slaves, but some enterprising slaves such as Frederick Douglass (see page 14) managed to escape to free states in the North.

When slavery began to disintegrate under the pressure of the Civil War, the migration of former slaves became an issue. While black Southerners dreamt of a better life away from the South and its memories, Northern whites feared a black influx into the North. Such fears were partly responsible for a **draft** riot in New York City in 1863.

Freedom after the Civil War

When slavery ended and Radical Reconstruction commenced, the incentive for black migration decreased. Not only was life in the South improving, but it was not easy for black people to leave: most had only basic agricultural skills and were illiterate. This made migration to Northern cities a frightening prospect, especially as Northern employers and unions excluded black labour.

When federal troops were withdrawn from the South in 1877 and Reconstruction came to an end, the development of Jim Crow accelerated migration northwards. For example,

- In 1879, 20,000 black Mississippian '**Exodusters**' left the South and went North to seek a better life in Kansas.
- After her attacks on lynching caused a white mob to burn down the office of her Memphis newspaper, Ida B. Wells migrated North to live in Chicago in 1892 (see page 47).
- Between 1880 and 1900, black migration from the South led Chicago's black population to rise from 6480 to 30,150 and New York City's from 65,000 to 100,000.

The significance of the slow drift North

Contemporaries recognised the significance of black migration from the South. It was investigated in 1880 by a Senate committee, concerned that 'it is currently alleged that they are induced to do so by the unjust and cruel conduct

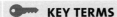

KEY TERMS

Draft Compulsory government call-up into the armed forces, known as conscription in Britain.

Exodusters Post-Reconstruction black migrants from the South to Kansas.

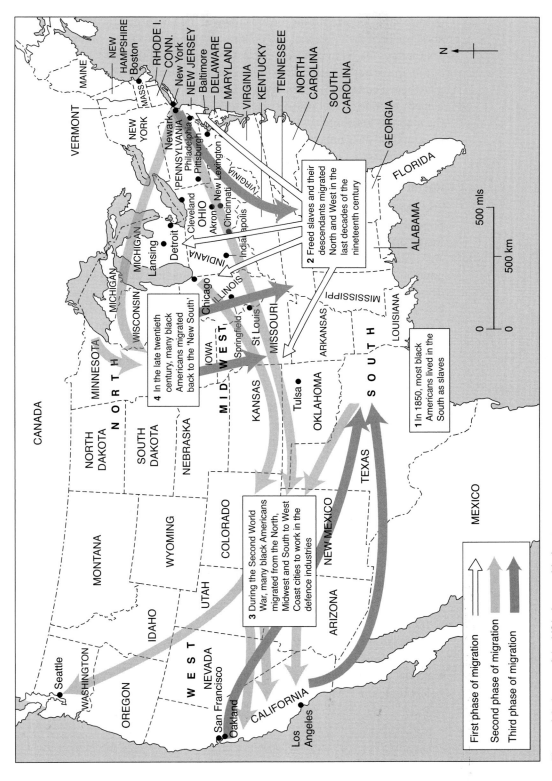

The following labels appear on the map:

N

CANADA

MAINE
NEW HAMPSHIRE
VERMONT
RHODE I.
CONN.
Boston
MASS.
NEW YORK
NEW JERSEY
New York
Newark
DELAWARE
MARYLAND
Baltimore
PENNSYLVANIA
Philadelphia
Pittsburgh
VIRGINIA
New Lexington
KENTUCKY
TENNESSEE
NORTH CAROLINA
SOUTH CAROLINA
GEORGIA
FLORIDA
ALABAMA

Cleveland
Akron
Cincinnati
OHIO
INDIANA
Indianapolis
Detroit
Lansing
MICHIGAN
WISCONSIN
Chicago
ILLINOIS
Springfield
St Louis
MISSOURI
MISSISSIPPI
LOUISIANA
ARKANSAS

N O R T H
M I D W E S T
S O U T H
W E S T

MINNESOTA
NORTH DAKOTA
SOUTH DAKOTA
NEBRASKA
IOWA
KANSAS
OKLAHOMA
Tulsa
TEXAS
NEW MEXICO
ARIZONA

MONTANA
WYOMING
COLORADO
UTAH
IDAHO
NEVADA
OREGON
WASHINGTON
Seattle
San Francisco
Oakland
CALIFORNIA
Los Angeles

MEXICO

500 mls
500 km
0
0

1 In 1850, most black Americans lived in the South as slaves

2 Freed slaves and their descendants migrated North and West in the last decades of the nineteenth century

3 During the Second World War, many black Americans migrated from the North, Midwest and South to West Coast cities to work in the defence industries

4 In the late twentieth century, many black Americans migrated back to the 'New South'

Key:
First phase of migration
Second phase of migration
Third phase of migration

Figure 4.1 A map of the USA showing black migration.

of their white fellow-citizens towards them in the South, and by the denial or abridgment of their personal and political rights and privileges'. Many white Southerners feared that the loss of black labour threatened the economy of the South. In contrast, the migrants were optimistic that migration North would give them a better life – and it often did. Another benefit was that the migration helped generate greater race consciousness and civil rights activism. However, the migrants encountered racial hostility in the North and West. The changing geographical distribution of black Americans had transplanted Southern racial tensions into other regions.

Racial tensions in the North

The *Tribune*, published in New Lexington, Ohio, encapsulated much Northern popular feeling when it bemoaned the 'horde of barbarian' black migrants. Rising black populations resulted in riots in many Northern cities such as New York. Although black Americans constituted only 1 per cent of New York's population between 1880 and 1900, white resentment at their presence was demonstrated in the great race riot of 1900. The wife of a black man was being bothered by a white man. The black man mortally wounded the white man with a knife. The white man was a police officer who had mistaken the wife for a prostitute. Within days, the *New York Times* recorded, a 1000-strong white mob 'started to clean the side streets of Negroes'. The predominantly Irish police force encouraged them. Black people fought back and the violence continued throughout the summer. In that same summer, a white mob in Akron, Ohio, attacked a black migrant accused of assaulting a four-year-old white girl. One of the worst riots occurred in Abraham Lincoln's birthplace, Springfield, Illinois, in 1908. By that time, black Americans were as likely to be lynched in the North and the West as in the South (see page 28).

Northern white methods of race control

Whites in the North had tactics other than violence for the control of the growing black population:

- city councils made black voting difficult: for example, in 1897, Boston's City Council redrew electoral district boundaries in order to dilute the black vote
- by 1891, 30 states in the North and West had adopted the secret ballot, partly because it was a means of preventing illiterate black voters from exercising the franchise
- white landlords and landowners usually refused to sell or rent property to blacks in areas inhabited by whites
- school boards promoted *de facto* segregation
- labour unions excluded black workers.

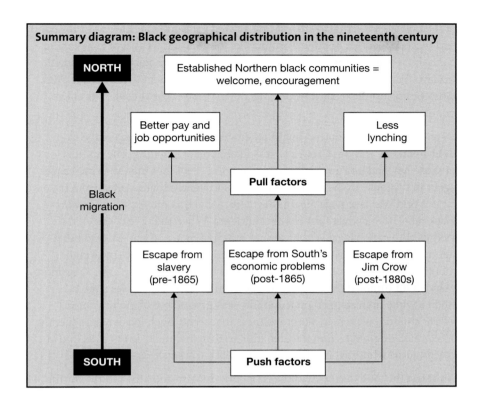

Summary diagram: Black geographical distribution in the nineteenth century

The Great Migration

▶ *What were the causes and consequences of the Great Migration?*

Between 1880 and 1910, 500,000 black Americans left the South. However, the 6 million who stayed constituted a large majority of the nation's black population, so the drift North was slow in the late nineteenth century. Before 1900, black migration was relatively small scale in comparison to the dramatic population movement that became known as the **Great Migration**. Between 1910 and 1970, over 6 million black people migrated from the rural South to the cities of the North, Midwest and West. In 1910, 89 per cent of black Americans lived in the South, but by 1970, the figure was only 53 per cent.

Causes of the Great Migration

There were many '**push and pull**' factors behind the Great Migration. Amongst the 'push' factors was the excessive dependence of the economy of some areas of the South upon the cotton crop. Overproduction led to frequent slumps in cotton prices, for example, in 1913–15 and in 1920. That meant lower wages for black cotton pickers. There were also years in which harvests were poor because

 **KEY TERMS**

Great Migration Between c.1910 and c.1970, over 6 million black Americans migrated from the South to the North or the West. Some historians subdivide this into two separate phases of migration.

Push and pull When people move to a different place, it is usually because there are attractions that pull them toward a new life, and factors that push them away from the old life.

of the boll weevil. This tiny insect first arrived in Texas from Mexico in 1892 and had reached Georgia and the Carolinas by the 1920s. It was capable of wiping out half the cotton crop. A ruined harvest caused 50,000 black cotton workers to leave South Carolina for the North between November 1922 and May 1923. One county lost 3600 black Americans in that time – 22 per cent of its entire population.

KEY TERM

Debt peonage White employers kept black farmers in virtual slavery by keeping them in debt, for example, by forcing them to pay inflated prices for materials such as seed.

Departure from the South brought other advantages, including escape from **debt peonage** and Jim Crow, and less likelihood of lynching. The numbers of those lynched had gradually fallen since the 1890s, but then they increased again in response to the increased black assertiveness that resulted from the First World War (see page 59). In May 1918, a Georgia mob lynched eleven black men after a white farmer was murdered. When the wife of one of the victims threatened legal action, several hundred men and one woman hung her upside down, doused her in gasoline, and set her alight. She was eight months pregnant, so one of the mob slashed her stomach open and, a reporter noted, 'Out tumbled the prematurely born child. Two feeble cries it gave … [then a white man stepped on it and] life was ground out of the tiny form.' White children were held aloft to witness that scene. Such incidents frequently accelerated migration from the area (that in turn invariably led to a decline in lynchings as whites worried about losing black workers).

Amongst the 'pull' factors was the economic dynamism of the North. During the late nineteenth and early twentieth centuries, the economy and society of the United States were revolutionised by rapid industrialisation and the great urban growth that resulted from it. Most of this change occurred outside the South. For example, between 1880 and 1920, New York City's population rose from 1.2 million to 5.6 million, Chicago's from 500,000 to 2.7 million, and Detroit's from 16,360 to 1 million. These cities seemed to offer black Americans more opportunities for economic advancement than the rural South, where 90 per cent of black Americans still resided in 1900. Detroit had a 300 per cent population increase, but 2400 per cent black population increase (see Table 4.1).

Table 4.1 Detroit population figures 1910–30

Year	Total population	Black population
1910	465,766	5,741
1920	993,675	40,838
1930	1,568,662	120,066

The North promised better employment opportunities and wages. This was especially the case during the First World War, when a factory worker in the North could earn up to $3.25 daily, compared to 75 cents for agricultural work in the South. The war disrupted travel and transportation and caused immigration from Europe to fall, but American industrial expansion proceeded apace. Northern employers were desperate for labour so they actively recruited black workers. Between 1915 and 1925, 1.25 million black Americans migrated from the South to the North and settled in cities such as New York, Cleveland, Detroit, Indianapolis, Philadelphia and Pittsburgh. The exodus was such that Florida Governor Sidney Catts begged black Americans to remain in the state. Migrants sent letters from the North to Southern friends and relations, telling of more pay, less prejudice and fewer lynchings. Such letters encouraged further migration. One Mississippi black man who migrated to Chicago during the First World War said, 'I should have been here 20 years ago. I just begin to feel like a man.' Black people could vote in the North, and they began to gain representation and greater local influence. For example, Oscar De Priest (1871–1951) gained election as Chicago's first black alderman in 1915. In 1920, he became the first black American to be elected to the US Congress in the twentieth century. The NAACP opined that 'the greatest significance of this migration is the increased political power of black men in America'. A final 'pull' factor was that a black community, once well established in any city outside the South, naturally attracted more immigrants. Harlem was a classic case of this (see page 60).

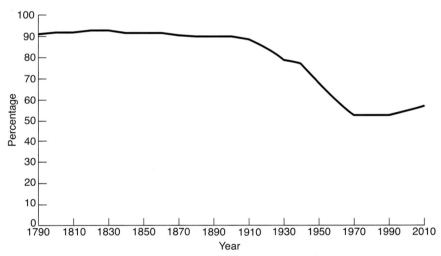

Figure 4.2 The percentage of black Americans living in the American South, 1790–2010.

Problems arising from the Great Migration

Migration to the North brought some problems. Departure from the South meant separation from friends, family and familiar surroundings. In the North, racial prejudice sometimes made it difficult to obtain employment, the cost of living was higher and urban accommodation was often hard to find, crowded and expensive. Northern **ghettos** had high rates of tuberculosis, juvenile delinquency and crime. In a 1989 study, the sociologist Carole Marks emphasised such problems, in contrast to the many historians who for years had automatically assumed life was better in the North.

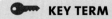

KEY TERM

Ghettos Areas inhabited mostly or solely by (usually poor) members of a particular ethnicity, nationality or religion.

The greatest problem arising from the Great Migration was increased racial tension. The black influx worsened race relations in Northern cities. Northerners were inspired to join the revitalised Ku Klux Klan (see pages 26–8), membership of which rose from 100,000 in 1921 to 4 million in 1924. Small, pre-war black communities had not always aroused fear and antagonism, but the influx increased the visibility of those communities and whites responded by trying to separate the races. As a result, black people were crowded into areas such as Harlem in New York City and Chicago's South Side. In 1911, Baltimore passed its first residential segregation law, and many Northern cities soon followed suit. A primarily Southern race relations problem had become a national one. Race riots grew more common, for example, in East St Louis, Illinois, in 1917. Thousands of black Southerners from Louisiana had found employment in East St Louis at factories, foundries, meatpacking houses, railroads and stockyards. White workers opposed the influx, especially when black migrants were used as strikebreakers. White gangs began to attack black residents and women and children also joined in this 1917 riot, in which over 40 blacks and 80 whites died.

After the First World War ended in November 1918 and black and white soldiers returned to the urban centres of the North and Midwest, the white soldiers resented what they perceived to be black competition for jobs and housing. There was also growing white resentment at the increase in black political influence in local elections. Racial jealousies led to race riots in which hundreds were killed in 25 cities across the nation. The worst riots were in Chicago.

The Chicago riots, 1919

Around 50,000 black Americans had moved into Chicago between 1910 and 1920. White residents particularly disliked their moving into white neighbourhoods. Between 1917 and 1921, 58 homemade bombs were thrown at the homes of black residents who had dared to move into white areas.

In 1919, a fifteen-year-old black boy accidentally crossed the dividing line on a segregated beach that extended into Lake Michigan. When whites stoned the boy, black Chicagoans protested and were arrested by the police. During two weeks of rioting, Irish and Polish workers supported by the police and the military, attacked black ghetto residents and committed appalling atrocities: 15 whites and 25 blacks were killed, 500 people were injured, and the homes of over 1000 black families were destroyed when white mobs set fire to them. The black community fought back.

KEY FIGURE

Walter White (1893–1955)

Born in Atlanta, Georgia, he joined the small staff of the NAACP in 1918 and led the organisation 1931–55. He exploited his white skin and blonde hair to work undercover with the Ku Klux Klan and expose their activities. He lobbied Congress for anti-lynching legislation and spoke out eloquently against discrimination.

The black American who was White

NAACP official **Walter White**, who considered himself black but looked white, was deliberately shot at by a black man as he walked through Chicago's South Side ghetto during the 1919 race riot: 'I ducked as a bullet whanged into the side of the building exactly where my head had been a fraction of a second before.'

A report commissioned by the Governor of Illinois called for desegregation. It blamed the riots on the unfair treatment of blacks by white law enforcers, ghetto living conditions, and the increasing black 'race consciousness' that developed with urban life.

The Tulsa race riot, 1921

In the late nineteenth century, Oklahoma offered plentiful cheap land and the greater political freedom that arose from territory status. This attracted both black and white migrants from the South. As many of the whites were former slaveholders from the South, lynching was not uncommon. When Oklahoma became a state in 1907, it introduced Jim Crow laws. A 1916 ordinance that made residential segregation mandatory was declared unconstitutional by the Supreme Court in 1917, but the ruling was ignored. Not surprisingly, many black Americans sought separation with as much enthusiasm as whites did. By 1910, black migrants had established 25 all-black towns in Oklahoma.

Race relations deteriorated after the First World War, when returning black veterans, who had been told that they were fighting to make the world safe for democracy, grew more assertive. One of the biggest clashes was in the city of Tulsa, Oklahoma. The Greenwood District of Tulsa contained the wealthiest black community in the United States and its main street was known as the 'Black Wall Street' (see page 64). In 1921, Tulsa was agog with rumours of a lynching after a young black male supposedly assaulted a young white female. An armed black mob, ready to defend the supposed assailant, inspired whites to arm themselves. Tensions rose and a white mob attacked the Greenwood District. Around 10,000 black people were left homeless after over 1000 black homes were burned down. It has been estimated that as many as 300 black people died, and as many as 800 white people were injured.

Compensation for the Tulsa riots

In 1996, the Oklahoma state legislature commissioned a report on the riots. Published in 2001, the report recommended some compensation for survivors and those affected by the riots. The black community was disappointed by the level of compensation.

The 1920s

Although lynchings declined across the nation after 1920, riots such as those in Chicago and Tulsa had demonstrated how migration and war could be a catalyst for change – sometimes positive, sometimes negative. The riots led to further racial tension, as shown in the consolidation of *de facto* segregation. For example, in 1921, Chicago **realtors** adopted 'restrictive covenants' that prohibited white buyers from reselling or renting to black people. Huge black ghettos were

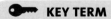

KEY TERM

Realtors Estate agents who deal in real estate (property) sale and rental.

developing in cities such as Chicago and Detroit (see page 56), because black Americans could not rent or buy housing elsewhere else. School enrolment naturally followed housing patterns and some cities even adopted school segregation as official policy. For example, 25 per cent of Philadelphia's black children attended schools officially designated 'Negro'. Wilfred Little, brother of Malcolm X (see page 131), described black lives in Lansing, Michigan, in the 1920s as 'the same as being in Mississippi … When you went into the courts and when you had to deal with the police, it was the same as being down South'.

Summary diagram: The Great Migration

Advantages	Disadvantages
No Jim Crow	White racism
Less lynching	Race riots, violence
More political influence	Discriminatory law enforcement
More jobs	White racism could make it difficult to get jobs
Better pay	Higher cost of living
Established black communities	Juvenile delinquency
Segregation = developing race consciousness, better in one's own community	Segregation = poorer schools and housing

Case study: Harlem

▶ *What was the significance of Harlem for black America?*

The impact and significance of the changing geographical distribution of the black American population are well illustrated by the history of the Harlem area of New York City.

Mass migration into Harlem from 1905

There had been black residents of Harlem from the seventeenth century, and by the late nineteenth century their numbers had reached tens of thousands. Most were migrants from the South. However, it was after 1905 that the mass black migration to the area began. This was because:

- a price crash made property cheap, so landlords were desperate for tenants of any colour
- black real estate entrepreneur Philip Payton Jr brought in black tenants through his Afro-American Realty Company
- many black New Yorkers sought new accommodation because of race riots in areas of New York City they had previously favoured, and because some black tenements had been demolished in order to make way for a railroad station.

The mass migration to Harlem after 1905 accelerated further during the First World War (1914–18). As American industry worked flat out to produce war materiel, tens of thousands of black migrants from Virginia, North Carolina, South Carolina and Georgia travelled to Harlem on the East Coast railroad line and sought employment in munitions factories. The well-established black community attracted further migration, mostly from the South but also from the West Indies. Between 1890 and 1920, New York City's black population increased from 70,000 to 200,000. As Harlem's black population grew, the white population shrank: between 1920 and 1930, nearly 100,000 black migrants arrived in Harlem, but over 100,000 white people left there.

Table 4.2 The percentage of black residents of Central Harlem 1910–50

Year	Percentage
1910	10 per cent
1920	32 per cent
1930	70 per cent
1950	98 per cent

The significance of Harlem

The concentration of large numbers of black Americans in an urban area generated a sense of togetherness and empowerment, as demonstrated when Harlem developed into a centre for black civil rights advocates. The Abyssinian Baptist Church in Harlem provided the location, money and leadership for civic clubs in which politics was discussed. By 1910, the NAACP (see page 48) was active in Harlem, and in 1916, Harlem became the headquarters of Marcus Garvey's United Negro Improvement Association (see below). Leading black activists such as A. Philip Randolph (see page 63) and the academic W.E.B. Du Bois (see page 48) lived in Harlem during the 1920s and the area developed into a great black cultural centre. During the 'Harlem **Renaissance**' of the 1920s, black intellectuals such as Du Bois and the poet Langston Hughes, and great jazz musicians such as 'Duke' Ellington, were active and much admired within the black community. Indeed, black music and dance ensured that Harlem's theatres, nightclubs and speakeasies attracted fashionable white patrons.

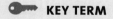 **KEY TERM**

Renaissance A revival or exceptionally productive period for culture.

Marcus Garvey and UNIA

Jamaican-born Marcus Garvey (1881–1940) established the United Negro Improvement Association (UNIA) in Jamaica in 1914. He emigrated to the United States in 1916 and settled in Harlem, convinced it was the best place for the headquarters of an ambitious black organisation that hoped to encourage the black population of the world to 'take Africa, organize it, develop it, arm it, and make it the defender of Negroes the world over'. His UNIA won the support of millions of the black American urbanites frustrated by the lack of black progress

KEY TERM

Self-help Booker T. Washington and Marcus Garvey emphasised black-owned businesses as typical of the self-help needed for black progress.

? What do you suppose was Marcus Garvey's purpose in engaging in pageantry as seen in Source A?

after the First World War. It attracted far more members than the NAACP. Garvey enthused supporters when he maintained that God was black and that 'black is beautiful'. His *Negro World* newspaper was the only black publication that rejected advertisements for 'race-degrading' products that lightened skin and straightened hair. Black Americans responded to his advocacy of **self-help**, armed self-defence and separation of races. Harlemites enjoyed his UNIA parades through their streets during the 1920s.

SOURCE A

Marcus Garvey in his 'President of Africa' uniform in a UNIA parade in Harlem in 1922.

Garvey frightened and alienated both black and white Americans. Other black leaders were more middle class and light skinned. They resented his success amongst the black American working classes and his claims that blacker was better, and they collaborated with the white authorities, who were keen to silence him. Although Garvey was deported in 1927, UNIA had a great and long-lasting impact upon black consciousness, as demonstrated by Malcolm X (see page 131).

A UNIA member's thoughts on the Great Migration

SOURCE B

From a July 1920 speech at a UNIA meeting in Washington by UNIA member Reverend Doctor J.G. Brooks of New York City. Quoted in Robert Hill, editor, *Marcus Garvey and Universal Negro Improvement Association Papers, Volume 2*, University of California Press, 1983, pp. 449–50.

This is from the Associated Negro Press: 'There is another mighty exodus of the Negroes from the South. The chief cause this time is not economic, although practically all who come are able to get work, but the movement is due to intimidation and lynching …'

… What means the coming of these thousands from the South? What means their moving North? Does it mean that there is a new heaven opened up for the Negro? No, sir. Does it mean that the folks North, East, and West are more gracious to us … [?] No, sir. It does not mean that, it is almost like jumping out of the frying pan into the fire… [For example] there are no houses to rent when they go North, East, and West …

According to Source B, what motivated black migration, and did it bring the expected improvements?

Marcus Garvey's choice of Harlem as the headquarters of UNIA showed how Harlem had become important not only to black American life, but also to black people worldwide. Harlem's contribution to black consciousness was also evident in the career of **A. Philip Randolph**.

A. Philip Randolph

Born in Florida, A. Philip Randolph migrated North to New York City in search of greater economic opportunities. He was politicised by attendance at free courses at Harlem's City College (nicknamed 'the poor man's Harvard'), which was full of socialists and labour unionists. Randolph believed that people could not be free if they were impoverished and he considered labour unions that negotiated for better wages and working conditions to be of vital importance in the battle against poverty. However, many white-dominated unions opposed black membership.

KEY FIGURE

A. Philip Randolph (1890–1979)

Randolph was a leading black activist who established the Brotherhood of Sleeping Car Porters, and used his union power base to exert national influence. He was important in President Roosevelt's establishment of the Fair Employment Practices Commission, and in the 1963 March on Washington.

Randolph set up an unemployment office in Harlem to help Southern migrants find jobs and join unions. In 1917, he organised elevator operators into a union, and in 1919 he became President of the National Brotherhood of Workers of America, which had many black members in the Virginia shipyards and docks. White labour opposition to that union helped bring about its demise in 1921, but in 1925 Randolph was asked to organise the long-suffering black porters who worked for the Pullman Railroad Company. The late nineteenth-century railroad boom had attracted many black Southern agricultural workers to the less arduous job of porter, but working conditions were often poor and wages were low. The Brotherhood of Sleeping Car Porters was the first significant black labour union, and through it, Randolph became one of the most influential voices in the black civil rights movement of the twentieth century (see Chapter 7). The union's headquarters was in Harlem. Harlem thus played a vitally important role in the career of Randolph and the development of black labour union power.

Harlem's problems

Despite its massive contribution to black consciousness and advancement, Harlem had its problems. Poor relations between the black community and the white police officers led to periodic race riots, most famously in 1935. There was considerable poverty. Most of Harlem's black population did unskilled work and low wages affected mortality rates. A black child born in Harlem was twice as likely to die in infancy as a white child born elsewhere in New York City. The city Housing Commission chairman believed 'the State would not allow cows to live in some of these apartments in Harlem'. Cocaine addiction, prostitution and homicides were common. Harlem's poverty was exacerbated by the Great Depression that followed the **Wall Street crash** of October 1929. However, that **Depression** brought about changed attitudes toward poverty that proved of great significance to black Americans.

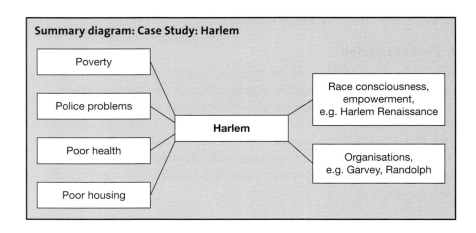

Summary diagram: Case Study: Harlem

Poverty — Police problems — Poor health — Poor housing → **Harlem** → Race consciousness, empowerment, e.g. Harlem Renaissance; Organisations, e.g. Garvey, Randolph

Chapter summary

In the years before the abolition of slavery, most black Americans lived as slaves in the South and lacked freedom of movement. The Civil War and emancipation gave them that freedom, and the slow drift North and West began and then accelerated when the development of Jim Crow destroyed the hopes born of Radical Reconstruction.

In the second decade of the twentieth century, the slow drift became a flood. By 1970, nearly 7 million people had left the South for other regions of America, a Great Migration that had dramatically increased racial tensions across the nation.

Between the 1880s and 1965, Jim Crow dominated the South and the motivation of black migrants was primarily to escape racism and inequality. There were also more and better employment opportunities in the North, especially during the two world wars. Northern migrants encouraged friends and relations from the South to come to join them in well-established communities such as New York City's Harlem and Chicago's South Side.

Migration posed challenges. It could mean a break with family members and a departure from the familiar. From the first, whites in the North and West resisted black migration. There were repeated and violent race riots. Whites were usually determined to live separately, and *de facto* segregation led to the development of overcrowded black ghettos characterised by poverty, poor health, poor housing, poor schools, poor community relations with the white police and high crime rates.

Harlem became the unofficial capital of black America and it illustrated the positives and the negatives of migration. The most significant positive was the cultural and activist dynamism that characterised Harlem by the late 1920s, as demonstrated in Marcus Garvey's UNIA, A. Philip Randolph's black labour union and the Harlem Renaissance.

Refresher questions

1 How was the black population distributed in 1850?

2 What was the significance of the Exodusters?

3 How did white Northerners control the growing black population?

4 Which are the most famous examples of race riots before 1930?

5 What caused the race riots?

6 Why might a black American want to migrate to the North or West in: (a) 1850? (b) 1862? (c) 1865? (d) 1890? (e) 1917? (f) The 1920s?

7 What were the advantages and disadvantages of life in Harlem?

8 What was unusual about the work of the sociologist Carole Marks in 1989?

9 What did the NAACP consider to be the most significant result of the Great Migration and why?

10 How did the First World War affect black Americans?

CHAPTER 5

The New Deal and race relations, 1933–41

Between 1880 and 1933, the federal government had little sympathy for the problems of black Americans, and the influence of white supremacist Southerners in the Democratic Party and in Congress made any black progress unlikely. However, during the 1930s, the United States suffered a particularly devastating economic depression that prompted unprecedented federal government assistance to the poor. Many black Americans were poor, so they benefited from this assistance, despite considerable discrimination against them in the New Deal agencies established by President Roosevelt and Congress to combat this 'Great Depression'. Roosevelt's New Deal convinced black Americans that the federal government was the key to progress and that Roosevelt's Democrats were the party most likely to help them.

These developments are covered in sections on

★ The influence of Southern whites in the Democrat Party

★ Franklin Roosevelt and the New Deal

★ Conclusions: the impact of the New Deal on black Americans

Key dates

1929		Wall Street crash triggered the Great Depression
1933	March	Roosevelt became President and initiated New Deal programmes; Civilian Conservation Corps (CCC) established
	May	Agricultural Adjustment Administration (AAA), Federal Emergency Relief Administration (FERA) and Tennessee Valley Authority (TVA) established
	June	National Recovery Administration (NRA) and Public Works Administration (PWA) established
1934	June	Federal Housing Administration (FHA) established
1935	April	Works Progress Administration (WPA) established
	July	Wagner Act
	Aug.	Social Security Act
1937	Sept.	Wagner–Steagall National Housing Act
1938	June	Fair Labor Standards Act
1941		Fair Employments Practices Commission established

1 The influence of Southern whites in the Democrat Party

▶ *How did Southern white influence in the Democratic Party affect black Americans?*

In the years between the end of Reconstruction (see page 29) and the **Great Depression** that followed the Wall Street crash of 1929, the three branches of the federal government gave little assistance to black Americans. The Supreme Court invariably endorsed Southern white behaviour (see page 37). Although most black Northerners voted for Republican candidates, the NAACP magazine, *The Crisis*, told readers in 1924 that 'Republican presidents are just about as bad as Democratic and Democratic presidents are little better than nothing.' Congress was similarly unhelpful, partly because of the influence of Southern whites in the Democratic Party.

In 1933, the Democratic Party was a loose coalition that included:

- the '**Solid South**'
- urban (mostly Catholic) ethnic voters in the North
- workers and middle-class liberals across the nation.

The Republican role in the Civil War era affected black and white voting for many decades. Republicans had initiated the end of slavery, led the North to victory over the South in the Civil War, then imposed Reconstruction on the South (see page 22). As a result, most black Americans favoured the Republican Party, while white Southerners invariably voted Democrat.

Southern whites were determined to maintain the social, economic and political inferiority of black Americans and their domination of the Democratic Party in the South helped them to do so. The South's single-party system led to the repeated re-election of the same Democrat candidates, so that long-serving Southern Democrat senators and representatives gained disproportionate influence in the US Congress under seniority rules that gave them over half the committee chairmanships and control of the key committees. Their importance in those committees enabled them to block any legislation they opposed. Most Southern Democrats were far more conservative and resistant to change than other Democrats, particularly with regard to race. One result of Southern white influence in the Democratic Party was the congressional failure to address black grievances.

Black grievances

In the decades after Reconstruction, black Americans had many grievances that were publicised by articulate representatives such as Ida B. Wells (see page 47)

 KEY TERMS

Great Depression
Exceptionally severe economic depression that hit the United States after the Wall Street crash of October 1929, and also affected many other countries.

Solid South Prior to the 1960s, voters in the South invariably voted Democrat. The vast majority of those voters were white.

and the NAACP (see page 48). The political, social and economic status of black Americans was markedly inferior to that of white Americans, particularly in the South (see Table 5.1).

Table 5.1 Black grievances in the first quarter of the twentieth century

	North	South
Political status	Black Americans could vote. A few black politicians such as Oscar De Priest (see page 57) were elected to office, but black Americans did not win state-wide office because many whites would only vote for white candidates.	Few black Americans were allowed to vote. First, white registrars set them impossibly difficult questions to meet literacy qualifications. Second, would-be voters had to pay a prohibitively expensive poll tax, and most black Southerners were poor. Third, 'uppity' blacks who tried to exercise the franchise risked violence and intimidation. Southern politics was dominated by the Democratic Party, which was steadfastly white and segregationist in the South.
Social status	*De facto* segregation kept the black urban population crowded into ghettos such as New York City's Harlem and Chicago's South Side.	Under the Jim Crow laws, black Americans suffered *de jure* segregation in public places such as schools, buses, railroad cars, hospitals, libraries, parks and restaurants. Black males avoided eye contact with white females lest they be accused of harassment, and black people were expected to step aside if a white person approached on the sidewalk.
Economic status	There was a slowly growing black middle class. For example, in 1914, A. Philip Randolph (see page 63) had married a wealthy widow who had graduated from one of the few black universities, Howard. Economic opportunities were better than in the South, although poor education limited the prospects of most of those who came North during the Great Migration (see page 55). Some migrants obtained relatively well-paid work in Detroit car factories or meatpacking houses in Chicago or East St Louis, but most black Americans in the North were poor and particularly badly affected by the Great Depression.	Many black Southerners worked in agriculture as sharecroppers or tenant farmers. Some were employed in industry, for example, in steelworks in Birmingham, Alabama. Poor education in segregated and underfunded schools made economic progress difficult. Black Americans across the nation constituted the majority of the workers in unskilled occupations such as domestic help, shoeshine boys, bellhops, railroad porters and waiters/waitresses.
Legal status	Lynching was not uncommon in the North. With regard to treatment in the courts and by the police, Malcolm X's (see page 131) brother Wilfred Little saw little difference between Michigan and the South in the 1920s and 1930s. The police gave black people little or no protection over lynchings and during race riots (see page 58).	Many whites considered violence and even lynching as an acceptable form of race control. Whites dominated law enforcement and because judges and juries were all-white, black citizens lacked effective protection under the law.

The failure to address the problem of lynching in the 1920s

The fate of anti-lynching bills in Congress in the 1920s is an excellent illustration of the influence of Southern whites in the Democratic Party.

Between 1901 and 1929, over 1200 black Americans were lynched in the South, mostly in Georgia (250) and Mississippi (255). The NAACP campaigned for congressional anti-lynching legislation. NAACP leader James Weldon Johnson recalled his lobbying efforts: 'I tramped the corridors of the **Capitol** and the two office buildings so constantly that toward the end, I could, I think, have been able to find my way about blindfolded.' He found a congressional ally in Republican Representative Leonidas Dyer, whose St Louis district contained increasing numbers of black Americans. Shocked by the 1917 riot in East St Louis, Dyer introduced an anti-lynching bill into the House of Representatives in 1918. His bill got nowhere in the Democrat-controlled Congress. However, in 1919 the Republicans gained control, and an NAACP report (*Thirty Years of Lynching in the United States, 1889–1919*) prompted further consideration of an anti-lynching bill in the House. Southern Democrats tried to stop debate. For example, they refused to come to the House Chamber, which prevented the necessary **quorum**. The Speaker of the House responded by ordering the chamber doors locked and sending the Sergeant at Arms to seek out members. Under pressure from the NAACP and the national publicity, the House passed the Dyer bill 231–119 in 1922, but Southern Democrat opposition in the Senate, particularly **filibuster** threats, killed off the bill. Dyer reintroduced his bill several times in the 1920s, but the Senate rejected it in 1922, 1923 and 1924. However, the publicity might have contributed to a decline in lynching in the 1920s.

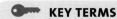

KEY TERMS

Capitol Building containing the Senate and the House of Representatives.

Quorum In this context, the minimum number required for the House of Representatives to conduct business.

Filibuster A procedure whereby the minority party in Congress can slow down proceedings so as to stop legislation being enacted.

> ### The Senate apology
>
> In 2005, the US Senate passed a resolution apologising for its historic inaction over lynching and 80 of the Senate's 100 members co-sponsored the resolution in order to emphasise their support. Two notable omissions from the list of co-sponsors were the two (white) senators from Mississippi.

The situation in 1929

Prior to the Great Depression, little was done to address black grievances because

- many white Americans were racist
- most Southern whites were determined to maintain white supremacy
- Southern white Democrats had considerable power in Congress, which made it impossible to get Congress to pass civil rights legislation
- there was as yet no well-established tradition of federal government intervention to assist the disadvantaged.

However, the Great Depression prompted unprecedented federal government intervention in the economy and society, and this had a considerable and beneficial impact on black Americans. Even then, Southern white Democrats worked frequently and effectively to ensure black Americans did not benefit from federal government measures.

The impact of the Great Depression on black Americans, 1929–33

The New York stock market collapse of 1929 triggered several years of economic depression. One black Georgian said, 'Most blacks did not even know the Great Depression had come. They had always been poor and only thought the whites were catching up.' Nevertheless, the Great Depression invariably hit blacks harder than whites:

- Tens of thousands of Southern black farmers left the land as crop prices plummeted.
- Many black farmers migrated to the cities, but urban black unemployment ranged between 30 and 60 per cent. The black unemployment rate was between four and six times higher than that of whites and desperate whites were moving into the low-paid jobs formerly dominated by black workers, such as domestic service, street cleaning, garbage collection and **bellhops**.
- Whites organised vigilante groups such as the Black Shirts of Atlanta to prevent black employment.
- Unskilled black workers were usually 'last hired and first fired'. There was no effective social security system, so disease and starvation frequently resulted.
- The black middle class was badly hit. For example, the percentage of black-owned property in Harlem fell from 35 per cent in 1929 to 5 per cent in 1935, while the median income for skilled workers fell by 50 per cent between 1929 and 1932.

A common black joke was that the long-running economic depression from which black workers suffered only became the 'Great' depression when it hit the white man. However, white suffering prompted congressional aid for the poor and unemployed – amongst whom were many black Americans.

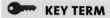 **KEY TERM**

Bellhops Porters.

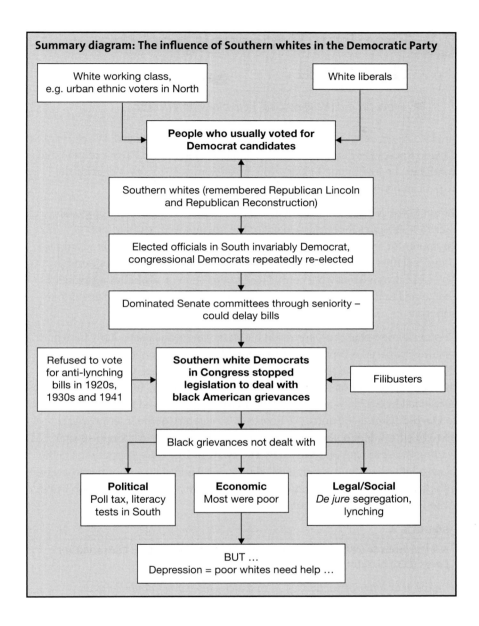

Summary diagram: The influence of Southern whites in the Democratic Party

White working class, e.g. urban ethnic voters in North

White liberals

People who usually voted for Democrat candidates

Southern whites (remembered Republican Lincoln and Republican Reconstruction)

Elected officials in South invariably Democrat, congressional Democrats repeatedly re-elected

Dominated Senate committees through seniority – could delay bills

Refused to vote for anti-lynching bills in 1920s, 1930s and 1941

Southern white Democrats in Congress stopped legislation to deal with black American grievances

Filibusters

Black grievances not dealt with

Political Poll tax, literacy tests in South

Economic Most were poor

Legal/Social *De jure* segregation, lynching

BUT … Depression = poor whites need help …

KEY TERMS

New Deal President Roosevelt's programme to bring the US out of the economic depression.

Alphabet agencies Federal government bodies, established to combat the Great Depression, that became known by their initials. For example, the AAA.

KEY FIGURES

Harold Ickes (1874–1952)

Pennsylvania-born reporter, lawyer, and Chicago politician Harold Ickes became Secretary of the Interior (1933–46) under Roosevelt, who wanted a progressive Republican in his cabinet. Ickes was important in the implementation of the New Deal.

Harry Hopkins (1890–1946)

Born in Iowa, he was a social services administrator in New York City who impressed Governor Roosevelt. As President, Roosevelt employed him to supervise New Deal programmes, notably FERA (see page 82), WPA (see page 81) and the NYA (see page 81). He was an important aide and advisor to Roosevelt during the Second World War.

? Judging from Source A, how did the views of Harold Ickes and Robert Fechner disagree with regard to black Americans?

 2 # Franklin Roosevelt and the New Deal

▶ *How far did the New Deal help black Americans?*

In 1932, 25 per cent of the American workforce was unemployed. When Franklin Delano Roosevelt (FDR) was nominated as the Democratic Party's presidential candidate, he told them, 'I pledge you, I pledge myself, to a new deal for the American people.'

When Roosevelt became President in March 1933, his **New Deal** proposals included subsidies for farmers, help for the unemployed, and welfare payments for the poor and the elderly. He sought and obtained from Congress unprecedented powers and money necessary to implement his programmes. The result was a (somewhat confusing) proliferation of '**alphabet agencies**' that aimed to lift the nation out of the economic depression and to ameliorate suffering.

Roosevelt knew that the Depression hit black Americans particularly hard and that they suffered exceptionally unfavourable social and political conditions in the South. In 1933, he appointed a liberal white Southerner, Clark Foreman, as his 'Special Adviser on the Economic Status of the Negro'. In 1934, Foreman was succeeded by his black assistant, Robert Weaver. Both owed their appointments to **Harold Ickes** (see Source A), Roosevelt's Secretary of the Interior, and erstwhile President of the Chicago branch of the NAACP. Although several leading Roosevelt appointees, led by **Harry Hopkins**, were sympathetic to the black plight, the administration relied upon local and state authorities to oversee and distribute federal government aid. This had an adverse impact upon black Americans in the South in particular.

SOURCE A

A letter from Secretary of the Interior Harold Ickes to Civilian Conservation Corps (CCC) director Robert Fechner, 20 September 1935.

I have your letter of September 24 in which you express doubt as to the advisability of appointing Negro supervisory personnel in Negro CCC camps. For my part, I am quite certain the Negroes can function in supervisory capacities just as efficiently as can white men and I do not think that they should be discriminated against mainly on account of their color. I can see no menace to the program that you are so efficiently carrying out in giving just and proper recognition to members of the Negro race.

Franklin Roosevelt

1882	Born to a wealthy family in New York State
1900–4	Studied law at Harvard
1905	Married distant cousin Eleanor Roosevelt
1913	Assistant Secretary of the Navy
1928–33	Popular Governor of New York State, unusually effective in combating unemployment
1933–7	First presidential term dominated by the Great Depression and the New Deal
1937–41	Second presidential term dominated by the deteriorating international situation
1941–5	Led the country through the Second World War in his third term
1945	Died in April, a few weeks into his fourth term

Background

Although Franklin Roosevelt had great personal wealth, he empathised with the less privileged, including black Americans. Many thought this owed much to the polio infection he contracted in 1921, which left him paralysed from the waist down. Throughout his political career, the American press respectfully hid his disability so that the general public never knew they had a disabled President who could only stand with the help of heavy metal braces and needed a cane or crutch to enable him to swing each leg forward and 'walk'.

Achievements

President Roosevelt used federal government power and expenditure to stimulate the economy during the Great Depression. The combination of his policies and wartime demand helped bring about economic recovery. Roosevelt led the nation through the war but died on the verge of victory.

Significance

Historians invariably rate Roosevelt one of the greatest American presidents. His presidency was a turning point in US history: it revolutionised the role of the federal government and saw the United States become the world's leading power. It was also a turning point for black Americans. It encouraged them to vote for Roosevelt's Democrat Party, and confirmed that pressure upon the federal government was the key to black progress.

The Agricultural Adjustment Administration (AAA)

The federal government considered overproduction the greatest problem in American agriculture and under the Agricultural Adjustment Act (May 1933), farmers were invited to voluntarily reduce their acreage and production in exchange for government subsidies. The **Agricultural Adjustment Administration (AAA)** paid farmers to decrease production of staples such as corn, cotton, milk, pigs, rice, tobacco and wheat.

At the local level, the AAA was invariably run by county committees dominated by the most powerful landowners, whose actions frequently harmed black Americans:

- When presented with the opportunity to receive money if they removed land from production, the powerful landowners did not hesitate to evict sharecroppers or tenants. In 1933, around 800,000 black Americans worked on farms in the South. Only 13 per cent of them owned their land. The rest were tenants and sharecroppers on white-owned land. Between 1933 and 1940, roughly 200,000 black sharecroppers were evicted.

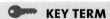 **KEY TERM**

Agricultural Adjustment Administration (AAA)
New Deal agency established in 1933 to aid farmers.

- Until 1936, the federal compensation due to evicted tenants and sharecroppers was distributed by white landowners, who frequently failed to pass it on to those for whom it was intended. After 1936, the federal government gave the large landowners cheques made out to individual black workers, but many landowners simply threatened the workers until they signed over the cheques.
- Many planters added to black economic problems when they used AAA money to buy machinery that replaced black farm workers.
- When the great landowners needed additional labour during planting and harvesting, they persuaded local relief administrators to remove black Americans from the welfare rolls. That created a labour surplus and workers willing to accept very low wages.

The AAA was of little help to Southern black farmers. In the face of determined resistance from the large landowners, AAA officials tried but failed to prevent evictions. The evicted sharecroppers or tenants sometimes attempted resistance. For example, the Communist-led Alabama Sharecroppers Union, established in 1931 and with 8000 members by 1934, resisted displacement. However, state officials condoned the use of violence against them by the landowners. Roosevelt did nothing about this: Southern Democrats had been amongst his staunchest supporters from the first and he wanted to reward them and be assured of their continued cooperation.

The Tennessee Valley Authority (TVA)

The Tennessee River ran through some of the poorest states in the United States, including Alabama, Mississippi and Tennessee. In May 1933, the federal government set up the **Tennessee Valley Authority (TVA)**, which constructed dams to control flooding and generated electricity. Black TVA workers were given segregated facilities and accommodation, restricted to unskilled jobs, given limited access to new housing, and excluded from model farm programmes (see Source B). Their situation improved somewhat when J. Max Bond, the TVA's black Supervisor of Negro Training, leaked information about discriminatory practices to the NAACP. When the NAACP published an exposé, it prompted a congressional committee to call for the improved treatment of black workers. After that, the TVA proceeded a little more carefully.

? According to Source B, in what ways were black Americans discriminated against by the TVA and in the Tennessee Valley?

SOURCE B

From an article by John Davis in *The Crisis*, the NAACP's official magazine, 1 October 1935, pp. 294–5 and 314 (available at: http://library.mtsu.edu/tps/lessonplans&ideas/Lesson_Plan--TVA_Opportunities_for_African_Americans.pdf).

… on TVA projects … Negroes were not employed in proportion to their numbers in the population and … received even less consideration in the matter of wage payments …

At Wilson Dam, Negroes are employed primarily in unskilled work … By reserving such occupations for Negroes, TVA effectively establishes a Negro differential, while at the same time loudly proclaiming: 'No discrimination is made between the races with reference to wages paid or hours of work.' … What is true of jobs at Wilson Dam is more or less true on other projects of TVA. Negro workmen have also been the victim of mis-classification, doing skilled work while receiving pay as unskilled workers … The men testified they were afraid to complain because the experience of other Negro workers had been that complaints about false classification led to dismissal.

… The failure to include a fair proportion of Negroes in skilled work … as well makes almost certain the gradual elimination of Negroes from employment by TVA. This is true because unskilled work is only necessary in the early stages of the dam projects …

The housing accommodations furnished Negro workers by TVA are notoriously inferior to those given whites … At Pickwick the Negro community is separated from that for the white workers by a deep ravine. Officials of TVA suggested the reason for the separation to be the need for keeping down racial outbreaks which 'would be occasioned if Negroes and whites live together.' … In addition at Pickwick Negroes can attend the white theatre, if they sit in a 'Jim-Crow' section …

We have the tragic picture of officials of the federal government, sworn to uphold the Constitution, teaching white citizens that Negroes are unfit to live in any but segregated communities …

Now what is the present plight of the Negro dwellers in the Valley? … Negroes in the area are especially the victims of inadequate relief, low wages, intolerable living conditions and complete lack of any type of labour organisation … For Negroes the introduction of cheaper electric rates into Lee County as result of the TVA power policy has meant nothing. Landlords … have not found it to their advantage to wire their Negro tenants' homes … Thus so far as TVA's electrification program is concerned the Negro family is still in outer darkness …

Civilian Conservation Corps (CCC)

The **Civilian Conservation Corps (CCC)** was established in March 1933 in order to create jobs for the unemployed. The Department of Labor recruited 17–24-year-old unemployed males to work in the CCC (the upper age limit was subsequently extended to 28 years). Around 250,000 worked on reforestation, soil conservation and forest management projects in 1933–4 and 500,000 in 1935. White Americans usually considered the CCC a great success, but black Americans were not always impressed (see Source C).

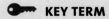 **KEY TERM**

Civilian Conservation Corps (CCC) New Deal agency established in 1933 to offer employment through public works.

What does Source C suggest about the NAACP?

SOURCE C

From the *Norfolk Journal and Guide* account of the firing of Eddie Simons, a Harlem youth, from the CCC camp at North Lisbon, New Jersey, 13 January 1934.

Simons was dishonorably discharged and his last month's pay withheld … when he refused to stand and fan flies from a white officer … Simons told the officer he did not think fanning flies was part of his duty … The N.A.A.C.P. immediately took up the case and protested to Robert Fechner … Three weeks later director Fechner again wrote the N.A.A.C.P. that he had directed that Eddie Simons be given an honourable discharge 'free from any charge of insubordination' and that 'he be paid all cash allowances and allotments due.'

The CCC was headed by Robert Fechner, a racially conservative Tennessean. Fechner did nothing to encourage black American recruitment until 1935, when the Roosevelt administration intervened and the CCC doubled black recruitment. Around 200,000 black Americans worked for the CCC during its nine-year existence, but they were often restricted to low-skilled jobs and although some camps were integrated in the early years, the combination of local complaints, and the beliefs and advice of the US Army and CCC administrators, caused Fechner to issue a directive ordering the 'complete segregation of colored and white enrollees' in July 1935.

What can you infer about the Civilian Conservation Corps from Source D?

SOURCE D

A CCC camp in Pennsylvania, 1933.

The CCC in the North

Although the South offers the best illustrations of racial tensions under the New Deal, there were also problems in the North, as demonstrated by events at Fort Dix, New Jersey.

Within two weeks of the establishment of the CCC, black recruits arrived at Fort Dix. Soon, 100 of them from Newark, New Jersey, went on strike. They said the food was scarce and poor. They claimed that they had been evicted from their barracks to make way for white recruits and then forced to give up their hot meals for raw potatoes. The white Army officers who ran the camp claimed that the recruits ate too much (the officers said one company of 200 men consumed 2200 hotcakes for breakfast) and that the strikers had gone joyriding in stolen cars.

Fort Dix's 180 black recruits from Harlem, known as Company 235-C (C for 'Colored'), were sent to upstate New York to plant trees at $30 per week. When their white major brought in 20 white recruits and replaced the company's black clerks, the Harlem recruits refused to work. State police arrested six 'ringleaders', who were sent home, but 35 Harlemites still refused to work. The major said, 'This camp is operated on merit and the Negro clerks are not capable of handling their jobs.' Only one Harlemite returned to work, the other 34 were sent home. The white recruits were transferred to another company, but trouble continued. CCC reports said the local white population was 'somewhat nervous' about the 'possibility of rape' by the black recruits, so Company 235-C was sent far away from white towns.

SOURCE E

From 'A Negro in the CCC,' by New Yorker Luther Wandall, published in the NAACP magazine *The Crisis*, August 1935, pp. 244 and 253–4.

During the two years of its previous existence I had heard many conflicting reports concerning the Civilian Conservation Corps, President Roosevelt's pet project … Some said that the colored got all the leftovers. Others said that everything was all right. But my brother, who is a World War veteran, advised me emphatically: 'I wouldn't be in anything connected with the Army.'

… We reached Camp Dix [New Jersey] about 7:30 that evening … And here it was that Mr. James Crow first definitely put in his appearance. When my record was taken at Pier I, a 'C' [for colored] was placed on it … But until now there had been no distinction made. But before we left the bus the officer shouted emphatically: 'Colored boys fall out in the rear.' The colored from several buses were herded together, and stood in line until after the white boys had been registered and taken to their tents. This seemed to be the established order of procedure at Camp Dix. This separation of the colored from the whites was completely and rigidly maintained at this camp …

> What does Source E see as the advantages and disadvantages of the CCC, and how would you explain the attitude of the 'colored people living on farms'?

We were finally led away to our tents. And such tents! They were the worst in Camp Dix ... you can imagine my feelings when an officer, a small quiet fellow, obviously a southerner, asked me how I would like to stay in Camp Dix permanently as his clerk! This officer was very courteous, and seemed to be used to colored people, and liked them. I declined his offer ...

[Then] We were taken to permanent camp ... in the upper South. This camp was a dream compared with Camp Dix. There plenty to eat, and we slept in barracks instead of tents. An excellent recreation hall, playground, and other facilities ... Our bosses are local men, [white] southerners, but on the whole I have found nothing to complain of. The work varies, but is always healthy, outdoor labor ...

There are colored people living on farms on all sides of this camp. But they are not very friendly toward CCC boys in general, and toward the northerners in particular ...

On the whole, I was gratified rather than disappointed with the CCC. I had expected the worst. Of course it reflects, to some extent, all the practices and prejudices of the U.S. Army. But as a job and an experience, for a man who has no work, I can heartily recommend it.

Fort Dix, New Jersey, was by no means the only Northern CCC camp where there was a problem with a 'somewhat nervous' local white population. There was similar problems in Ohio (see Source F).

SOURCE F

From CCC director Robert Fechner's letter to Ohio Senators Robert Bulkley and Vic Donahey, 4 June 1936 (available at: http://newdeal.feri.org/aaccc/).

Whether we like it or not, we cannot close our eyes to the fact that there are communities and States that do not want and will not accept a Negro Civilian Conservation Corps company. This is particularly true in localities that have a negligible Negro population. There were so many vigorous complaints and protests that I felt it was necessary to direct Corps Area Commanders to find a location within their State of origin for all Negro Civilian Conservation Corps Companies ... Even this did not solve the situation because there was great difficulty in finding a community that was willing to accept a Negro company of its own citizens. In your own state we had a good example ...

There has been no discrimination against Negro enrollees but to the contrary ... The total percentage of Negro enrollees at the present time is larger than at any time since this work started.

> ? What does Source F's contention that it was very difficult to find 'a community that was willing to accept a Negro company of its own citizens' suggest to you?

When the two Ohio senators interrogated CCC director Robert Fechner on the treatment of black Americans in the CCC in their state, it demonstrated considerable contemporary concern over black Americans working for New Deal agencies. There was obviously a growing sensitivity over black inferiority. This growth in awareness and sensitivity owed much to the NAACP and to President

Roosevelt. In September 1935, Roosevelt sent a brief handwritten letter to TVA director Robert Fechner that revealed that there was both promise and prejudice in the President's attitude toward black Americans:

> *In the CCC Camps, where the boys are colored, in the Park Service work, please try to put in colored foremen, not of course in technical work but in the ordinary manual work.*

Roosevelt continued to press Fechner over his treatment of black Americans (see Source G).

SOURCE G

From a letter from CCC director Robert Fechner to Thomas Griffith, President of the NAACP, 21 December 1935 (available at: http://newdeal.feri.org/aaccc/).

The President has called my attention to the letter you addressed to him on September 14, 1935, in which you ask for information relating to the policy of segregation in CCC camps.

The law enacted by Congress setting up Emergency Conservation Work specifically indicated that there should be no discrimination because of color. I have faithfully endeavored to obey the spirit and letter of this, as well as all other provisions of the law.

At the very beginning of this work, I consulted with many representative individuals and groups who were interested in the work, and the decision to segregate white enrollees, negro enrollees, and war veterans, was generally approved …

While segregation has been the general policy, it has not been inflexible, and we have a number of companies containing a small number of negro enrollees. I am satisfied that the negro enrollees themselves prefer to be in companies composed exclusively of their own race.

This segregation is not discrimination and cannot be so construed. The negro companies are assigned to the same types of work, have identical equipment, are served the same food, and have the same quarters as white enrollees. I have personally visited many negro CCC companies and have talked with the enrollees and have never received one single complaint.

> To what extent do you trust the claims made about segregation in Source G?

The National Recovery Administration (NRA)

In June 1933, Congress passed the National Industry Recovery Act, which set up the **National Recovery Administration (NRA)**. The NRA aimed to assist the recovery of businesses and manufacturing through a variety of measures, one of which was codes that encouraged employers to establish minimum wages and maximum hours for workers. Companies that adopted the codes were allowed to display the government seal of approval, a blue eagle symbol. However, some workers benefited more than others. NRA codes allowed regionally differentiated wage rates and excluded workers in agriculture and in domestic

KEY TERM

National Recovery Administration (NRA)
New Deal agency established in 1933 to help business and manufacturing.

service, areas in which three-quarters of black workers were employed. In 1934, a group that christened itself the National Association for Domestic Workers, based in Jackson, Mississippi, with branches in St Louis, Knoxville, Baltimore and Washington, wrote to the NRA and pointedly drew up a code for domestic workers, who were excluded from New Deal legislation.

Black workers in industries that were covered by the codes often had their job classification redefined so that employers could avoid the set wage levels. The NRA was famous amongst the black population for its unfairness, which prompted many jokes as to what the initials NRA stood for.

> ### Black suggestions as to what the initials 'NRA' stood for
>
> - Negro-Run-Around
> - Negroes Roasted Again
> - Negroes Rarely Allowed
> - Negro Removal Act.

Southern Democrats, wages and labour unions

In 1935, the Supreme Court declared the NRA unconstitutional, so Congress assisted workers by passing

- the Wagner Act (July 1935), which forced employers to allow unions and collective bargaining
- the Fair Labor Standards Act (1938), which fixed the minimum wage at 25 cents per hour and set a maximum number of hours weekly for workers (44 hours) in several industries. As a result, 300,000 workers had an immediate wage increase and 1.3 million had their work hours reduced.

However, in order to get Southern Democrats to accept this legislation, Roosevelt had to make crucial exemptions. Waiters, cooks, janitors, domestic and farm workers were excluded from the provisions of the Wagner Act and the Fair Labour Standards Act – and most of those workers were black. Furthermore, many unions excluded black workers and NAACP lobbying failed to persuade Congress to include a non-discrimination clause in the Wagner Act.

? What point was Source H making and how effectively did it make it?

> ### SOURCE H
>
> **In September 1933, the 100 or so black employees of a pencil factory in Atlanta, Georgia, received notice of the end of their employment in their pay envelope, along with a warning (available at: www.pbs.org/wgbh/americanexperience/features/primary-resources/fdr-square-deal/).**
>
> *If the 'false friends' of the colored people do not stop their propaganda about paying the same wages to colored and white employees this company will be forced to move the factory to a section where the minimum wage will produce the greatest production. Stop your 'friends' from talking you out of your job.*

The Public Works Administration (PWA)

The National Industry Recovery Act also set up the **Public Works Administration (PWA)**, headed by Harold Ickes (see page 72). With $3.3 billion of federal funding, the PWA employed hundreds of thousands of workers who constructed roads, schools, hospitals and dams. It was particularly helpful to black Americans:

- It spent over $65 million on the construction and improvement of black schools, homes and hospitals.
- Its Housing Division used quotas to ensure construction jobs for black workers, and by 1940, black Americans occupied over 30 per cent of PWA-constructed housing.
- Ickes ensured that black PWA workers got equal pay.

Works Progress Administration (WPA)

In April 1935, the Emergency Relief Appropriation Act set up the **Works Progress Administration (WPA)**, which was given $45.5 billion (worth around $500 billion today) to spend on public works. At any given time, the WPA employed roughly 2 million workers. The $52 monthly wage was greater than relief, although a lower wage than in industry. The WPA built 8000 schools and hospitals, 1000 airport landing fields and 12,000 playgrounds.

The WPA employed an average of 350,000 black Americans in each year of its four-year existence (1936–40). Some employers protested that the WPA pay was so high that black Americans were no longer willing to pick cotton at the normal rate. WPA education programmes employed over 5000 black teachers and taught over 250,000 black Americans how to read and write. The WPA imposed racial quotas on contractors whom it employed and doubled its percentage of black workers from 8 to 15 per cent within two years. However, only 5 per cent of black WPA workers had supervisory roles in the North, and in May 1940, only 11 of the 10,344 WPA supervisors in the South were black.

The WPA was responsible for the **National Youth Administration (NYA)**, which assisted students and provided them with part-time jobs while they completed their education.

The National Youth Administration (NYA)

Educator **Mary McLeod Bethune**, the fifteenth child of former slaves, established the National Council of Negro Women in 1935. It aimed to voice black concerns to New Dealers. She lobbied the NYA to give greater aid to black Americans and was appointed to work for the agency. In 1938, she became the NYA's Director of the Division of Negro Affairs. One black contemporary said she possessed the 'most marvelous gift of affecting feminine helplessness in order to attain her goals with masculine ruthlessness'. She was famously persuasive, as when she prodded Texas NYA state administrator Lyndon Baines

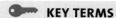

KEY TERMS

Public Works Administration (PWA)
New Deal agency established in 1933 to offer employment through public works.

Works Progress Administration (WPA)
New Deal agency established in 1935 to offer employment through public works.

National Youth Administration (NYA)
New Deal agency established in 1935 to help the young unemployed.

KEY FIGURE

Mary McLeod Bethune (1875–1955)
South Carolina-born Bethune was an educator and civil rights activist, appointed by President Roosevelt to head the Negro Division of the NYA. She was a leading member of Roosevelt's so-called 'Black Cabinet' (see page 93).

Johnson (see page 126) to increase the number of black youths in the NYA programme.

During the Depression, black youth unemployment was higher than white youth employment. As many as 40 per cent of black youths were unemployed. Bethune had her own fund for black students, and she encouraged state officials to ensure that black youths signed up for programmes. Bethune worked at the NYA until its demise in 1943, and was one of the highest-ranking black Americans in the Roosevelt administration (she became a close friend of Eleanor Roosevelt). The NYA gave aid and taught skills to 500,000 young black Americans. It was exceptionally fair in its distribution of money, but it accepted segregation.

> ## Black employment in entertainment and scholarship
>
> The New Deal provided jobs in the world of entertainment and culture, giving some black scholars the opportunity to increase black consciousness by getting black history and contemporary living conditions into the New Deal's state guidebooks. Black songs and oral reminiscences of slavery and hardship were recorded for posterity. Black authors such as Zora Neale Hurston and Richard Wright benefited from the Federal Writers' Project.
>
> Government sponsorship of culture was inevitably controversial. Many congressmen were convinced that those people who worked in the Theater Project and the Writers' Project were Communists. In 1939, the House Un-American Activities Committee criticised federally funded **biracial** theatrical productions because they encouraged black and white colleagues to go out on dates.

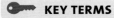 **KEY TERMS**

Biracial Black and white together.

Welfare Government payments to relieve poverty.

Federal Emergency Relief Administration (FERA) New Deal agency established in 1933 to help the unemployed through relief and job creation.

The benefits of welfare to black workers and their families

Extreme poverty amongst the elderly, poor and unemployed in the Depression years made many Americans reconsider the role of government in relation to **welfare** payments.

The Federal Emergency Relief Administration (FERA)

In May 1933, the Federal Emergency Relief Act established the **Federal Emergency Relief Administration (FERA)**. Under Harry Hopkins (see page 72), FERA spent over $4000 million to help the unemployed through relief and work projects. Overall, FERA's effectiveness was limited because:

- Many state authorities considered poverty the result of idleness and were reluctant to assist the unemployed (the Governor of Georgia recommended the unemployed be given a dose of castor oil – a laxative).
- FERA's funds were limited. In 1935, it paid an average of $25 per month to a needy family, while the subsistence wage was around $100.
- FERA officials were often overburdened (many had to deal with thousands of needy workers).

In some ways, FERA served black Americans well. Prior to the New Deal, state and local welfare agencies had usually ignored black needs but one-third of black Americans benefited from FERA: in 1935, 3.5 million received help from it. However, the distribution of FERA relief was frequently characterised by discriminatory practices at local level. White officials in the South made it harder for the black unemployed to get on the welfare rolls and paid black welfare recipients less than whites, arguing that as black people had a lower standard of living, they could survive on less money. Atlanta gave monthly relief checks of $32.66 to whites but $19.29 to blacks. In some rural areas in Georgia and Mississippi, black relief payments were 30 per cent lower than those of whites. FERA was closed down in 1935, but the WPA continued some of its work.

Social Security Act

Under the Social Security Act of August 1935, insurance for the unemployed and pensions for the elderly were to be funded by contributions from employers and employees. The Act also established aid programmes for the physically disadvantaged and for families with dependent children.

These **social security** provisions were no cure-all. First, the payments were low:

- Pensions ranged from $10 to $85 monthly, depending on how much the recipient had contributed to the scheme. The first payments were not made until 1940 (by that time contributions would have been made).
- The unemployment benefit was a maximum $18 weekly and for 16 weeks only.
- The amount paid to families with dependent children varied according to the wealth, inclination and generosity of each individual state. For example, while Massachusetts paid poor children $61 monthly, Mississippi paid $8.

Second, many black Americans were waiters, cooks, janitors, domestic and farm workers, and although they were probably the workers who most needed help, they were excluded from social security coverage. However, the exclusion of agriculture and domestic workers was not necessarily a deliberate act of racism: countries other than the United States had similar exclusions, because such employment was often seasonal or temporary and it was considered that employers would probably struggle to pay the contributions and that there would be unmanageable collection problems.

Third, the American Medical Association vehemently opposed health insurance and ensured that it was excluded from these New Deal measures.

Although top NAACP lawyer Charles Houston said that the Social Security Act was 'like a sieve with holes just big enough for the majority of Negroes to fall through', the Social Security Act represented a radical change in the role of the federal government and created the first national system of benefits.

KEY TERM

Social security Welfare benefits for the needy, for example, the old, sick or unemployed.

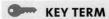 **KEY TERM**

Federal Housing Administration (FHA)
New Deal agency established in 1934 to help homeowners.

Housing

Many homeowners struggled to pay their mortgages during the Depression, so the **Federal Housing Administration (FHA)** was established in June 1934 to help homeowners pay the lower-interest, long-term mortgages provided by the government since June 1933 for those buying new homes. These measures proved of little help to the impoverished inner-city areas where many black families lived, and the federal government refused to guarantee mortgages for houses purchased by black families in white neighbourhoods. Federal housing loans deliberately preserved the racial composition of neighbourhoods.

The Wagner–Steagall National Housing Act (September 1937) aimed to build new low-rent housing to replace slums, but Congress underfunded it, and only 160,000 homes had been built by 1941.

Summary diagram: Franklin Roosevelt and the New Deal

New Deal agency or measure	Aim	Black Americans
AAA	Stop overproduction	200,000 black sharecroppers evicted, rarely got the compensation due
TVA	Provide employment and electricity and improved farming methods	Got jobs but discriminated against
CCC	Create jobs for young	200,000 worked for it, but discrimination
NRA	Help business and industry recover	Excluded agricultural and domestic workers (most were black) and wages lower than whites
PWA	Create jobs through public works programmes	Equal pay and in 1940 occupied 30% of PWA-built homes
WPA	Create jobs through public works programmes	Average 300,000 employed annually. Taught 250,000 to read and write. Supervisory roles: only 5% in North, and 11 out of 10,344 in South
NYA	Help unemployed youths	500,000 got aid and were taught skills. Fair distribution of funds. Accepted segregation
FERA	Relief and work projects for poor	One-third benefited – something new BUT Southern administrators unfair
Social Security Act	Insurance for unemployed, pensions for elderly	Excluded service industry and farm workers (many black). Money not generous
FHA	Help homeowners	Little help for ghetto-dwellers

Conclusions: the impact of the New Deal on black Americans

▶ *How did the New Deal affect black Americans?*

Roosevelt and his New Deal affected black Americans in ways both negative and positive.

The impact of New Deal agencies upon black poverty

New Deal agencies such as the AAA (see page 73), the CCC (see page 75) and the TVA (see page 74) often discriminated against blacks. Sometimes aid did not reach the people for whom it was intended, particularly in the South where aid was distributed by whites. A 1936 NAACP report said the 6 million black workers engaged in agriculture received no help from the federal government, although that situation improved. Black complaints were plentiful. A group of Chicago workers wrote to President Roosevelt, 'The officials of the W.P.A. are not treating us as God's children, but as God's step-children.' S.D. Redmond, a black Republican from Mississippi, told black political scientist Ralph Bunche, 'The New Deal agencies haven't meant a goddamned thing to the Negroes.' A petition seeking federal aid for anyone wanting to emigrate to Africa received 2 million signatures and one Illinois petitioner said he would 'rather be any place but here, working on W.P.A. and starving to death'. In 1938, Mary McLeod Bethune told an audience of black educators, 'We are losing our homes and our farms and jobs … We are scorned of men; they spit in our faces and laugh. We cry out in this awesome darkness.'

On the other hand, while it was sometimes hard for blacks to make effective protests about unfairness in the administration of the New Deal, New Dealers were often responsive to criticism and even protest, as seen in the letters of Harold Ickes and President Roosevelt to Robert Fechner (see pages 72 and 79), and in the 1935 Harlem riot. In that riot, one black died and 200 were injured in clashes with the police, whom they believed to have beaten or possibly killed a young black shoplifter. While the tabloids tried to blame Communist agitators, an investigatory commission blamed Harlem's poverty and discrimination in relief given to blacks. Racist officials were transferred from Harlem and more Harlemites were employed to administer relief.

Indeed, there were many positives for black Americans in the New Deal, the programmes of which were racially inclusive if not racially equal. Even discriminatory aid was better than none, and agencies such as the NYA in particular were of great help to black Americans. While the federal government had appeared uninterested in black Americans prior to 1933, New Deal programmes helped them by providing a million jobs, nearly 50,000 public housing units, and financial assistance and skilled occupations training for half a

SOURCE I

? What point is Source I making?

Margaret Bourke-White's photograph showing black victims of the Kentucky flood of February 1937. They are standing in front of an advertising sign that says 'World's highest standard of living – There's no way like the American way'.

million black youths. As a result of federal assistance, many black sharecroppers became independent farmers. Finally, New Deal welfare payments were invaluable for many impoverished families.

The New Deal and civil rights

Although the New Deal was important in improving the economic status of black Americans, the influence of Southern white Democrats ensured that there was no civil rights legislation to improve the social, legal and political status of black Americans in the South in the New Deal years.

The exclusion of black voters

Most black Americans remained unable to exercise the vote in the South between 1933 and 1941. In 1941, only 3 per cent of eligible black voters were registered in the South. Southern white registrars used literacy tests and the poll tax to deter any black American brave enough to risk the violence and intimidation likely to result from attempts to register.

In 1937, Nolan Breedlove, a 28-year-old white man, tried but failed to get the Supreme Court to outlaw the poll tax. Breedlove was not allowed to vote because he had declined to pay the state of Georgia's poll tax ($1 per annum). He lost the case: the Supreme Court upheld the Georgia state voting law in *Breedlove v. Suttles* (1937). Rosa Parks (see page 113) was an intelligent, politically knowledgeable black woman, but in 1943 she 'failed' the literacy test in

Montgomery, Alabama. She finally managed to register in 1945, but even then the $16.50 poll tax was expensive for a part-time seamstress. President Roosevelt criticised the poll tax but ignored NAACP calls to do something to end it.

Without the ability to vote for and elect sympathetic public officials, black Americans in the South depended upon congressional legislation to combat their social inequality. However, Congress remained unsympathetic.

The continuation of Jim Crow laws

President Roosevelt kept a low profile on the Jim Crow laws, although his wife frequently signalled her disapproval (see page 90). Even the Southern white liberals who campaigned for state anti-lynching legislation, a fairer legal system, and better public services for black Americans, did not challenge segregation.

The Jim Crow laws were a daily reminder of black inferiority. When the young son of Atlanta's most respected black Baptist minister went into downtown Atlanta in the New Deal years, he would have to travel from 'nigger town' at the back of the bus. He could not buy a soda or hot dog at a downtown store lunch counter. If a white drugstore served him, they would hand him his ice cream through a side window and in paper cups so no white would have to use any plate that he had used. He had to drink from the 'colored' water fountain and use the 'colored' restroom. He had to sit in the 'colored' section at the back of the balcony in the movie theatre. That young boy, Martin Luther King Jr, subsequently recalled that it made him 'determined to hate every white person'.

President Roosevelt's lack of support for civil rights legislation was due to his reluctance to alienate Southern white Democrat voters. Although Roosevelt was the first President since the 1870s to denounce lynching as murder, he never fully supported the anti-lynching bills of 1934, 1935 and 1937–8. The defeat of those bills demonstrated yet again the disproportionate power of Southern Democrats in Congress.

The failure of anti-lynching bills in the New Deal era

In 1934, the NAACP supported Senators Costigan of Colorado and Wagner of New York in their introduction of an anti-lynching bill. However, Southern Democrats in the Senate organised a filibuster and the bill died. In that year, there was nationwide coverage of the lynching of black American Claude Neal in Florida. Neal suffered two hours of torture in front of a celebratory white crowd. He was forced to eat his severed penis, repeatedly stabbed in the stomach, and several of his fingers and toes were cut off. This led to a second Costigan–Wagner bill. The Roosevelt administration, fearful for the passage of New Deal relief legislation, did nothing to support the bill. Southern Democrats organised another filibuster, lasting seven weeks. In the meantime other legislation could not be passed, and as a result the anti-lynching bill was dropped. Another such bill met a similar fate in 1937.

? How persuasive are the arguments in Source J?

SOURCE J

President Franklin Roosevelt's explanation to NAACP leader Walter White as to why he could not support the anti-lynching bill in Congress, 1934. Quoted in Kevin McMahon, *Reconsidering Roosevelt on Race*, University of Chicago Press, 2010, p. 15.

I did not choose the tools with which I must work. Had I been permitted to choose them, I would have selected quite different ones. But I've got to get legislation passed by Congress to save America. The Southerners by reason of the seniority rule in Congress are chairmen or occupy strategic places on most of the Senate and House committees. If I come out for the anti-lynching bill now, they will block every bill I ask Congress to pass to keep America from collapsing. I just can't take the risk.

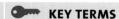

KEY TERMS

Executive powers
The Constitution gave the President 'Executive Power', a vague phrase that enabled successive presidents to act without Congress in certain areas.

Fair Employment Practices Commission (FEPC) Federal agency set up by President Roosevelt in 1941 to promote racial equality in defence industries.

On the other hand, although there was no civil rights legislation in the Roosevelt era, the President used his **executive powers** to establish the **Fair Employment Practices Commission (FEPC)**.

The Fair Employment Practices Commission (FEPC)

During the Second World War (1939–45), American industry focused on the production of military equipment. The resultant demand for black labour gave black workers greater bargaining power. A. Philip Randolph (see page 63) threatened to bring Washington DC to a standstill unless there was equality within the armed forces and the workplace. Impatient at the lack of progress on the anti-lynching bills, NAACP leader Walter White was supportive. Advised by his generals that it would disrupt the war effort, Roosevelt refused to integrate the armed forces, although he left black leaders with the impression that he might do so in the future. However, he set up a federal agency called the Committee on Fair Employment Practices (FEPC) to promote equality in defence industries, in which 2 million black Americans were eventually employed.

The FEPC had mixed success. Two-thirds of the 8000 job discrimination cases referred to the FEPC were dismissed and only one-fifth of Southern cases were black victories. Southern Democrat congressmen successfully decreased FEPC's funding after it was given greater power in 1943. FEPC accomplished too little to be considered a great success, but enough to show the importance of federal aid. There, in the increased federal involvement in the lives of black Americans, lay the key to further progress.

A New Deal and a new black relationship with the federal government

In spite of the lack of civil rights legislation and the fact that Roosevelt had to be forced into establishing the FEPC, the New Deal helped make civil rights a national political issue and familiarised Americans with federal government intervention in state issues. Several prominent black Americans praised

Roosevelt and the New Deal: W.E.B. Du Bois (see page 48) said Roosevelt 'gave the American Negro a kind of recognition in political life which the Negro had never before received', while Ralph Bunche (see page 85) said the New Deal 'represented a critical break with the past' for black Americans. White Southerners noticed increased black assertiveness and blamed Roosevelt. One said, 'You ask any nigger in the street who's the greatest man in the world. Nine out of ten will tell you Franklin Roosevelt. That's why I think he's so dangerous.' The New Deal served to reinforce the contention of some black activists that the federal government was the key to improvements in the black situation and it revolutionised black political affiliations.

The impact of the New Deal on voting patterns

The New Deal caused a voting revolution in that black voters in the North switched to the Democratic Party. In 1932, around 70 per cent of black voters supported the Republican presidential candidate Herbert Hoover, but in 1936, 76 per cent of black Americans assured pollsters they planned to vote for the Democrat Franklin Roosevelt. In 1936, 1940 and 1944, the majority of black voters supported Roosevelt. In 1940 he won 85 per cent of the vote in Harlem.

Roosevelt and the Democrats recognised the increasing importance of the black vote. In 1936, Roosevelt addressed an all-black audience for the first time, and promised 'no forgotten men and no forgotten races' in his term.

Songs and slogans designed to encourage black voters to vote Democrat during the Depression

The Democratic Party came out with slogans such as: 'Abraham Lincoln Is Not A Candidate In The Present Campaign' and 'Let Jesus Lead You and Roosevelt Feed You'.

Black author Richard Wright (see page 82) heard this song sung on the streets of Harlem in 1940:

Roosevelt! You're my man!
When the time come
I ain't got a cent
You buy my groceries
and pay my rent.
Mr. Roosevelt, you're my man!

Table 5.2 The number of **wards** that Roosevelt won out of 15 black wards in nine major cities

Year	Number won
1932	4 out of 15
1936	9 out of 15
1940	15 out of 15

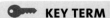 **KEY TERM**

Wards Urban electoral districts.

Why black American voters changed from Republican to Democrat

Black Americans were changing their voting allegiance because

- Many benefited from New Deal relief measures and believed that Roosevelt really cared about them.
- Many New Deal administrators, including top ones such as Harry Hopkins (head of FERA) and Harold Ickes (Secretary of the Interior and head of

the PWA), were notably keen to assist black Americans. Over 100 black Americans held quite important administrative posts in New Deal agencies. In the NYA, black officials were usually appointed in predominantly black areas. Roosevelt dramatically increased the number of black employees in the federal bureaucracy from around 50,000 in 1932 to 150,000 in 1941.

- The Democratic Party responded to the growing importance of the black American vote. For example, at the 1936 Democrat Convention, there were 30 black delegates, one of whom, Arthur Mitchell, was granted the honour of delivering the opening address.
- First Lady Eleanor Roosevelt devoted much time and effort to assisting black Americans.

The work of Eleanor Roosevelt

In order to get New Deal legislation through Congress, Roosevelt needed Southern white congressional votes, so he left it to his wife to take a very public interest in black affairs. Eleanor Roosevelt ensured that prominent black Americans such as NAACP chief Walter White frequently met with her husband. She regularly met and was photographed with black Americans, attended black functions, and made her own position clear on countless occasions:

- In 1938, she attended the Southern Conference of Human Welfare (SCHW) in Birmingham, Alabama. The SCHW was a biracial group and it wanted the meeting to be fully integrated. Birmingham's racist police chief Eugene 'Bull' Connor (see page 122) tried to enforce local segregation laws at the meeting, but could not stop the First Lady sitting next to black delegates (she particularly wanted to sit alongside her close friend Mary MacLeod Bethune). The meeting did not condemn Jim Crow outright, but declared support for equality before the law, voter registration for the poor, and funding for black graduate students.
- In 1936, Eleanor Roosevelt invited black singer Marian Anderson to sing at the White House. In 1939, the Daughters of the American Revolution (DAR) refused to allow Anderson to sing before an integrated audience at their Constitution Hall in Washington DC in 1939 (the nation's capital was segregated). Walter White lobbied Eleanor Roosevelt and Harold Ickes, who arranged for Anderson to perform before an integrated crowd of 75,000 at Washington's Lincoln Memorial. Eleanor Roosevelt attended Anderson's performance and resigned from the DAR. She explained why in her 'My Day' column, which was published in 90 newspapers across the nation in that year, and reached a potential audience of 4 million Americans. She received more mail in support of this than on any other political issue on which she expressed an opinion in 1939.
- In 1940 alone, she promoted National Sharecroppers Week and the National Committee to Abolish the Poll Tax.

Eleanor Roosevelt

1884	Born to a wealthy family in New York City
1905	Married Franklin Roosevelt
1921	Encouraged her disabled husband to remain in politics
1933–45	First Lady
1934	Lobbied for the Costigan–Wagner anti-lynching bill
1939	Resigned from the Daughters of the American Revolution over racial discrimination
1943	Blamed by many for the Detroit race riot
1947	Helped draft the **United Nations**' Universal Declaration of Human Rights
1961	Chaired President John Kennedy's Presidential Commission on the Status of Women
1962	Died

Background

Born to two wealthy New York City socialites, Eleanor Roosevelt lost both her parents and brother to illness before she reached her teens. Despite the strong opposition of his possessive mother, Sara, Eleanor married her fifth cousin Franklin Roosevelt, and was given away in the ceremony by her uncle, President Theodore Roosevelt. Her ever-present mother-in-law made Eleanor's life a misery and precipitated a nervous breakdown. 'I did not like to live in a house which was not in any way mine … Franklin's [six] children were more my mother-in-law's children than they were mine.' Multiple bereavements, her difficult mother-in-law, and her 1918 discovery of Franklin's love affair with her social secretary, perhaps explain Eleanor's subsequent commitment to helping improve the lives of others. Sara successfully persuaded Franklin not to divorce Eleanor, but could not get him to retire from politics after he contracted polio in 1921. It was Eleanor who persuaded him to continue his political career. When he was Governor of New York State, she travelled the state and reported back on what she had seen to him.

Significance

As First Lady, from 1933 to 1945, Eleanor Roosevelt was revolutionary in her activism. That aroused considerable criticism. She was 'the eyes and ears' of Roosevelt's New Deal and worked particularly hard to promote equality of opportunity for black Americans. After Franklin's death, she was important in the early years of the United Nations and its commitment to human rights.

- During the Second World War, she made clear her support for the black Tuskegee airmen, whose aerial prowess was doubted by white racists.
- She repeatedly publicised the contrast between the American myth of freedom and equality and the situation of black Americans. For example, in a 1942 article in the *New Republic,* she said Americans needed to acknowledge that 'one of the main destroyers of freedom is our attitude toward the colored race'.

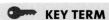 **KEY TERM**

United Nations
International organisation established after the Second World War to combat conflict, deprivation and discrimination.

Privately, Mrs Roosevelt tried to persuade her husband to endorse the anti-lynching legislation, and urged New Deal officials to provide non-discriminatory aid for blacks, especially in the South. In 1934, she read an article entitled 'NRA Codifies Wage Slavery' and pointedly passed it on to the NRA (see page 79). Her stance was exceptionally liberal for a time when her husband told racist jokes in private, and even her liberal friend Lorena Hickok saw fit to write to her after a visit to the South, 'SUCH Negroes … Many of them look and talk and act like creatures barely removed from the Ape.' Mrs Roosevelt did not go so far as to advocate integration: in an essay entitled 'If I Were Negro', she advised that 'things such as social relationships might well wait'.

What does Source K suggest about those liberal on race in the Roosevelt administration?

Roosevelt administration liberals and race

Within the Roosevelt administration, even those most sympathetic to black Americans did not advocate an end to segregation, as seen in Source K.

SOURCE K

From a letter in 1937 from Harold Ickes to Senator Josiah Bailey, a North Carolina Democrat who had accused him of trying to destroy the segregation laws.

As a matter of fact, I think it is up to the states to work out their social problems if possible, and while I have always been interested in seeing that the Negro has a square deal, I have never dissipated my strength against the particular stone wall of segregation. I believe that wall will crumble when the Negro has brought himself to a high educational and economic status. After all, we can't force people on each other who do not like each other, even when no question of color is involved … Moreover, while there are no segregation laws in the north, there is segregation in fact and we might as well recognize this.

The President's willingness to use his wife to help with black issues was evidenced in 1941. Back in 1939, Eleanor Roosevelt had helped Walter White mobilise support against an anti-DAR demonstration. In 1941, when A. Philip Randolph, Walter White and Mary McLeod Bethune threatened a March on Washington in protest against racial discrimination in the defence industries and the military, President Roosevelt sent his wife to negotiate with them. She reported back that only an anti-discrimination ordinance would halt the March, so President Roosevelt signed Executive Order 8802, which created the Fair Employment Practices Commission (see page 88).

However, the President and his aides sometimes felt irritation at Eleanor's interventions. The aides were particularly furious when she pressured the President to support the Costigan–Wagner anti-lynching bill (see page 87) and to defend the integration of the Sojourner Truth housing development for defence workers in Detroit. When there was a race riot in Detroit after the black families moved into that development, several aides blamed her and agreed with those in the Southern and Northern press who cried, 'There's blood on your hands, Mrs Roosevelt.' The Southern press were deeply hostile to Eleanor Roosevelt. For example, the *Alabama Sun* had a whole issue on what it called 'Eleanor and Some Niggers'. President Roosevelt was naturally anxious about her alienation of white Southerners, whose attacks upon her reflected upon him and caused him embarrassment with leading Southern Democrats such as Georgia Governor Eugene Talmadge, who led state critics of Mrs Roosevelt's support for the NAACP and in 1935 helped saturate Georgia newspapers with photographs of the First Lady with black Americans. There was much talk that she must have black blood, and she responded to enquiries about the issue by saying that her family had lived in the United States for so long that she could not be sure whether or not she did. Those rumours were perhaps the most conclusive proof that she was considered a great help to black Americans.

A Black Cabinet?

The nearly 50 black Americans with relatively senior positions in government departments and agencies were nicknamed the 'Black Cabinet' because of their frequent meetings and concerted pressure on the administration over the implementation of New Deal programmes. Mary McLeod Bethune was the leading figure in the group. Other members included William Hastie and Robert Weaver, both of whom worked in the Department of the Interior, and Robert Vann, who edited the *Pittsburgh Courier*. However, their influence should not be exaggerated.

Summary diagram: Conclusions: the impact of the New Deal on black Americans

Positives	Negatives
Many employed, received welfare	Discriminated against by agencies, Southern white administrators
Much black praise – voting revolution showed gratitude	Much black criticism, e.g. NRA jokes
FEPC on the national political agenda – this was new	No civil rights legislation

Chapter summary

Memories of the Republican role in the Civil War and Reconstruction encouraged most Southern whites to vote Democrat. Southern Democrats had disproportionate power in Congress because they constituted a solid voting bloc with control of major important committees (due to the seniority rules). They successfully opposed legislation to help black Americans, for example, the anti-lynching bills in the 1920s and 1930s. Then the Great Depression began to change the black situation.

In 1933, the Roosevelt administration introduced a New Deal to help the poor during the Depression. As so many black Americans were poor, they too benefited, although there were many negatives. There was racial discrimination in many New Deal agencies (for example, the CCC) and in the new social security measures (New Deal aid for workers often specifically excluded domestic service and agricultural workers, in which black Americans constituted the majority). The NRA allowed differential wage rates that disadvantaged black workers. On the other hand, most New Deal agencies and policies helped black Americans in some way, whether through providing employment, equal wages, training programmes or financial aid for the unemployed and elderly. Particularly helpful New Deal agencies included the PWA, where black workers got equal pay, the WPA, which employed many black workers, and the NYA, which offered many young black Americans education and training. Federal government aid to the poor, whether black or white, was unprecedented, and it helped revolutionise black voting. Black voters turned from the Republican Party to the Democratic Party.

Although the New Deal was often a great help to black Americans, there was no civil rights legislation under Roosevelt. Southern white Democrat power remained great in Congress, and Roosevelt did not want to risk losing New Deal relief programmes by promoting civil rights legislation. He therefore offered no support to anti-lynching bills or the NAACP campaign against the poll tax. However, under pressure of the Second World War, A. Philip Randolph forced Roosevelt to introduce the Fair Employment Practices Commission. The FEPC promoted equality in the defence industries, which employed 2 million black Americans.

The new relationship between black Americans and the federal government and the Democratic Party was emphasised in the words and deeds of First Lady Eleanor Roosevelt, who took an unprecedented and very public stance against black inequality, sometimes to the exasperation of the President's aides. Although neither Eleanor Roosevelt nor anyone else in the administration campaigned for an end to segregation in the South, the overall impact of the Roosevelt administration upon black Americans was beneficial.

Refresher questions

1 Why did the Great Depression hit black Americans particularly hard?

2 Why did anti-lynching bills fail in the 1930s?

3 How did the AAA hurt black Americans?

4 In what ways did the TVA both help and hinder black Americans?

5 What problems did black Americans face in the CCC?

6 Why did black Americans make jokes about the NRA?

7 What was the significance of the Wagner Act and the Fair Labor Standards Act for black Americans?

8 Why was the PWA particularly useful to black Americans?

9 How did the WPA impact upon black Americans?

10 What was the significance of Mary McLeod Bethune?

11 In what ways did Southern white officials ensure that white Americans benefited more than black Americans from New Deal policies and agencies?

12 Why did President Roosevelt introduce the FEPC?

13 What was the significance of Marian Anderson's 1939 concert in Washington DC?

14 How did Americans react to Eleanor Roosevelt's activism?

15 What was the 'Black Cabinet' and how important was it?

 Question practice

SOURCE ANALYSIS QUESTIONS

1 Assess the value of Source B (page 74) for revealing the responses of black Americans to the New Deal and the relationship of black Americans with white Americans in the 1930s. Explain your answer, using the source, the information given about its origin, and your own knowledge about the historical context.

2 Assess the value of Source E (page 77) for revealing the attitudes of black Americans to the New Deal and the impact of employment by New Deal agencies upon black Americans. Explain your answer, using the source, the information given about its origin, and your own knowledge about the historical context.

ESSAY QUESTIONS

1 'The New Deal unquestionably improved the lives of black Americans in the years 1933–41.' How far do you agree with this statement?

2 To what extent was Eleanor Roosevelt responsible for the change in black American voting habits in the years 1933–41?

CHAPTER 6

The Second World War and the changing geography of black America

The Second World War accelerated the Great Migration of black Americans to the cities of the North, West and Midwest. That acceleration increased urban racial tensions. One white response was an exodus to the suburbs. This changed pattern of settlement promoted the development of large black ghetto areas in many cities and is vital to the understanding of the events covered in Chapter 7. This chapter explores the changing geography of black American settlement through the following sections:

★ Migration North and West, 1941–5

★ The post-1945 Northern white exodus to the suburbs

Key dates

1941	June	Roosevelt established the Fair Employment Practices Commission	1947	Construction of first Levittown began
	Dec.	Japanese attacked Pearl Harbor, USA entered Second World War	1948	Supreme Court ruling against restrictive covenants generally ignored
1943		Notable race riots in Detroit and Harlem	1949	Congressional urban renewal programme
1945		Second World War ended	1951	Housing riots in Cicero, Chicago

1 Migration North and West, 1941–5

▶ *What was the impact of black migration during the Second World War?*

The Second World War had a dramatic impact on black Americans. Around 2 million black Americans migrated from the South to seek employment in defence industries in Northern cities such as New York, Midwestern cities such as Detroit and West Coast cities such as Oakland. As black migrant workers obtained new jobs in industry, it helped average black income rise faster in the 1940s than in any other decade of the twentieth century.

This migration impacted upon race relations in several ways. First, the denser concentration of population in urban areas and the need for workers in defence industries perceived as vital to the nation's safety, contributed to greater black political power and community consciousness and assertiveness. For example, in 1941, black labour leader A. Philip Randolph threatened to bring Washington DC to a standstill unless there was equality within the armed forces and the defence industries. Aware that the United States might soon find itself at war, President Roosevelt needed black workers, so in Executive Order 8802 he established the Fair Employment Practices Commission (FEPC) to promote equality in the defence industries in which 2 million black Americans were employed (see page 88). In summer 1942, 3 per cent of those employed in defence industries were black; by 1944, it was 8 per cent.

SOURCE A

From Executive Order 8802, 25 June 1941, in which President Franklin Roosevelt prohibited discrimination in the defence industries.

Whereas it is the policy of the United States to encourage full participation in the national defense program by all citizens of the United States, regardless of race, creed, color, or national origin, in the firm belief that the democratic way of life within the Nation can be defended successfully only with the help and support of all groups within its borders; and

Whereas there is evidence that available and needed workers have been barred from employment in industries engaged in defense production solely because of consideration of race, creed, color, or national origin, to the detriment of workers' morale and of national unity:

Now ... as a prerequisite to the successful conduct of our national defense production effort, I do hereby reaffirm the policy of the United States that there shall be no discrimination in the employment of workers in defense industries or government ... and I do hereby declare that it is the duty of employers and of labor organizations ... to provide for the full and equitable participation of all workers in defense industries ...

All contracting agencies of the Government of the United States shall include in all defense contracts hereafter negotiated by them a provision obligating the contractor not to discriminate against any worker because of race, creed, color, or national origin ... a Committee on Fair Employment Practice ... shall receive and investigate complaints of discrimination in violation of the provisions of this Order and shall take appropriate steps to redress grievances which it finds to be valid ...

Franklin D. Roosevelt

> **?** Using both the source and your own knowledge, what is the value of Source A for revealing President Roosevelt's attitude toward racial equality?

A second way in which the migration impacted upon race relations was a result of the dramatic changes in the racial composition of the population of cities such as Detroit and Chicago (see Figure 6.1, page 98). Chicago's black population rose from 250,000 in 1940 to 500,000 by 1950. The influx of black migrants and wartime overcrowding served to increase racial tensions. This led to race riots and eventually to a dramatic change in the pattern of settlement in the great American cities.

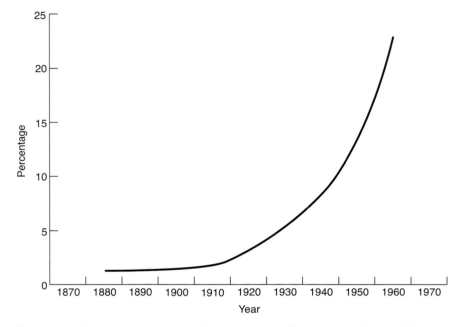

Figure 6.1 The rising percentage of black Americans in Chicago's population 1870–1960.

Wartime urban riots

Great tensions arose from what some historians have called 'defence migration': in 1943, black researchers recorded 242 major racial clashes, mostly in the North and West. The influx of black migrants made whites uneasy. As San Francisco's black population quadrupled, its mayor called for an end to the 'Negro invasion'. A liberal editor in Hartford, Connecticut, told British journalist Alistair Cooke, 'We want to keep our reputation as abolitionists and humanitarians with a conscience about the Southern Negro, but the new Negroes in town constitute a nuisance.' The speed and intensity of the 'defence migration' surpassed that of the earlier phase of the Great Migration (see page 55) and as white workers grew anxious about their jobs, neighbourhoods, schools and daughters, riots broke out.

The Detroit riots, 1943

The Midwestern city of Detroit was an excellent example of the tensions that resulted from 'defence migration'. Detroit was a centre of defence industries and employment opportunities abounded. However, when black migrants turned up for work at the Packard aircraft factory, it prompted a 'hate strike' by 25,000 white workers. In 1943, whites across the nation saw blacks as rivals for homes and employment, but the worst riots were in Detroit. When nine whites and 25 blacks died, and 800 people were injured, Detroit Mayor Edward Jeffries blamed 'Negro hoodlums' and denounced 'the mingling of Negroes and whites in the same neighborhoods' (he won re-election). Black Americans called the Detroit riots the 'Black Pearl Harbor' and the NAACP criticised the Detroit police force as the '**Gestapo** of Detroit'. One federal official said Detroit 'closely resembles bombed-out London', while his colleagues calculated that the Detroit riots lost industry over a million man-hours.

KEY TERM

Gestapo Infamous Nazi secret police.

SOURCE B

During the 1943 Detroit race riot, a black man tries to flee the white mob that has attacked him.

What do you suppose motivated the person who took the photograph shown in Source B?

The Harlem riot, 1943

On the eve of the American entry into the Second World War in December 1941, only 142 black Harlemites were working in the 30,000 war-related jobs available in New York City (this had been a major factor in encouraging Randolph's threatened March on Washington, and skilled and semi-skilled employment opportunities did improve after Executive Order 8802). One-third of Harlemites were unemployed or on relief in 1941. A Harlem resident was four times more likely to catch tuberculosis than a white inhabitant of New York City. Harlem schools were overcrowded and decayed. Harlem rents were higher than in white working-class neighbourhoods, even as housing conditions deteriorated. A 1941 survey of West Harlem found 1979 of 2191 buildings had few operational windows, lacked hot water, or were overrun by rats. Several commentators thought trouble was inevitable.

In August 1943, rumours circulated in Harlem that a white police officer had shot a black soldier in the back, in front of his mother, because the soldier was trying to protect a black woman. In truth, a white police officer had arrested a black prostitute. A black soldier had tried to help her. He had hit the officer, then fled, and got shot in the shoulder. Thousands of ordinary Harlemites gathered in the streets. Some armed black men had been waiting for such an incident, claiming, 'We'll give them Detroit in reverse.' Harlem erupted amidst cries of 'Get the white man!' What black New York City Baptist minister Adam Clayton Powell Sr described as 'criminal subhuman savages' began looting and vandalising. After order was eventually restored, around 1000 had been arrested and 700 injured, including 400 police officers. The floor of Harlem Hospital was covered in blood.

The increased racial tensions that resulted from the Second World War and 'defence migration' contributed to the phenomenon known as white flight, the white exodus from America's great cities to the suburbs.

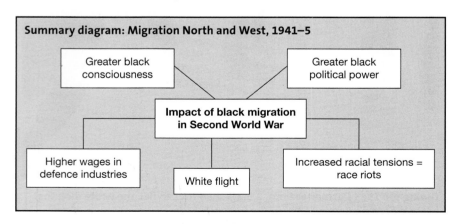

Summary diagram: Migration North and West, 1941–5

Greater black consciousness — Greater black political power — Impact of black migration in Second World War — Higher wages in defence industries — White flight — Increased racial tensions = race riots

The post-1945 Northern white exodus to the suburbs

▶ *What caused the great post-war changes in American cities?*

Suburbs were nothing new: 17 per cent of Americans lived in them in 1920. However, their growth greatly accelerated after the mid-1940s. Out of the 13 million homes built between 1948 and 1958, 11 million were in the suburbs. By 1960, 33 per cent of Americans were suburbanites and most of them were white and middle class.

There were several reasons for the explosive growth of suburbia:

- The post-Second World War housing shortage prompted the Federal Housing Administration and Veterans Administration to offer mortgages on excellent terms.
- Land and new homes were cheaper in suburban areas than in cities.
- Increased car ownership and federal highway construction made it easy for suburbanites to commute to work.
- More affluent whites sought to escape the cities, with their higher tax rates, noise, congestion and inner-city populations of poorer white and black Americans. The escapees sought spacious and comfortable homes in racially and economically homogeneous suburban neighbourhoods.

Levittowns and developments in *de facto* segregation

The most famous builders in the suburbs were the Levitt brothers, who built over 10 per cent of suburban houses. The massive suburban estates that they constructed provide a good illustration of the development of *de facto* segregation in the North.

In 1947, construction began on the first Levittown. It was situated in Hempstead, Long Island, in New York State. Built primarily for young veterans, Hempstead had 17,000 homes, 80,000 residents, seven village greens and shopping centres, nine swimming pools and two bowling alleys. Residents were expected to conform to rules stipulating weekly lawnmowing, no fences and no washing hung out at weekends.

People literally queued to buy Levittown homes: priced at around $8000 (only two and a half times the median family income), they were well-constructed with central heating and built-in closets on 60 foot by 100 foot lots that were twice the usual size. Most suburban Americans loved their spacious homes with modern bathrooms, gadget-filled kitchens and attached garages.

Levittowns were racially exclusive. Contracts for the purchase of a New York Levittown home stipulated, 'No dwelling shall be used or occupied by members of other than the Caucasian race, but the employment and maintenance of other than Caucasian domestic servants shall be permitted.' One journalist described Levittowns as 'nothing less than Jim Crow with a two-car garage'. Rocks were thrown at a black family that tried to move into a Pennsylvania Levittown in 1957. One white resident said the black owner was 'probably a nice guy, but every time I look at him I see two thousand dollars drop off the value of my house'. The NAACP won a legal case against the Pennsylvania Levittown, but the white hostility was such that the black family moved away in 1961. It was 1960 before a first Levittown house was sold to a black family in New Jersey. In the early 1950s, William Levitt defended the exclusion of black Americans from Levittowns by saying that white Americans simply did not want to live near them. In the mid-1960s, Levitt was still defending segregated housing in a Maryland development. Interestingly, the Jewish Levitts excluded Jews from their Long Island development.

How does Source C help explain the post-war growth of suburbia?

SOURCE C

From a statement by William Levitt to a reporter in the early 1950s, date unknown. Quoted in David Halberstam, *The Fifties*, Random House, 1993, p. 141.

[It was] not a matter of prejudice, but one of business … The Negroes in America … are trying to do in 400 years what the Jews in the world have not wholly accomplished in 600 years. As a Jew I have no room in my mind or heart for racial prejudice. But … I have come to know that if we sell one house to a Negro family, then 90 or 95% of white customers will not buy into the community. That is their attitude, not ours … As a company our position is simply this: We can solve a housing problem, or we can try to solve a racial problem, but we cannot combine the two.

As the most successful suburban builders, the Levitt brothers came in for great criticism. The NAACP complained to President Eisenhower (see page 111) about 'Jim Crow Levittowns', but the rest of what some cynics called 'segreburbia' was also very white. Tennessee Governor Frank Clement, tired of Northerners attacking Southern race customs, triumphantly and rightly pointed out, 'Levittowns … and other localities have proved … that the problem of mixed races living in a single place is not a Southern problem.'

The changing nature of cities

The black American Great Migration (particularly the 'defence migration'), along with the development of *de facto* segregated white suburbs, contributed to great changes in American cities such as Detroit, Chicago and Los Angeles. Black ghettos expanded dramatically in such cities. Black people lived in crowded ghettos partly out of personal choice (migrants tended to prefer areas where they already had family or acquaintances), but also because of white racism.

While black Americans in the South suffered *de jure* segregation, black migrants experienced *de facto* segregation in the North. In 1944, black journalist Louis

Martin wrote, 'the Negro has lost ground during the war period despite the surface gains in employment … [The] solution which seems most acceptable to the white majority is the Jim-Crow pattern of the South'. By the end of the war, over 75 per cent of white Americans supported residential segregation and the percentage was higher in the North than in the South.

The white contribution to ghetto growth

Northern whites assisted the growth of large, urban ghettos through violence and force, devices such as restricted covenants, and white flight. Federal government policies also played a part.

White violence and force

Frequent white use of violence and force contributed to the growth of America's black ghettos. During 1944–6, there were 46 reported fire-bombings of black homes in white neighbourhoods in Chicago. That city had 175 'neighbourhood protective associations' policing racial boundaries during the Second World War. Such associations mushroomed. For example, in 1949, the 'White Circle League' was established to 'keep white neighbourhoods free of Negroes'. Sometimes whites staged 'housing riots', as in 1951 in the Chicago suburb of Cicero, where several thousand working-class whites used looting and burning to drive out the sole black family.

Restrictive covenants and other devices

Whites used **restrictive covenants** to exclude black Americans from white neighbourhoods. For example, in post-war Chicago, 90 per cent of all housing was subject to such covenants. In New York City, housing officials used tax exemptions and land grants to support the Metropolitan Life Insurance Company's plan to build homes for 24,000 white people. The company President explained that it was not a question of white supremacy, simply that 'whites and blacks don't mix. Perhaps in 100 years they will.' White officials often managed to keep whole communities white. For example, popular Mayor Orville Hubbard of Dearborn, Michigan, was determined to exclude members of the poor population of nearby Detroit: 'Housing for Negroes is Detroit's problem. When you remove garbage from your backyard, you don't dump it in your neighbour's.' While Hubbard steadfastly refused to build public housing in Dearborn, other local governments followed existing patterns of racial population distribution when they spent federal funds (see page 84) on public housing projects. Poor whites would be housed in all-white projects in areas traditionally populated by whites, and poor blacks in all-black projects in the areas they traditionally inhabited. As a result of such white attitudes, black tenants paid high rents for poor accommodation in overcrowded ghettos.

A considerable number of black litigants took the case against racial covenants to court. In 1945, the Shelley family purchased a house in St Louis, Missouri, unaware that there had been a restrictive covenant on the property since 1911

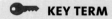 **KEY TERM**

Restrictive covenant
A clause in a property deed limiting certain uses.

that barred 'people of the Negro or Mongolian Race' from occupying the house. Louis Kraemer, who lived ten blocks away, sued to restrain the Shelley family from moving in. The Supreme Court of Missouri ruled in favour of the covenant, but the Supreme Court looked at this case and also at a Detroit case, *McGee v. Sipes*. The NAACP's top lawyer, **Thurgood Marshall**, argued the case for the McGees. In *Shelley v. Kraemer* (1948), the Supreme Court ruled that courts could not enforce restrictive covenants. However, white opposition ensured that the ruling proved ineffective in practice. Realtors, lending institutions, developers and city officials continued to make it difficult for black Americans to buy decent housing.

White flight

Whites who could afford it fled the nearby overcrowded black ghettos in cities. For example, many whites who lived in Oakland, California, moved to the nearby suburb of Hayward. Safely in the suburbs, they were unwilling to pay the increased taxes needed to assist inner-city areas. As a result, the physical fabric of the ghettos went into a spiral of decline.

Southern cities faced similar urban crises as black pressure for desegregation grew during the period 1955–63 (see Chapter 7). For example, Atlanta, Georgia, was experiencing large-scale white flight by the mid-1960s.

The federal government and urban decay

Federal government policies played a big part in changing the nature of American cities. When the Federal Housing Administration (FHA) distributed billions of dollars of low-cost mortgages from the late 1940s, it openly excluded applicants considered 'risks' – these were mostly black Americans, Jews or other 'un-harmonious racial or nationality groups'. In effect, residential segregation was the public policy of the US government. Furthermore, federally constructed highways enabled suburbanites to commute to city jobs.

Federal policies clearly bore considerable responsibility for urban decline. Although in 1949 Congress authorised the construction of 810,000 subsidised public housing units and the purchase of slum areas for redevelopment, it was commonly said that 'urban renewal equals Negro removal'. Chicago politicians, businessmen and developers manipulated zoning regulations and used federal funds for urban renewal to tear down black neighbourhoods and replace them with commercial buildings or more expensive housing for whites.

The federal government's attempt to alleviate the black housing shortage was ineffective. Only 200,000 federal housing units had been built by 1955, and 325,203 by 1965. One famous public housing project was Pruitt-Igoe, in St Louis, where 33 apartment buildings were constructed in 1954–6: the eleven-storey buildings incorporated 2800 units, open galleries, laundries, play areas and a 'river of trees'. By 1963, the open spaces had become scrubby and littered, and muggings and rapes were common in the corridors and the rare elevator that worked. Pruitt-Igoe's architect said, 'I never thought people were that destructive.' Some said that such projects failed because they were too big, too high-rise, and too sterile, and because the housing authorities were starved of money for maintenance and security.

Generally, both black and white Americans blamed each other for the changed the nature of American cities, and as a result **black separatist** radicalism gained in popularity (see page 129). Black ghetto discontent would be demonstrated in the multiple riots of the long, hot summers of 1964–8 (see page 142).

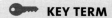
KEY TERM

Black separatists Black people who desired to live apart/away from whites.

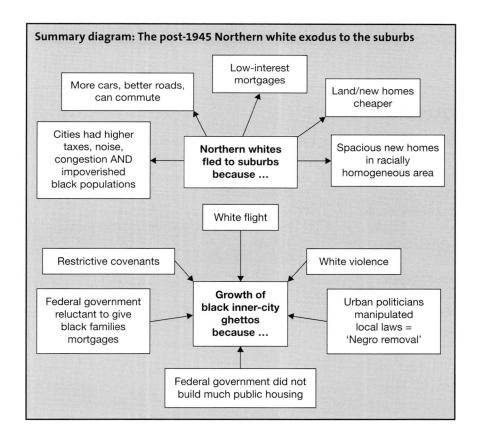

Summary diagram: The post-1945 Northern white exodus to the suburbs

Chapter summary

The Second World War saw the great black 'defence migration' to Northern and Western cities. The results included higher wages for black Americans, but also increased racial tensions and riots in many cities, including Detroit and New York. This helped to promote white flight to the suburbs.

Suburbia grew dramatically because it offered cheaper and bigger homes, an increasingly easy commute, and escape from inner-city problems. Those problems included higher taxes, noise, congestion, and black Americans. Suburban developments often excluded the black population, for example, Levittowns.

The growth of suburbia was paralleled by the dramatic growth of large black ghettos, for example, in Chicago's South Side. That growth was due to white flight, white violence, restrictive covenants, and federal government policies on mortgages and roads. This would soon lead to black alienation and militancy.

 ## Refresher questions

1 What did Executive Order 8802 say?

2 What was the significance of the Detroit riots of 1943?

3 What were the results of defence migration?

4 Why did suburbia grow so dramatically after the Second World War?

5 How did William Levitt justify his exclusion of black families?

6 How did white citizens contribute to ghetto growth?

7 How did the federal government contribute to ghetto growth?

8 What was the significance of *Shelley v. Kraemer*?

9 Why was Thurgood Marshall important?

10 How did local government officials contribute to ghetto growth?

11 How and with what success did the federal government attempt to alleviate the black housing shortage?

12 What explanations were offered for the decay of the Pruitt-Igoe projects?

CHAPTER 7

I have a dream, 1954–68

Black civil rights activism had a long history, but the decade after 1954 is frequently seen as its high point. Black organisations and black leaders were particularly dynamic in this period, and their activism gained unprecedented sympathy from white Americans and the federal government. President Lyndon Johnson (1963–9) was determined to end *de jure* segregation and black disfranchisement in the South. This was accomplished with the Civil Rights Act (1964) and the Voting Rights Act (1965), the passage of which owed much to Johnson, black activism and changing white opinion. This legislation revolutionised the South, but did little to help the ghettos of the North, Midwest and West. Malcolm X helped draw national attention to the ghetto problems from which the Black Power movement developed, but Johnson, King and the Black Power movement found those problems insoluble.

These issues are covered in sections on:

★ The NAACP, Earl Warren and the Supreme Court

★ The Montgomery bus boycott, 1956

★ The work and impact of Martin Luther King Jr, SCLC, SNCC and CORE, 1957–63

★ The Civil Rights Act and the Voting Rights Act

★ The role of Malcolm X

★ King, the ghettos and black divisions

★ Black Power

Key dates

1954		Supreme Court's *Brown* ruling	
1956		Montgomery bus boycott	
1957		King established SCLC	
1960		SNCC established after sit-ins	
1961		Freedom Rides	
1963	Summer	SCLC's Birmingham campaign; March on Washington; Kennedy promoted civil rights bill	
	Nov.	Johnson became President	
1964		SNCC's 'Mississippi Freedom Summer'	

1964–8		Annual ghetto riots	
1964		Civil Rights Act	
1965	Jan.–Feb.	King's Selma campaign	
	Aug.	Voting Rights Act; Watts riots	
1966		King's Chicago campaign	
	July	Meredith March	
		CORE and SNCC increasingly advocated Black Power	
	Oct.	Black Panthers established	
1967	July	Newark riots	
1968	April	King assassinated; Fair Housing Act	

The NAACP, Earl Warren and the Supreme Court

▶ *Why was the Supreme Court so important to black Americans?*

Some historians have criticised the NAACP (see page 48) as excessively bureaucratic and conservative, but it was behind the first major events of the productive decade that began in 1954: the *Brown* ruling and the Montgomery bus boycott.

From its foundation in 1909, the NAACP used several tactics to achieve its aim of black equality. These included lobbying (see page 69), publicity (see page 74), boycotts (see page 113), and litigation. The litigation strategy had many successes. In 1950, in response to the work of brilliant NAACP lawyers such as Thurgood Marshall (see page 104), the Supreme Court ruled against segregated universities and railroad dining cars and almost overturned *Plessy v. Ferguson* (see page 40). However, the most important Supreme Court ruling against segregation was the *Brown* ruling.

Brown v. Board of Education (1954)

Kansas was one of seventeen states with legally segregated schools. Oliver Brown, a church minister in Topeka, Kansas, could not send his daughter to a whites-only school five blocks away. She had to walk across railroad tracks to reach the all-black school twenty blocks away. Brown decided to challenge the segregated school system. The NAACP supported him, in the belief that there was a good chance of success because Kansas was not a Southern state.

Marshall argued before the Supreme Court that segregation was against the 14th Amendment. In *Brown v. The Board of Education, Topeka, Kansas* (1954), Chief Justice Earl Warren and the Supreme Court adjudged that even if facilities were equal (they never were), separate education was psychologically harmful to black children.

Results and significance of *Brown*

The *Brown* ruling was highly significant:

- It was a great triumph for the NAACP's long legal campaign against segregated education, because it seemed to remove all constitutional sanctions for racial segregation by overturning *Plessy v. Ferguson*.
- The victory was not total: the Supreme Court gave no date by which desegregation had to be achieved and said nothing about *de facto* segregation.
- The NAACP returned to the Supreme Court and obtained the *Brown II* (1955) ruling that integration be accomplished 'with all deliberate speed', but there was still no date for compliance. Warren believed that schools and administrators needed time to adjust. The white reaction suggests he was right.

SOURCE A

A school for black children in Ruleville, Sunflower County, Mississippi, in 1950.

- White Citizens' Councils were quickly formed throughout the South to defend segregation. By 1956, they boasted around 250,000 members. The Councils challenged desegregation plans in the law courts and Southern politicians were supportive. The Ku Klux Klan was revitalised.
- Acceptance of *Brown* varied. Desegregation was introduced quite quickly in the peripheral and urban South: 70 per cent of school districts in Washington DC, and in the border states of Delaware, Kentucky, Maryland, Missouri, Oklahoma and West Virginia, desegregated schools within a year. However, in the Deep South, in Georgia, South Carolina, Alabama, Mississippi and Louisiana, schools remained segregated. Some school boards maintained white-only schools by manipulating entry criteria. From 1956 to 1959, white 'massive resistance' campaigners in Virginia closed some schools rather than desegregate. Virginia labour unions financed segregated schools when the public schools were closed.
- *Brown* inspired further activism. NAACP activist Rosa Parks (see page 113) recalled, 'You can't imagine the rejoicing among black people, and some white people.'

> What can you infer from Source A about the educational opportunities for black children in Mississippi in 1950?

The role of Earl Warren and the Supreme Court

Although the Supreme Court had no powers of enforcement, its rulings had considerable prestige and moral force. The Warren court's responsiveness to NAACP litigation was vital to black progress, especially in *Brown*. There were four main reasons for the Supreme Court's *Brown* ruling.

First, the NAACP was persistent and effective in its litigation. It was the NAACP that responded to the black plaintiffs in the five conflated cases from five different areas (Delaware, Kansas, South Carolina, Virginia and Washington DC) that became known as the *Brown* case, and Marshall was one of the most persuasive litigants in Supreme Court history.

❓ What is the main thrust of the Truman administration's argument in Source B, and why do you suppose the administration chose to emphasise it?

Second, President **Harry Truman** (1945–53) supported black equality and when the school segregation cases were first brought before the Supreme Court in December 1952, the Truman **administration**'s lawyer argued persuasively against discrimination (see Source B).

SOURCE B

From the government's brief in the *Brown* case, December 1952. Quoted in Peter Irons, *Jim Crow's Children*, Penguin, 2002, pp. 135–7.

The problem of racial discrimination is particularly acute in the District of Columbia, the nation's capital. This city is the window through which the world looks into our house. The embassies, locations, and representatives of all nations are here … Foreign officials and visitors naturally judge this country and our people by their experiences and observations in the nation's capital …

[A black visitor to Washington faces humiliation:] With very few exceptions, he is refused service at downtown restaurants, he may not attend a downtown movie or play, and he has to go into the poorest section of the city to find a night's lodging. The Negro who decides to settle in the District must often find a home in an overcrowded, sub-standard area. He must often take a job below the level of his ability. He must send his children to the inferior public school set aside for Negroes and entrust his family's health to medical agencies which give inferior service. In addition, he must endure the countless daily humiliations that the system of segregation imposes upon the one-third of Washington that is Negro …

Capital custom not only humiliates colored citizens, but is a source of considerable embarrassment … Foreign officials are often mistaken for American Negroes and refused food, lodging and entertainment … [As **Secretary of State** *Dean Acheson wrote last week] 'As might be expected, Soviet spokesmen regularly exploit this situation in propaganda against the United States, both within the United Nations and through radio broadcasts and the press, which reaches all corners of the world … The segregation of schoolchildren on a racial basis is one of the practices in the United States that has been singled out for hostile foreign comment in the United Nations and elsewhere. Other peoples cannot understand how such a practice can exist in a country which professes to be a staunch supporter of freedom, justice, and democracy … [Racial discrimination] remains a source of constant embarrassment to this Government in the day-to-day conduct of its foreign relations; and it jeopardizes the effective maintenance of our moral leadership of the free and democratic nations of the world.'*

Third, the majority of the Supreme Court justices in the years 1952–4 were Democrat appointees, and although several were Southerners, they disliked Jim Crow schools. The justices all took the liberal view that racism could be overcome by integration. They were impressed when the NAACP argued that when ten black South Carolina children chose white rather than black dolls in a test, it proved that segregated schools produced inferiority complexes.

Fourth, Chief Justice **Earl Warren** played a vital role in the *Brown* ruling. After hearings in late 1953, Warren worked hard to get consensus on the *Brown* ruling, believing that Supreme Court unanimity would help persuade the nation to accept the principle and practice of integrated schools. He compromised, cajoled and charmed his fellow justices for five months, in order to obtain consensus. President **Eisenhower** (1953–61) had appointed Warren and he tried but failed to dissuade him from supporting integrated schools: after all, the President said, Southern whites were not 'bad people … All they are concerned about is to see that their sweet little girls are not required to sit in school alongside some big overgrown Negroes.' Eisenhower recognised Warren's role in the *Brown* ruling and called his nomination the 'biggest damn fool mistake' he had ever made.

Problems implementing *Brown*

The difficulties involved in the implementation of Supreme Court rulings were well illustrated in the city of Little Rock, Arkansas, in 1957. Little Rock planned full compliance with *Brown* by 1963 and began with the integration of Central High School. Nine black students reported there in September 1957. Arkansas Governor Orval Faubus decided to exploit white racism to ensure his re-election. Declaring it his duty to prevent the disorder that would arise from integration, he ordered the Arkansas **National Guard** to keep black students out of Central High.

President Eisenhower had said he could never envisage sending in federal troops to enforce *Brown*, which doubtless encouraged Governor Faubus. Eisenhower did not believe in federal government activism, but Little Rock's mayor told him the mob was out of hand and begged him to act. Furthermore, the Constitution and federal law seemed threatened. Eisenhower said he had an 'inescapable' responsibility for enforcing the law against 'disorderly mobs' and 'demagogic extremists', and that Soviet propaganda about Little Rock damaged America's international 'prestige and influence'.

Melba Pattillo

One of the 'Little Rock nine', Melba Pattillo, wrote about her experiences years later in her book *Warriors Don't Cry*. She had volunteered to be a guinea-pig when asked by the NAACP and church leaders. Her father was opposed, saying it endangered both her and his job, but she was inspired by the 'self-assured air' of Thurgood Marshall, and the support of her mother and grandmother, many blacks and a few whites. When she walked into Central High, a white man violently assaulted her crying, 'I'll show you niggers the Supreme Court cannot run my life.' Others cried 'Two, four, six, eight, we ain't gonna integrate', 'Keep away from our school', 'Go back to the jungle', 'Lynch the niggers'. One white befriended her at school. She trusted him, in spite of the warnings of her family. Most white students were actively hostile: she was pushed down the stairs and had burning paper and chemicals thrown at her. Subsequently she wondered 'what possessed my parents and the adults of the NAACP to allow us to go to school in the face of such violence'.

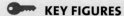

KEY FIGURES

Earl Warren (1891–1974)

A lawyer, Warren was Governor of California (1943–53), and then appointed as Chief Justice of the Supreme Court by President Eisenhower. The Warren Court (1953–69) was known for its liberalism, notably in the *Brown* ruling against segregated schools.

Dwight D. Eisenhower (1890–1969)

General Eisenhower was a career soldier whose role in winning the Second World War made him universally popular. As President (1953–61), he was reluctant to intervene in the segregated South. He disliked the *Brown* ruling, but eventually tried to help enforce it at Little Rock in 1957. Concerned about the black vote and white violence against black Americans, his administration supported two feeble Civil Rights Acts (1957 and 1960) designed to promote black voting.

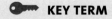

KEY TERM

National Guard State-based US armed forces reserves.

So, to Southern cries of 'invasion', Eisenhower sent in troops to protect the black children.

Results and significance of Little Rock

Little Rock showed how *Brown* met tremendous grassroots resistance in practice, although the Supreme Court ploughed on, ruling in *Cooper v. Aaron* (1958) that any law seeking to keep public schools segregated was unconstitutional.

Neither local nor national authorities were keen to enforce *Brown*. As Eisenhower feared, Faubus closed the schools rather than integrate (he was re-elected four times). Eisenhower did not respond. It was 1960 before Central High School was integrated and 1972 before other Little Rock schools were. However, cities such as Atlanta desegregated to avoid Little Rock-style violence and publicity.

The black struggle made for dramatic pictures and Little Rock demonstrated the increased importance of the media to black progress. The image of black children being harassed and spat at by aggressive white adults in Little Rock influenced moderate white Americans. On-site television reporting was pioneered at Little Rock, which drew national television crews.

Perhaps the most significant result of Little Rock was that it confirmed the belief of some black Americans that they could not rely upon court decisions, but needed to do more of the direct, non-violent action that had been successful during the Montgomery bus boycott.

? Why do you suppose images of the 'Little Rock Nine' walking toward Central High amidst hostile white crowds affected Northern white opinion?

SOURCE C

Elizabeth Eckford, one of the 'Little Rock nine', trying to enter Central High School in Little Rock, Arkansas in 1957.

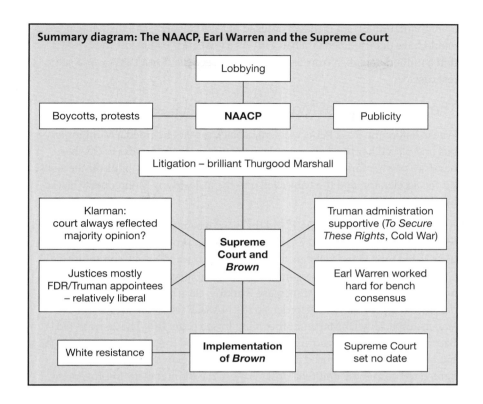

Summary diagram: The NAACP, Earl Warren and the Supreme Court

② The Montgomery bus boycott, 1956

▶ *What was the impact of the Montgomery bus boycott?*

In December 1955, Rosa Parks caught the bus home after a hard day's work as a seamstress in a department store in Montgomery, Alabama. The bus filled up and a white man was left standing. The driver ordered four black passengers to move. Parks refused. She was arrested and charged with a violation of the Montgomery city bus segregation ordinance that forbade black passengers sitting parallel with whites.

Many writers portray 42-year-old Parks as a tired old lady who had been exhausted by the day at work and could not take any more, but she was an NAACP activist. After joining the organisation in 1943, she became Montgomery branch secretary and worked very closely with branch leader E.D. Nixon, a railroad porter inspired by and close to A. Philip Randolph (see page 63). The branch had been looking to challenge Montgomery's bus segregation laws and contemplated using Claudette Colvin, arrested in March 1955 for refusing to give up a seat to a white passenger. However, Colvin was a pregnant, unmarried teenager accused of assault. Parks said the white press would have depicted her as 'a bad girl'. As a challenge could cost the NAACP half a million dollars, Nixon decided that 'respectable' Rosa Parks was a safer test case.

The mobilisation of Montgomery's black community

Weeks before the Rosa Parks incident, a black mother boarded a Montgomery bus and placed her two babies on the front 'white' seats in order to free her hands to pay her fare. The driver yelled, 'Take the black dirty brats off the seats', hit the accelerator, and the babies fell into the aisle. Many Montgomery blacks had had enough.

After Parks' arrest, the NAACP and the black teachers and students of Alabama State College organised a day-long bus boycott in protest. Students copied and distributed propaganda leaflets to elicit support from the black community. Churches could contribute organisation, location, inspiration and financial aid, and their involvement would increase working-class black participation and decrease the possibility of disorder, so the NAACP worked with local church leaders, especially Dr Martin Luther King Jr (see page 115). The 26-year-old Baptist minister had already rejected an offer to lead the local NAACP branch, but he let his church be used as a meeting place to plan the boycott and agreed to head a new umbrella organisation, the Montgomery Improvement Association (MIA).

Boycotts hit white pockets and were a traditional and effective mass weapon. Black passengers boycotted streetcars throughout the South between 1900 and 1906 and used their economic power (most passengers were black) to try to gain bus seating on a **first-come, first-served** basis in Baton Rouge, Louisiana, in 1953. These Baton Rouge tactics were now adopted in Montgomery. Montgomery's black community successfully boycotted buses on the day of Rosa Parks' trial, demanding 'first-come, first-served', courteous drivers and the employment of black drivers. When the city commissioners rejected these proposed changes, the one-day boycott became a year-long one, and the aim became the integration of the buses.

A successful long-term boycott required unanimity and sacrifice among Montgomery's 50,000 black population. For the most part, it was achieved. On one occasion during the boycott, a black man used the bus. As he got off, an elderly black woman with a stick raced toward the bus. 'You don't have to rush, **auntie**', said the white driver. 'I'll wait for you.' 'In the first place, I ain't your auntie', she said. 'In the second place, I ain't rushing to get on your bus. I'm jus' trying to catch up with that nigger who jus' got off, so I can hit him with this here stick.'

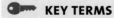

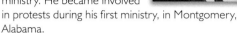

Martin Luther King Jr

1929	Born in Atlanta, Georgia
1944–8	Studied at Morehouse College, Atlanta; ordained as a minister
1948–51	Attended Crozer Theological Seminary in Pennsylvania
1951–4	Doctorate at Boston University's School of Theology; married Coretta Scott
1954	Pastor of Dexter Avenue Baptist Church, Montgomery, Alabama
1956	Headed Montgomery Improvement Association (MIA) during Montgomery bus boycott
1957	Founded Southern Christian Leadership Conference (SCLC); spoke at Prayer Pilgrimage for Freedom in Washington DC
1959	Moved to Atlanta, headquarters of SCLC
1960	Encouraged sit-ins
1963	Initiated Birmingham campaign; 'I have a dream' speech during March on Washington; *Time* magazine's man of the year
1964	Nobel Peace Prize
1965	Led Selma, Alabama, voting campaign
1966	Chicago ghetto campaign
1967	Criticised Vietnam War
	Initiated Poor People's Campaign
1968	Assassinated in Memphis, Tennessee

Born into a reasonably prosperous black family in Georgia, King followed his father and grandfather into the ministry. He became involved in protests during his first ministry, in Montgomery, Alabama.

King's inspirational oratory and charisma made him the leading spokesman for black Americans in the years 1956–65. His 'I have a dream' speech was the highlight of the March on Washington (1963). His Birmingham campaign (1963) contributed to the passage of the Civil Rights Act (1964), and his Selma campaign was vital to the passage of the Voting Rights Act in 1965. He was far less successful when he turned his attention to ghetto problems.

King's 'dream' was of integration, and he made a very important contribution to greater integration in the South. He maintained considerable white support for his campaigns to end *de jure* segregation and black disfranchisement in the South, but lost it when he focused on the ghettos. He was criticised by many black Americans, notably those who advocated the greater assertiveness that characterised Black Power. Some Black Power advocates considered him an Uncle Tom (see page 157), but he was a radical in the context of the South at that time and in his calls for redistribution of American wealth.

Black vs white

The *Brown* ruling inspired the establishment of White Citizens' Councils throughout the South and Montgomery's White Citizens' Council organised the opposition to the bus boycott. Its membership rose from 6000 to 12,000 during February and March 1956. The Council was dominated by leading city officials, and they ordered harassment of black activists. In January 1956, King was arrested for driving at 30 mph in a 25 mph zone. His house was bombed. When his family urged him to quit, he subsequently admitted he was tempted but felt called by God to continue. His inspirational words even appealed to some whites:

If we are wrong, the Supreme Court of this nation is wrong. If we are wrong, the Constitution of the United States is wrong. If we are wrong, Jesus of Nazareth was merely a … dreamer.

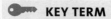

KEY TERM

Passive resistance Non-violent refusal to comply with a particular policy.

King stressed this was 'non-violent protest', but it was not **passive resistance**, it was 'active non-violent resistance to evil'.

When Montgomery whites used Alabama's anti-boycott law against the black community, their mass indictments attracted national media coverage and inspired Northern donations to the MIA. King was the first boycott leader to be tried. He was found guilty and chose a fine rather than 368 days in jail.

White hostility encouraged the MIA to up the stakes. After litigation partly funded by the NAACP, the Supreme Court cited *Brown* when it ruled segregated buses unconstitutional in *Browder v. Gayle* (1956). In December 1956, desegregated buses began operating and the boycott was called off.

The impact of the Montgomery bus boycott

Bus boycotts were not new, but there had never been a boycott as long, well organised, well supported and well publicised as the Montgomery one. Rosa Parks' defiance and the boycott were very much a product of the whole black community of Montgomery. 'Every day in the early 1950s we were looking for ways to challenge Jim Crow laws', she said. The boycott demonstrated the power of a whole black community using direct non-violent action. Montgomery whites could not believe local blacks had started and sustained the movement ('We know the niggers are not that smart'), but as Claudette Colvin said, 'Our leaders is just we ourselves'. The boycott showed the importance and potential of a sustained demonstration of black economic power. Black shoppers could not get downtown without the buses, so businesses lost $1 million. White businessmen began to work against segregation. Furthermore, while black churches were sometimes reluctant to engage in activism, Montgomery demonstrated how church involvement greatly assisted the fight for equality. Although the boycott showed the continuing effectiveness of the NAACP strategy of working through the law courts (it took the *Browder* decision to finally get the buses desegregated), its greatest impact lay in that it advertised an effective alternative to NAACP's litigation tactic.

In Montgomery itself, the impact of the boycott was limited. The buses were desegregated, but nothing else was. Still, black morale was boosted and when the Ku Klux Klan responded to *Browder v. Gayle* by sending 40 carloads of robed and hooded members through Montgomery's black community, the residents did not retreat behind closed doors as usual, but came out and waved at the motorcade, showing how black morale had been boosted.

The regional and national impact of the boycott was greater. It inspired

- similar successful bus boycotts in twenty Southern cities
- individuals such as Melba Pattillo (see page 111)
- more Northern white support
- more cooperation between black Northerners and Southerners.

Perhaps most importantly, it brought King, with all his inspirational rhetorical gifts, to the forefront of the movement. In 1957 he established a new organisation, the Southern Christian Leadership Conference (SCLC) (see page 118). This was important because the NAACP had been persecuted in the Deep South since *Brown*. However, it aroused jealousy among King's colleagues and other black leaders and organisations. A friend noted that:

> *King's colleagues felt that he was taking too many bows and enjoying them … he was forgetting that victory … had been the result of collective thought and collective action.*

King felt the need to reassure people:

> *I just happened to be here … If M.L. King had never been born this movement would have taken place … there comes a time when time itself is ready for change. That time has come in Montgomery, and I had nothing to do with it.*

One local activist agreed: it was 'a protest of the people … not a one-man show … the leaders couldn't stop it if they wanted to'. King claimed the boycott signalled the emergence of 'the new Negro', but NAACP leader Roy Wilkins disagreed.

SOURCE D

NAACP leader Roy Wilkins, talking in 1956 about the 'New Negro', quoted in Robert Cook, *Sweet Land of Liberty*, Longman, 1998, p. 39.

The Negro of 1956 who stands on his own two feet is not a new Negro; he is the grandson or the great grandson of the men who hated slavery. By his own hands, through his own struggles, in his own organized groups – of churches, fraternal societies, the NAACP and others – he has fought his way to the place where he now stands.

Using the content of Source D and your own knowledge, what reasons can you suggest that help to explain Wilkins' viewpoint?

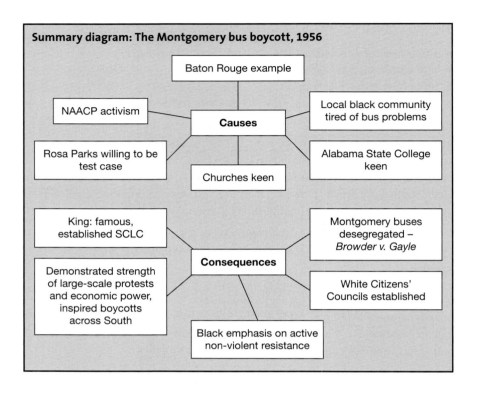

Summary diagram: The Montgomery bus boycott, 1956

- Baton Rouge example
- NAACP activism
- Local black community tired of bus problems
- Rosa Parks willing to be test case
- **Causes**
- Alabama State College keen
- Churches keen

- King: famous, established SCLC
- Montgomery buses desegregated – *Browder v. Gayle*
- **Consequences**
- Demonstrated strength of large-scale protests and economic power, inspired boycotts across South
- White Citizens' Councils established
- Black emphasis on active non-violent resistance

③ # The work and impact of Martin Luther King Jr, SCLC, SNCC and CORE, 1957–63

► *What was the impact of King, SCLC, SNCC and CORE to 1963?*

The NAACP had focused on litigation, but the organisations established after the Montgomery bus boycott emphasised different tactics.

SCLC, 1957–60

The Southern Christian Leadership Conference (SCLC) was established because King considered an organisation that focused upon the South a necessity while the national organisations were weakened: the NAACP was persecuted in the South because of *Brown* and the Congress of Racial Equality (CORE) (see page 120) lacked dynamism. King also hoped that a religious organisation would suffer less persecution and he felt that new tactics were needed because while the NAACP's legal challenges had demolished 'separate but equal' in the law courts, *de jure* segregation continued in the South. The Montgomery bus boycott had shown that direct non-violent action could effect change.

King sought to draw attention to abuses and the easiest method was to organise a march. His 1957 march in Washington DC attracted around 20,000 people. However, even King admitted that the SCLC achieved little else in its first three years of existence: its Crusade for Citizenship, a grassroots campaign designed to encourage black voting, was poorly organised and lacked a salaried staff or mass support. Furthermore, SCLC aroused antagonism. 'Jealousy among black leaders is so thick it can be cut with a knife', said the black *Pittsburgh Courier*. NAACP leader Roy Wilkins disliked King and favoured litigation, while King preferred mass action. A new organisation, the Student Nonviolent Coordinating Committee (SNCC, pronounced SNICK), preferred empowerment of local communities.

Sit-ins and the birth of the SNCC, 1960

In 1960, four black college students spontaneously ignored a request to leave the all-white Woolworth's cafeteria in Greensboro, North Carolina. Other students took up and retained the seats, day after day, forcing the lunch counter to close. This prompted 'sit-ins' across the South that were joined by 70,000 students, better educated than their parents and more impatient with the slow progress towards equality. Sit-ins had been pioneered by CORE (see page 120) in Chicago in the Second World War, but as King said, 'What is new in your fight is the fact that it was initiated, fed, and sustained by students.' Unprecedented media interest was also new.

King assured the students of full SCLC support, and Atlanta students persuaded him to join them in sit-ins. Although critics such as disgruntled SCLC employee Ella Baker implied that King always had to be in the forefront, King's leadership was characterised by a willingness to be led by others when their methods were effective.

The significance of the sit-ins

The sit-ins helped to erode Jim Crow: loss of business made Woolworth's desegregate all its lunch counters by the end of 1961, and 150 cities soon desegregated various public places. The sit-ins confirmed that direct action was the new focus of black activism. However, when the black students set up SNCC, inter-organisational strife increased. Top NAACP lawyer Thurgood Marshall said he did not want to represent 'a bunch of crazy colored students', while SNCC accused SCLC of keeping donations intended for SNCC, and King's public acknowledgement of NAACP/SCLC divisions infuriated Roy Wilkins.

Encouraged by Ella Baker, the students felt their actions had rendered King's 'top-down' leadership obsolete. Between 1961 and 1964, SNCC worked to empower and mobilise ordinary black Americans in places like Danville (Virginia), Lowndes County (Alabama), Albany (Georgia), Pine Bluff (Arkansas) and the Mississippi Delta.

CORE and the Freedom Rides, 1961

The Congress of Racial Equality was established in Chicago in 1942 by James Farmer, amongst others. The leaders believed in passive resistance to segregation, and held wartime sit-ins in protest against segregated restaurants in Chicago. In 1947, CORE tested Supreme Court rulings against segregation on interstate transport (*Morgan v. Virginia*, 1946) and on interstate bus facilities (*Boynton v. Virginia*, 1960) in a 'Journey of Reconciliation' through several Southern states. CORE repeated that tactic in 1961, but now called it a Freedom Ride.

This time, CORE's 'Freedom Rides' electrified the civil rights movement and were successful. A small, integrated group rode buses across the South. CORE's director James Farmer explained that:

> *We planned the Freedom Ride with the specific intention of creating a crisis. We were counting on the bigots in the South to do our work for us. We figured that the government would have to respond if we created a situation that was headline news all over the world, and affected the nation's image abroad.*

As expected, racists attacked black passengers. In Anniston, Alabama, they used clubs and chains and burned the buses. SNCC sent in reinforcement riders.

The Freedom Rides publicised Southern white racism and lawlessness in the South and led Attorney General **Robert F. Kennedy** and the Interstate Commerce Commission to try to enforce the Supreme Court rulings on desegregated interstate travel in November 1961. However, black divisions continued. CORE insisted SCLC announce that CORE had originated the Freedom Ride!

KEY FIGURE

Robert Fitzgerald Kennedy (1925–68)

Appointed Attorney General by his brother, President John F. Kennedy. One of Kennedy's preoccupations as Attorney General (1961–4) was civil rights issues. He was elected to the US Senate in 1965, but was assassinated during what seemed likely to be a successful presidential election campaign in 1968.

? What can you infer about the Freedom Riders and their motives from Source E?

SOURCE E

From original recordings of interviews with some of the Freedom Riders (no date given) (available at: http://clio.lib.olemiss.edu/cdm/search/collection/freeriders/).

1. Charles Person, African American:

I grew up in Atlanta ... at a time when America needed scientists ... My [test] scores and my [grades] were good enough to get me accepted at MIT [Massachusetts Institute of Technology], but Georgia Tech was also the number one engineering school in the South, so I applied to Georgia Tech, and of course rejected my application. So I could not understand, here we were competing with the Russians, because the Russians had launched Sputnik, and we say we needed scientists, yet I was being denied an opportunity to go to a school which I was eminently qualified to go to, so that gave me the impetus to get involved in all the civil rights activities that were happening on campus ... So this was a great time, the energy on campus with all the kids being involved in all those kind of activities, it just snowballed. Once I got involved, it was infectious.

2. Sandra Nixon, African American:

I grew up in New Orleans … I was … in college at Southern University in New Orleans and met some … members of the Congress on Racial Equality. After listening to them talking about the social injustices that were going on in the city of New Orleans, I decided to become a member of … CORE.

3. Joan Trumpower Mulholland, white

I was born in Washington, DC … My involvement came about from my religious conviction, and the contradiction between life in America with what was being taught in Sunday School. I was at Duke University in Durham [North Carolina], which was the second city to have sit-ins, and the Presbyterian chaplain arranged for the students … to come over and talk with us about what the sit-ins were about and the philosophical and religious underpinnings … At the end, they invited us to join them on sit-ins in the next week or so, and that started a snowball effect.

4. Albert Gordon, white:

Why some of us have been ready to do things, and others not? In my own past, I was born in Europe, and I did see the Nazis, and most of my family was killed by the Nazis during World War II in the concentration camp, because I was Jewish … So those things can explain in part my social conscience, but by no means all together … When I saw the young people first in the first sit-ins and the courage that they had to have, and then saw a couple of years later the bus in Anniston, and Jim Peck being so brutally beaten, I thought I just had to do something, and simply volunteered and proceeded.

SCLC and Birmingham, 1963

King and SCLC had accomplished little that was effective until their spring 1963 concentration upon segregation and unequal opportunities in Birmingham, Alabama. King chose Birmingham because:

- SCLC felt it needed to demonstrate that it could be dynamic and successful in the face of competing civil rights organisations and the increasing attractiveness of black nationalism (see page 129).
- The NAACP and SNCC were relatively inactive in Birmingham, where the local black leader was affiliated to the SCLC and King's own brother was a pastor.
- Although white extremists had recently castrated a black American, prohibited the sale of a book that featured black and white rabbits, and campaigned to stop 'Negro music' being played on white radio stations, influential white businessman felt racism held the city back, so white divisions looked promising.

- King described Birmingham as 'by far' America's 'worst big city' for racism. Under the hot-tempered Public Safety Commissioner 'Bull' Connor, Birmingham was likely to produce violent white opposition that would gain media attention and hopefully win national sympathy. 'To cure injustices', said King, 'you must expose them before the light of human conscience and the bar of public opinion'.
- Although President **John F. Kennedy** (1961–3) had suggested that he would prove helpful to black Americans if elected, he had demonstrated little enthusiasm for a civil rights bill as President. King hoped Connor would force a response from Kennedy: 'The key to everything is federal commitment.'

Events in Birmingham

The Birmingham campaign was King and SCLC's first great triumph, but he miscalculated at first. The SCLC failed to recruit enough local demonstrators, because many felt that the recent electoral defeat and imminent retirement of Connor made action unnecessary. King admitted to 'tremendous resistance' in the black community to his demonstrations. The SCLC had to use demonstrators in crowded areas to give the impression of mass action and to encourage onlookers to participate.

Then, as expected, Connor attracted national attention. His police and their dogs turned on black demonstrators. King defied an injunction and marched, knowing his arrest would gain national attention. Kept in solitary confinement and without private meetings with his lawyer or sufficient writing paper, his inspirational 'Letter from Birmingham Jail', written partly on prison toilet paper, eloquently defended direct action. His wife Coretta's phone call to President Kennedy obtained his release.

It remained difficult to mobilise sufficient demonstrators. 'You know, we've got to get something going', said King. 'The press is leaving.' The SCLC enlisted black schoolchildren, some as young as six, but this aroused considerable local opposition. King himself had doubts about the morality of the policy and the black separatist Malcolm X (see page 131) said, 'Real men don't put their children on the firing line'. Still, the policy was successful: soon, 500 young marchers were in custody and Birmingham was headlines again. Connor's high-pressure water hoses tore clothes off students' backs and SCLC succeeded in its aim of 'filling the jails'. A leading SCLC official 'thanked' 'Bull' Connor for his violent response, without which there would have been no publicity.

An agreement was reached to improve black opportunities in Birmingham, but the Klan tried to sabotage it, bombing King's brother's house and King's motel room. That caused black riots. A policeman was stabbed, and Birmingham degenerated into chaos that President Kennedy described as 'damaging the reputation' of Birmingham and the United States. Attorney General Robert Kennedy feared Birmingham could trigger off national violence, and urged his

KEY FIGURE

John Fitzgerald Kennedy (1917–63)

Kennedy's Second World War record, charm, and family wealth, helped ensure his election to the House of Representatives (1947–53), Senate (1953–60) and the White House. President Kennedy (1961–3) wooed black voters in his 1960 campaign, but was slow to help them when President. He finally reacted to black pressure and supported a civil rights bill in 1963. His real preoccupation was the Cold War.

brother to protect the Birmingham agreement: 'If King loses, worse leaders are going to take his place.'

Results and significance of Birmingham

Birmingham was the first real success of King and SCLC. King had correctly anticipated the reactions of Connor and the media. 'There never was any more skillful manipulation of the news media than there was in Birmingham', gloated one leading SCLC staffer. King had shown that he could lead from the front and force desegregation, if through rather artificially engineered violence. He recognised that non-violent demonstrations 'make people inflict violence on you, so you precipitate violence', but he excused it: 'We are merely bringing to the surface the tension that has always been at the heart of the problem.' One critic said, 'He marches for peace on one day, and then the very next day threatens actions we think are coldly calculated to bring violent responses from otherwise peaceful neighborhoods.'

Little changed in Birmingham itself, but SCLC's campaign inspired protests throughout the South and demonstrated segregation at its worst to the United States and the world. The Kennedy administration admitted that Birmingham persuaded it to push the bill that eventually became the 1964 Civil Rights Act. 'We are on the threshold of a significant breakthrough', said King, 'and the greatest weapon is the mass demonstration'.

The March on Washington, 1963

A. Philip Randolph (see page 63) masterminded the August 1963 March on Washington, which aimed to encourage passage of the civil rights bill and promote black employment opportunities. Malcolm X's rise to prominence (see page 133) made King fearful that black Americans might reject non-violence, so he was desperate for the March to succeed. It did. Roughly 25 per cent of the predominantly middle-class crowd of around 250,000 were white and King's memorable speech made a powerful appeal to white America when it referred to the Declaration of Independence and the Bible, and emphasised the Old Testament God who freed his enslaved people. This was King the leader at his best, involved in an action the morality of which could not be doubted, and the effectiveness of which he increased when he helped persuade a reluctant Roy Wilkins (see page 117) to participate and made his superb 'I have a dream' speech.

The March on Washington was the first (and only) time the major civil rights leaders collaborated on a national undertaking. It impressed television audiences worldwide. Historians disagree over the extent to which its emotional impact helped the passage of civil rights legislation: while many contemporaries were thrilled by the march, the *New York Times* described Congress as unmoved. Malcolm X was unimpressed: 'the Negroes spent a lot of money, had a good time, and enjoyed a real circus or carnival type atmosphere', he mocked, but he questioned how 'a one-day "integrated" picnic' was suddenly going to change white racism. 'Now that the show is over, the black masses are still without land, without jobs, and without houses. Their Christian churches are still being bombed, their innocent little girls murdered. So what did the March on Washington accomplish? Nothing.'

SNCC and Mississippi

The SNCC's finest hour was the Black Freedom Movement in Mississippi. In 1960, only 5.2 per cent of black adults in Mississippi could vote (the Southern average was over 30 per cent). White voter registrars set impossible questions and opened offices at inconvenient hours to stop black voter registration. Although half of Mississippians were black, there had been no elected black official since 1877. With black people politically powerless, Mississippi whites spent three times more on white students and 70 per cent of Mississippi's black population were illiterate. Mississippi had few black doctors and segregated hospitals, and this, in combination with black poverty, ensured that black babies were twice as likely to die as white babies. Half a million black Mississippians had migrated North to escape to a better life. King's close associate Andrew Young confessed that the SCLC 'knew better than to try to take on Mississippi'. In 1961, increasingly victimised NAACP activists called for help from the SNCC, knowing that SNCC's white volunteers would attract media attention to Mississippi's racist horrors.

With no federal government protection against white extremists, SNCC worked at the local community level, establishing Freedom Schools to educate would-be voters and get them registered. It was poorer black people such as sharecropper Fannie Lou Hamer rather than the black middle class who responded to SNCC's 1964 voter registration drive (the Mississippi Summer Project, or **Freedom Summer**). Northern volunteers, most of whom were white, poured into Mississippi to help and America took notice when three young activists, two white, one black, were murdered by segregationists (the 1988 movie *Mississippi Burning*, discussed on page 181, would be based upon this incident). SNCC helped to politicise many poor black Mississippians (especially women), develop new grassroots leaders, and bring black Mississippi suffering to national attention.

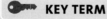

KEY TERM

Freedom Summer SNCC voter registration campaign in Mississippi in 1964.

Summary diagram: The work and impact of Martin Luther King Jr, SCLC, SNCC and CORE, 1957–63

Date	Organisation	Event	Impact
1957	NAACP	Little Rock	Great publicity, forced federal government intervention, BUT showed strength of white resistance
1957	SCLC	Washington March	Not much
1960	Student sit-ins	Greensboro	Inspired sit-ins across South and establishment of SNCC BUT inter-organisational rivalry
1961	CORE	Freedom Rides	JFK administration ordered desegregated interstate transport
1963	SCLC	Birmingham	Good national publicity, helped civil rights bill, not so good for Birmingham
1963	All black organisations	March on Washington	Brilliant publicity, possibly helped civil rights bill
1964	SNCC	Mississippi Freedom Summer	Culmination of 3-year campaign to empower local communities through vote – good political education but whites still stopped most blacks voting

The Civil Rights Act and the Voting Rights Act

▶ *How, why and with what results were the Civil Rights Act and Voting Rights Act passed?*

When President Kennedy was assassinated in November 1963 and Vice President Lyndon Johnson became President, *de jure* segregation remained in operation in many areas of life in the South. Although Kennedy had finally championed the civil rights bill, it was stuck in Congress. However, the South was soon transformed by the Civil Rights Act (1964) and the Voting Rights Act (1965).

Lyndon Johnson's role in the passage of the 1964 Civil Rights Act

The civil rights bill faced considerable opposition in Congress, but finally became an act because:

● Black activists had drawn the nation's attention to injustices. Johnson said, 'The real hero of this struggle is the American Negro'.

Lyndon Baines Johnson

1908	Born in Texas
1935–7	Headed Texas NYA
1937–61	Congressman then senator
1961–3	Vice President
1963–9	President
1964–5	Important to passage of Civil Rights Act and Voting Rights Act
1973	Died

Lyndon Baines Johnson ('LBJ') spent his life in public service: teacher (1929), congressional aide (1931–5), Texas state director for Roosevelt's National Youth Administration (1935–7), Congressman (1937–49), Senator (1949–61), Vice President (1961–3) and President (1963–9). He loved power, but claimed it was because of what it enabled him to do for others.

Senator Johnson demonstrated unparalleled mastery of the American legislative process. As President, he obtained unprecedented social reform legislation but his '**Great Society**' programmes had varied success. From 1965 he was increasingly focused on the Vietnam War, his escalation of which made him unpopular.

Johnson's presidency was highly significant for black Americans through the 1964 Civil Rights Act, the 1965 Voting Rights Act, subsidised medical care, unemployment programmes, and welfare payments. He remained dissatisfied ('So little have I done. So much have I yet to do.'), but when his body lay in state in Congress, it was mostly black Americans who queued to pay their respects.

- The NAACP, labour unions and churches lobbied Congress incessantly, and by January 1964, 68 per cent of Americans favoured the bill. Congress could not afford to ignore this marked swing in public opinion.
- The nation was saddened by Kennedy's death. Passing his bill seemed an appropriate tribute.
- Important congressional leaders such as Hubert Humphrey worked hard on the bill.
- President Johnson was determined to get the bill passed.

Johnson envisaged an American 'Great Society' in which there would be 'an end to poverty and racial injustice'. He described how, when his black cook drove to Texas, she could not use the whites-only facilities in a petrol station:

> When they had to go to the bathroom, they would … pull off on a side road, and Zephyr Wright, the cook of the vice-president of the United States, would squat in the road to pee. That's wrong. And there ought to be something to change that.

Johnson believed reform would help the economic, political and spiritual reintegration of the South within the nation. When Johnson told the NAACP leader Roy Wilkins he was 'free at last' from his Texas constituency and could finally promote equality as President, Wilkins considered him 'absolutely sincere'.

Johnson's role in the passage of the Civil Rights Act was crucial. One aide believed the bill would not have passed without him. He forced it past the white Southern Democrats in Congress. He devoted a staggering amount of his time, energy and political capital to breaking the Senate filibuster, made emotive appeals to Kennedy's memory and national traditions and ideals, and won over some Southerners by appealing to their self-interest. When addressing Southerners, he emphasised how the bill would help to get blacks and **Hispanics** working:

> I'm gonna try to teach these nigras that don't know anything how to work for themselves instead of just breedin'; I'm gonna try to teach these Mexicans who can't talk English to learn it so they can work for themselves … and get off of our taxpayer's back.

The importance of the Civil Rights Act of 1964

The 1964 Civil Rights Act prohibited discrimination in public places, furthered school desegregation, gave the federal government the legal tools to end *de jure* segregation in the South, and established an Equal Employment Commission. It would help revolutionise the South.

However, there were problems. First, the act did little to facilitate black voting. Second, black Americans in ghettos across the nation were resentful that it did nothing to combat the poverty and discrimination from which they suffered. Within weeks of the passage of the Act, there were riots in the black ghettos of many East Coast cities. Johnson was hurt and angry but he ploughed ahead, repeatedly requesting voting rights legislation from Congress. Congress remained unmoved – until Martin Luther King Jr's campaign in Selma.

King's Selma campaign

Despite the 1964 Civil Rights Act, little changed in Selma, Alabama. Roughly half of Selma's 29,000 population was black but, despite a SNCC campaign, there were only 23 registered black voters. **Justice Department** lawsuits remained bogged down in the courts.

King chose to campaign in Selma because he

- considered Selma 'a symbol of bitter-end resistance to the civil rights movement in the Deep South'
- hoped to exploit the divisions within the white community
- was convinced Selma's Sheriff Jim Clark could be trusted to react violently and expose Southern racism at its worst
- hoped to revitalise the SCLC and the whole civil rights movement after a year in which he said he and the others had 'failed to assert the leadership the movement needed'.

King led would-be voters in unsuccessful attempts to register at Selma's County Court. Several incidents made headlines. A state trooper shot a black youth who was trying to shield his mother from a beating. Whites threw venomous snakes at blacks trying to register. Keen for the media to expose brutality and

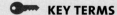

KEY TERMS

Hispanics Spanish-speaking people in the USA, usually of Latin American origin.

Justice Department Branch of the federal government in Washington DC with special responsibility for enforcing the law and administering justice.

unfairness, King held back men who tried to stop Clark clubbing a black woman then got himself arrested for marching and told the media, 'This is Selma, Alabama. There are more Negroes in jail with me [3400 in February 1965] than there are on the voting rolls.'

The SCLC and SNCC organised a march from Selma to Montgomery (Alabama's capital) to publicise the need for a Voting Rights Act. Eighty Alabama whites joined the march. Television viewers saw state troopers attack the marchers with clubs and tear gas in a 'Bloody Sunday' that aroused nationwide criticism of Selma's whites. Under pressure from President Johnson to stop the marches, King got the marchers to approach the state troopers then retreat. His failure to inform SNCC of these tactics embittered SCLC–SNCC relations.

King and Johnson's roles in the passage of the Voting Rights Act

King thought the nationwide criticism of 'Bloody Sunday' and the sympathetic interracial marches in cities such as Chicago, Detroit, New York and Boston constituted 'a shining moment in the conscience of man'. 'Bloody Sunday' prompted Congress to pass the Voting Rights Act (August 1965). Johnson made one of his best speeches in support of the legislation – King said it brought tears to his eyes. Jim Crow would no doubt have been legislated out of existence eventually, but President Johnson and Martin Luther King Jr ensured that it was done in 1964–5.

SOURCE F

> **From President Lyndon Johnson's address to Congress, 15 March 1965 (available at: https://en.wikisource.org/wiki/We_Shall_Overcome).**
>
> … *in Selma, Alabama … long-suffering men and women peacefully protested the denial of their rights as Americans. Many were brutally assaulted … Rarely are we met with a challenge … to the values and the purposes and the meaning of our beloved Nation. The issue of equal rights for American Negroes is such an issue … The command of the Constitution is plain … It is wrong – deadly wrong – to deny any of your fellow Americans the right to vote in this country … A century has passed, more than a hundred years, since the Negro was freed. And he is not fully free tonight … A century has passed, more than a hundred years, since equality was promised. And yet the Negro is not equal … The real hero of this struggle is the American Negro. His actions and protests, his courage to risk safety and even to risk his life, have awakened the conscience of this Nation … He has called upon us to make good the promise of America. And who among us can say that we would have made the same progress were it not for his persistent bravery, and his faith in American democracy?*

> Why do you suppose the words in Source F were considered effective?

The importance of the Voting Rights Act 1965

The Voting Rights Act provided for federally appointed registrars to combat Southern white devices such as literacy tests (see page 68). It had a dramatic effect on the South. By late 1966, only four of the old Confederate states had fewer than 50 per cent of their eligible black voters registered. By 1968, even Mississippi was up to 59 per cent. In 1980, the proportion of registered black voters was only seven per cent less than the proportion of whites. The number of black Americans elected to office in the South increased six-fold between 1965 and 1969, then doubled between 1969 and 1980. The South was transformed.

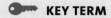

KEY TERM

Black nationalist Favouring a separate black nation either within the USA or in Africa.

Summary diagram: The Civil Rights Act and the Voting Rights Act

Act	How/why passed	What it said	Results, significance
1964 Civil Rights Act	• Black activism, e.g. Birmingham • Hard work by Johnson and Congressional Democrats • Changing public opinion, e.g. churches • Feeling that owed it to JFK	• Gave federal government tools to end *de jure* segregation in the South • Further school desegregation • Established Equal Employment Commission	Finished off Jim Crow BUT little to help black voting
1965 Voting Rights Act	• King's Selma campaign, especially Bloody Sunday • Johnson's pressure on Congress	Federal registrars, no more tricks such as poll tax (forbidden by the 24th Amendment 1964), literacy tests	Revolutionised politics in South – many black officials elected

---

 ## 5 The role of Malcolm X

 ► *How and why was Malcolm X important?*

While organisations such as the SCLC and SNCC focused upon the problems of the South, a separatist **black nationalist** religion, the Nation of Islam (NOI), gained members in the ghettos of the North and Midwest. Its most famous convert was Malcolm X.

Elijah Muhammad and the Nation of Islam

The Nation of Islam (a name designed to suggest a nation within the American nation) was founded by Wallace Fard in Detroit in 1930. After Fard mysteriously disappeared in 1934, **Elijah Muhammad** led the NOI from 1934 to 1975. Although Elijah Muhammad said he was the prophet of Allah, the 'Messenger of Islam', his teachings differed from those of orthodox Islam. For example, he

KEY FIGURE

Elijah Muhammad (1897–1975)

Born Elijah Poole to a Georgia sharecropper family that joined the first Great Migration and eventually settled in Detroit, 'Elijah Muhammad' joined Marcus Garvey's UNIA (see page 61), but was more impressed by the Nation of Islam, which he led from 1934 until his death. The organisation grew dramatically under his leadership, although that probably owed more to Malcolm X.

claimed that Allah originally created people black, and that other races were created by an evil scientist, Yakub, whose last evil creation was the white race. Whites would rule the world for several thousand years, but then Allah would return and end their supremacy.

The NOI aimed to

- provide an alternative to the white man's Christian religion
- persuade members to live a religious life
- increase black self-esteem
- keep blacks and whites separate
- improve the black economic situation.

From the 1930s to the 1950s, the NOI set up temples in ghettos in cities such as Detroit, New York, Chicago, Boston and Philadelphia. In the 1950s, the NOI's most effective preacher, Malcolm X, attracted the attention and devotion of frustrated ghetto-dwellers when he rejected integration, bitterly attacked white Americans and Christianity's 'turn the other cheek' philosophy, and advocated **separatism** and armed self-defence against white aggression. Estimates of NOI membership vary. It was possibly as high as 100,000 in 1960, and perhaps 250,000 by 1969. The NOI newspaper *Muhammad Speaks* had a weekly circulation of 600,000 by the mid-1970s.

KEY TERM

Separatism Desire for black Americans to live separate but equal lives from whites, in all-black communities or even a black state or in Africa.

Achievements of the NOI

Assessment of the Nation of Islam's achievements varied. Critics pointed out that some NOI solutions to black problems (a return to Africa or a separate black state in the Deep South) were unrealistic and that NOI teachings exacerbated divisions between blacks and whites and between blacks. While the NOI derided Martin Luther King Jr as an Uncle Tom, a 'fool' who humiliatingly begged for access to a white-dominated world and urged non-violence on his defenceless followers, King described the NOI as a 'hate group'.

On the positive side, the NOI attracted and inspired ghetto-dwellers because of its self-confidence and emphasis on racial pride and economic self-help. Elijah Muhammad created many businesses, such as restaurants, bakeries and grocery stores, which gave rare employment opportunities in the ghettos. The NOI expected converts to live a religious life, and it emphasised marital chastity and the rejection of alcohol, tobacco and flamboyant clothing. When Elijah Muhammad died in 1975, the white press was often surprisingly generous, saying he was 'a kind of prophetic voice in the flowering of black identity and pride' (*Newsweek*) who inculcated 'pride in thousands of black derelicts, bums, and drug addicts, turning outlaws into useful, productive men and women' (*Washington Post*).

Malcolm X

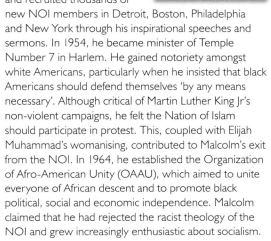

1925	Born in Omaha, Nebraska
1941	Moved to Boston
1946–52	Imprisoned; joined the Nation of Islam (NOI)
1950s	The Nation of Islam's most effective preacher and recruiter
1959	Attracted national and international attention after television programme, *The Hate That Hate Produced*
1963	Criticised King's 'non-violence'
	Suspended by Elijah Muhammad
1964	Left the NOI, established Organization of Afro-American Unity (OAAU)
1965	Assassinated by NOI gunmen

Nebraska-born Malcolm Little's father supported Marcus Garvey's separatism and nationalism. Malcolm blamed his father's death in 1931 on white supremacists. Unable to cope with Depression-era poverty, Malcolm's mother was committed to an insane asylum in 1939. Malcolm left school full of resentment: he claimed that a white teacher told him his ambition to become a lawyer was not a 'realistic goal for a nigger'. Malcolm subsequently described his white foster parents as patronising. He moved to Boston's black ghetto, and worked as a shoeshine boy and railroad waiter. In his autobiography, he claimed that he became involved in a great deal of crime, including drug dealing, pimping and burgling. He joined the Nation of Islam while in prison, adopted the name Malcolm X (the X replaced the African name taken from his enslaved ancestors), and recruited thousands of new NOI members in Detroit, Boston, Philadelphia and New York through his inspirational speeches and sermons. In 1954, he became minister of Temple Number 7 in Harlem. He gained notoriety amongst white Americans, particularly when he insisted that black Americans should defend themselves 'by any means necessary'. Although critical of Martin Luther King Jr's non-violent campaigns, he felt the Nation of Islam should participate in protest. This, coupled with Elijah Muhammad's womanising, contributed to Malcolm's exit from the NOI. In 1964, he established the Organization of Afro-American Unity (OAAU), which aimed to unite everyone of African descent and to promote black political, social and economic independence. Malcolm claimed that he had rejected the racist theology of the NOI and grew increasingly enthusiastic about socialism.

Malcolm drew attention to ghetto problems. He became a black icon and role model for black youth, particularly through his exploration of his feelings of rejection and his search for his identity in his 1965 *The Autobiography of Malcolm X*.

Malcolm inspired a new generation of black leaders such as SNCC's Stokely Carmichael and CORE's Floyd McKissick, along with the **Black Power** movement in general, but he alienated white America.

Malcolm X

Malcolm converted to the NOI while in prison. It taught him that the 'white man is the devil' – 'a perfect echo' of his 'lifelong experience', he said. His sermons and talks and especially his criticism of non-violence attracted national and international attention. He scoffed at the 'American dream' ('What is looked upon as an American dream for white people has long been an American nightmare for black people') and at King's call for integration ('Imagine, you have the chance to go to the toilet with white folks!') He mocked Christianity, a religion 'designed to fill [black] hearts with the desire to be white … A white Jesus. A white virgin. White angels. White everything. But a black Devil of course.'

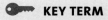

KEY TERM

Black Power
A controversial term, with different meanings, such as black pride, black economic self-sufficiency, black violence, black separatism, black nationalism, black political power, black working-class revolution, black domination.

Malcolm's split from the NOI

In late 1963, Malcolm was suspended by Elijah Muhammad for making unpopular remarks about the assassination of President Kennedy. In March 1964, Malcolm announced his split with the NOI, disappointed by Elijah Muhammad's expensive lifestyle, romantic affairs and rejection of political involvement. 'We spout our militant revolutionary rhetoric', said Malcolm, but 'when our own brothers are … killed, we do nothing'.

On an April 1964 pilgrimage to Mecca, Malcolm established good relations with white Muslims and rejected the NOI's racial theology (see page 131). Opinions vary as to whether Malcolm's development was genuine or whether his sudden realisation of the 'true' Islam was a ploy to re-create his public image. In May, he established the Organization of Afro-American Unity (OAAU), which aimed to unite all people of African descent and promote black political, social and economic independence. Like King, he increasingly criticised economic inequality in the United States ('You show me a capitalist and I'll show you a bloodsucker').

In February 1965, Malcolm was assassinated by NOI gunmen.

The aims, methods and achievements of Malcolm X

Malcolm X aimed to improve black American lives. His main methods were to advertise and encourage critical thinking on race problems, and, some would say, to encourage racial hatred and violence. While in Washington DC for the passage of the 1964 Civil Rights Act, Malcolm claimed, 'I'm here to remind the white man of the alternative to Dr King.'

Malcolm's achievements are controversial. Thurgood Marshall (see page 104) criticised the NOI ('run by a bunch of thugs') and Malcolm ('what did he achieve?'). Black baseball player Jackie Robinson commented that King and others put their lives on the line in places like Birmingham, but Malcolm did not. Many considered his suggestions that black Americans were frequently left with no alternative other than violence to be negative, irresponsible and unhelpful. *Time* magazine described him as 'an unashamed demagogue whose gospel was hatred and who in life and in death was a disaster to the civil rights movement'.

On the other hand, Malcolm drew attention to the dreadful conditions in America's ghettos, brought America's black population in closer contact with oppressed black people throughout the world, and inspired the new generation of black leaders such as SNCC's Stokely Carmichael and CORE's Floyd McKissick and the Black Power movement in general (see page 142). He was the first prominent advocate of separatism and what subsequently became known as Black Power during the great civil rights era.

SOURCE G

From Martin Luther King Jr's interview with Alex Haley in *Playboy* magazine, January 1965. King talks about Malcolm X (available at: https://en.wikiquote.org/wiki/Martin_Luther_King,_Jr.).

Maybe he does have some of the answers. I don't know how he feels now, but I know that I have often wished that he would talk less of violence, because violence is not going to solve our problem. And in his litany of articulating the despair of the Negro without offering any positive, creative alternative, I fear that Malcolm has done himself and our people a great disservice. Fiery, demagogic oratory in the black ghettos, urging Negroes to arm themselves and to prepare to engage in violence, as he has done, can reap nothing but grief.

Paying attention to the provenance, does Source G give a fair assessment of Malcolm X?

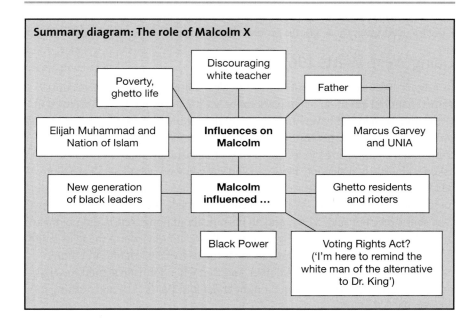

Summary diagram: The role of Malcolm X

King, the ghettos and black divisions

▶ *When and why did black divisions become prominent?*

By 1965, black divisions had increased. The SNCC resented King's prominence, accused the SCLC of 'leader worship' of King, and publicly criticised the SCLC as perpetually leaving behind 'a string of embittered cities' that they had used to make a point then left. They cited Selma activists who felt betrayed when the SCLC raised a great deal of money while Selma was headline news, then left and spent the money in the North (see page 127). There were also divisions resulting from the role of Malcolm X in relation to ghetto problems.

Ghetto problems

The great civil rights movement of 1955–65 helped transform the South, but did nothing for the ghettos that had mushroomed as a result of the Great Migration and the Second World War (see Chapter 6). Ghetto life was soul destroying. Housing was poor, amenities were few. It was difficult to break out of the cycle of poverty. Ghetto schools did not provide a solid educational foundation for good jobs and only 32 per cent of ghetto pupils finished high school, compared to 56 per cent of white children. In the 1950s and 1960s, automation decreased the number of factory jobs for unskilled workers. That led to a disproportionate amount of black unemployment. In the early 1960s, black Americans constituted around 10 per cent of the population but 46 per cent of the unemployed. Ghettos such as Chicago's had 50–70 per cent black youth unemployment. After Selma, King focused upon these ghetto problems.

Going West: Watts 1965

In August 1965, riots broke out in Los Angeles' Watts ghetto. The Watts riots gained national attention when black mobs set fire to several blocks of stores in Watts and 34 died, 1000 were injured, 3500 rioters and looters were arrested, and over $40 million damage was done to largely white-owned businesses. Local churchmen sought King's help. The scenes of devastation shocked him. He asked some Watts residents, 'How can you say you won, when 34 Negroes are dead, your community is destroyed, and whites are using the riots as an excuse for inaction?' They replied, 'We won because we made them pay attention to us.' One Watts resident said, 'King, and all his talk about nonviolence, did not mean much. Watts had respect for King, but the talk about nonviolence made us laugh. Watts wasn't suffering from segregation, or the lack of civil rights. You didn't have two drinking fountains.' Another said that when Johnson signed the civil rights bill in 1964, 'Nobody even thought about it in Watts … It had nothing to do with us.'

KEY TERM

Socialism Political philosophy that society should be as equitable as possible in terms of economic and social standing.

King told the press Watts had been 'a class revolt of underprivileged against privileged … the main issue is economic'. King had thought of 'freedom' in terms of ending segregation and exercising the vote, but he now began to define it in terms of economic equality. He was turning to **socialism**, calling for 'a better distribution of the wealth' of America. Bayard Rustin, King's ex-Communist friend, recalled how the Watts riots impacted upon King, who was:

> absolutely undone, and he looked at me and said, 'You know, Bayard, I worked to get these people the right to eat hamburgers, and now I've got to do something … to help them get the money to buy it' … I think it was the first time he really understood.

Going North: Chicago

Watts convinced King that he needed to focus upon the ghettos and do something to stop the increasing tendency towards violence and radicalism amongst some black groups. He decided upon a Chicago campaign because:

- 700,000 of Chicago's 3 million people were black. Concentrated in the South Side and West Side ghettos, they suffered employment, housing and education problems. Chicago's black schools were so overcrowded that students attended in half-day shifts.
- Other great Northern cities were effectively shut off to King. Harlem Congressman Adam Clayton Powell told him to keep out of New York City and the local NAACP leader told him to keep out of Philadelphia.
- Chicago had a tradition of sporadic protest. In 1961, there were 'wade-ins' in protest against the customary segregation of South Side beach. In October 1963, over half of Chicago's 500,000 black students boycotted their inferior segregated schools for a day in protest (no improvement resulted).
- Chicago's influential religious community supported the civil rights movement.
- Chicago's Mayor Daley relied heavily on black voters and was not racist.

Throughout the winter of 1965–6, King was unsure of what to do in Chicago, but in late spring 1966, SCLC finally focused on discrimination in housing sales, which stopped blacks moving out of ghetto slums.

King and life in Chicago

SCLC rented a West Side ghetto flat for King during the campaign. When the landlord found out who his new tenant was, an army of repairmen moved in to make it habitable. Chicagoans joked that the easiest way for King to improve ghetto housing would be for him to move from building to building. King led reporters around rat-infested, unheated ghetto dwellings. He and his aides dramatically seized a Chicago slum building and, dressed in work clothes, began repairing it. King told the press that SCLC had collected the tenants' rents to finance this. His claim that moral questions were more important than legal ones in this case generated media criticism.

The campaign went badly. Local Chicago activists and SCLC members squabbled and the lack of a clearly defined issue did not help. The July 1966 Chicago rally turnout was only 30,000. King said Mayor Daley did too little, Daley said he did his best. King's family neared disintegration as they sampled Chicago ghetto life. Without pools or parks in which to escape the suffocating heat of their small, airless flat, and with surrounding streets too crowded and dangerous to play in, King's children screamed and fought as never before. With the temperature near 100°F (38°C), the police shut off the water spouting from a fire hydrant black youths had been using to cool themselves. After some youths were arrested, angry blacks ran through the streets. King persuaded the police to release the youngsters and encouraged ministers to join him in walking the ghetto streets to try to calm people. Black crowds derided and walked away from him, but he persuaded Daley to make fire hydrants and pools available.

De facto segregated housing

Chicago whites feared black neighbours would hit property values, increase crime and threaten cultural homogeneity, so when 500 CORE marchers defied King and provocatively entered the white working-class suburb of Cicero to publicise the fact that they could not reside there, they were greeted with rocks, bottles and racist abuse. The police, shocked by cries of 'nigger lovers' from fellow whites, did little to protect marchers. When a rock hit King, it made national headlines and the marches became more peaceful. On one occasion, 800 policemen protected 700 marchers.

The riots caused $2 million worth of damage. Many influential whites blamed King and invited him to leave. King blamed Daley and said, 'A nonviolent movement cannot maintain its following unless it brings about change.' He warned that discriminatory house-selling practices would lead to 'Negro cities ringed with white suburbs' and that dangerous hatred and fear developed when people were separated. The *Chicago Tribune* denounced King as a 'paid professional agitator' and asked how he could justify demonstrations that turned violent. He said demonstrations might stop greater violence and that the problem was not the marches but the conditions that caused people to march.

Assessment of SCLC in Chicago

Most contemporaries felt King had achieved little in Chicago. The *New Republic* said, 'so far, King has been pretty much of a failure at organizing' and one of King's closest admirers described the Chicago venture as a 'fiasco' and 'disaster'. It failed because:

- SCLC could not effect a social and economic revolution in Chicago within months. Ella Baker (see page 119) always said SCLC's failure to develop grassroots participation often led to disaster. She felt King hoped to effect a miraculous transformation without educating and organising black Chicagoans for a long-term haul after he and the media had gone. King was in fact realistic about the prospects in the ghettos, saying in 1968, 'It's much easier to integrate lunch counters than it is to eradicate slums. It's much easier to guarantee the right to vote than it is to guarantee an annual minimum income and create jobs.'
- In contrast to Montgomery (see page 116), Chicago's black population was too large to mobilise. Furthermore, it was divided. The NAACP, some of the local black churches, radical Black Muslims (see pages 129–31), and black conservatives who loathed SCLC's attempt to recruit and convert violent young gang members, were unhelpful. Black Congressman William Dawson had represented Chicago since the Second World War. He opposed mass action, believing it caused trouble. Most slum landlords were black and they resented King's criticism of them.

- Mayor Daley outwitted King. Daley's police protected the marchers. He stopped the marches by threatening fines (which the SCLC could not afford) rather than filling the jails.
- National press coverage of King's Chicago Freedom Movement was unsympathetic toward black marches in white neighbourhoods. Black entry into a white neighbourhood would cause property prices to plummet and black schoolchildren from deprived backgrounds might damage the educational and employment prospects of white children. Whites were tired of black protests and ghetto riots (see page 142) and resistant to radical change that affected their property rights.
- The anti-Vietnam War movement was leeching funds and energy from the civil rights movement. President Johnson was politically close to Mayor Daley and alienated by King's criticism of the Vietnam War, so the federal government did not support the Chicago Freedom Movement.

Martin Luther King Jr's stance on the Vietnam War

The United States became involved in Vietnam as a result of the Cold War: because the Vietnamese Communists led the struggle for Vietnamese independence from France, President Truman (1945–53) helped the French. When the French left Vietnam, President Eisenhower (1953–61) promoted an anti-Communist regime in South Vietnam that struggled to cope with the threat from Communist North Vietnam. By the end of Kennedy's presidency (1961–3), the United States had around 15,000 'advisers' helping the South Vietnamese regime, which still could not defeat the Communists. So, from 1965, President Johnson sent in hundreds of thousands of American ground troops and bombed the Communists.

Some black Americans resented the disproportionate number of black casualties in the Vietnam War and felt kinship with the poor, non-white Vietnamese. In January 1967, a picture of Vietnamese children with burn wounds from American bombs made King publicly critical. He said that President Johnson's Great Society (see page 126) poverty programme had raised hopes for the inhabitants of the inner-city ghettos, but that now the funds were being diverted to the war.

Sixty per cent of African Americans believed King's opposition to the war hurt the civil rights movement, and 48 per cent disapproved of this alienation of President Johnson. 'I know it can hurt SCLC, but I feel better', said King. 'I was politically unwise, but morally wise.'

SOURCE H

From Martin Luther King Jr's 'Beyond Vietnam' speech at Riverside Church Meeting, New York, 4 April 1967. Quoted in Clayborne Carson *et al.*, *Eyes on the Prize*, Penguin, 1991, pp. 387–93.

Over the past two years, as I have moved to break the betrayal of my own silences and to speak from the burnings of my own heart, as I have called for radical departures from the destruction of Vietnam, many persons have

What arguments does Source H give against black participation in the Vietnam War?

questioned me about the wisdom of my path … Why are you speaking about war, Dr. King? Why are you joining the voices of dissent? Peace and civil rights don't mix, they say. Aren't you hurting the cause of your people? they ask … I have several reasons for bringing Vietnam into the field of my moral vision … [First] A few years ago … it seemed as if there was a real promise of hope for the poor – both black and white – through the [Great Society] Poverty Program … Then came the build-up in Vietnam and I watched the program broken and eviscerated … and I knew that America would never invest the necessary funds or energies in rehabilitation of its poor so long as adventures like Vietnam continued to draw men and skills and money … So I was increasingly compelled to see the war as an enemy of the poor and to attack it as such.

[Second] We were taking the black young men who had been crippled by our own society and sending them eight thousand miles away to guarantee liberties in Southeast Asia which they had not found in Southwest Georgia and East Harlem. So we have been repeatedly faced with the cruel irony of watching Negro and white boys on TV screens as they kill and die together for a nation that has been unable to seat them together in the same schools. ..

My third reason … grows out of my experience in the ghettos of the North over the last three years … As I have walked among the desperate, rejected and angry young men I have told them that Molotov cocktails and rifles would not solve their problems. I have tried to offer them my deepest compassion while maintaining my convictions that social change comes most meaningfully through non-violent action. But they asked – and rightly so – what about Vietnam? … Their questions hit home, and I knew that I could never again raise my voice against the violence of the oppressed in the ghettos without having first spoken clearly to the greatest purveyor of violence in the world today – my own government.

King departed Chicago in autumn 1966, leaving dynamic young Jesse Jackson in charge of 'Operation Breadbasket', which successfully used economic boycotts to help increase black employment. The threat of black marches into racist white areas had made Daley agree to promote integrated housing in Chicago, but the agreement was a mere 'paper victory' (*Chicago Daily News*). Although SCLC obtained a $4 million federal grant to improve Chicago housing and left behind a significant legacy of community action, the local black community felt SCLC had 'sold out'. An SCLC staffer in Chicago said the voter registration drive there was 'a nightmare', 'largely because of division in the Negro leadership' and partly because black Chicagoans were uninterested: 'I have never seen such hopelessness … A lot of people won't even talk to us.' Many disillusioned residents turned to Black Power, which gained prominence during the Meredith March.

Black divisions on the Meredith March

In 1962, James Meredith gained fame as the University of Mississippi's first black student. In June 1966, he began a 220-mile walk from Memphis, Tennessee, to Jackson, Mississippi. His aim was to encourage black people to vote. When he was shot on the second day and temporarily immobilised, black organisations continued his walk. By the third day, King and twenty others had been joined by 400 marchers, including **Stokely Carmichael**, the new SNCC leader.

Black divisions damaged the march. The NAACP sought to focus national attention on a new civil rights bill and withdrew when Carmichael criticised the bill. SNCC had become increasingly militant following the lack of federal protection for their voter registration projects in the 'Mississippi Freedom Summer' of 1964 (see page 124), and while King welcomed white participants, SNCC rejected them. As white bystanders waved Confederate flags, shouted obscenities and threw things at the marchers, SNCC people sang:

> Jingle bells, shotgun shells, Freedom all the way
> Oh what fun it is to blast, A [white] trooper man away.

Carmichael was arrested. Upon release, he urged burning 'every courthouse in Mississippi' and demanded 'Black Power' (see page 142). His followers chanted 'BLACK POWER', while King and SCLC, fearing that would alienate whites, encouraged rival chants of 'FREEDOM NOW'. Although he had reluctantly agreed to the black paramilitary group Deacons for Defense providing security, King urged blacks to avoid violent retaliation against tear gas. As in Selma (see pages 127–8), Johnson ignored King's pleas to send in federal troops to protect black marchers.

Meanwhile, Meredith felt excluded and began a march of his own. Some SCLC leaders joined him to disguise the split. The 15,000 main marchers ended at Jackson with rival chants of 'BLACK POWER' and 'FREEDOM NOW'.

Results and significance of the march

King despaired: 'I don't know what I'm going to do. The government has got to give me some victories if I'm going to keep people non-violent.' He felt he could no longer cooperate with SNCC, and told the press, 'Because Stokely Carmichael chose the march as an arena for a debate over black power, we did not get to emphasize the evils of Mississippi and the need for the 1966 Civil Rights Act.' He admitted that black Americans were 'very, very close' to a public split. NAACP no longer wanted to cooperate with SCLC or SNCC and it seemed that leadership might pass into the hands of extremists such as Carmichael who rejected non-violence.

 KEY FIGURE

Stokely Carmichael (1941–98)

Born in the West Indies, raised in Harlem, and educated at historically black Howard University, Carmichael participated in CORE's Freedom Rides and SNCC's voter registration campaigns in Mississippi. When SNCC became more militant, he was elected as its leader (1966). He publicised 'Black Power' during the Meredith March and his celebrity led other SNCC members to christen him 'Stokely Starmichael'. His disillusionment with SNCC and the Black Panthers (see page 145), coupled with a total of 36 arrests, led him to emigrate to Africa.

Where Do We Go From Here?

By late 1966, King was depressed, unsure what to do next and marginalised by black radicals such as Carmichael, who called for black and white separation and said blacks should use 'any means necessary' to obtain their rights. It seemed that black extremists, the white backlash and the distraction of white liberals by the Vietnam War had caused the collapse of what had been a productive civil rights coalition.

In his book *Where Do We Go From Here?* (1967), King highlighted the problem: it cost nothing to give black Southerners the vote, but ghetto improvements would be expensive. No one wanted higher taxation. King urged demonstrations to seek **affirmative action**: 'A society that has done something against the Negro for hundreds of years must now do something special for him, in order to equip him to compete on a just and equal basis.' King also urged blacks to bring Hispanics, Native Americans and poor whites together in a Poor People's Campaign. He planned to bring Washington DC to a standstill by having thousands of poor people camp out there, but admitted, 'It just isn't working. People aren't responding'. Adam Clayton Powell christened him 'Martin Loser King'.

> ### KEY TERM
>
> **Affirmative action** Help for those who have had a disadvantageous start in life, also known as 'positive discrimination'.

King's assassination and its immediate effects

In March 1968, King visited Memphis, Tennessee, to support black sanitation workers faced with discrimination from the city authorities. King joined a protest march. When a radical Black Power minority got violent and broke shop windows, King was exhausted, confused, frightened and in despair:

> *Maybe we just have to admit that the day of violence is here, and maybe we have to just give up and let violence take its course. The nation won't listen to our voice. Maybe it will heed the voice of violence.*

Within hours, he was shot and killed by a white racist.

The immediate effect of King's assassination was nationwide ghetto riots. Civil rights leaders called for calm, although Carmichael sought a more emphatic response. There were mixed feelings in white America: some grief, some guilt, some joy. President Johnson declared a day of national mourning and Congress was inspired to pass the Fair Housing Act (see below). In death, King became a somewhat sanitised hero, whose economic radicalism and faults such as womanising were swept under the carpet.

The 1968 Civil Rights Act

After the 1965 Voting Rights Act, Johnson continued to propose legislation helpful to black Americans, but voter opposition made Congress reluctant. For example, in 1966, Congress rejected a Johnson civil rights bill, one aim of which was to prohibit housing discrimination. Polls showed 70 per cent of white voters opposed large numbers of black residents in their neighbourhood, especially after the Watts riots and Stokely Carmichael's call for 'black power' (see page 139). Johnson's proposed bill resulted in some of the worst hate mail of his presidency. One immediate effect of King's assassination was the feeling in Congress that some kind of tribute was due. The result was the 1968 Fair Housing Act, which prohibited discrimination in housing sales and rentals. However, this Civil Rights Act proved difficult to enforce owing to white resistance. Basically, Johnson found it hard to sustain national and congressional support for further aid for black Americans. He was angry with congressmen who jokingly called his rat extermination bill a 'civil rats bill' and suggested he send in a federal cat army. Johnson pointed out that slum children suffered terribly from rat bites.

The work and impact of Martin Luther King Jr: conclusions

With his protests and inspirational and organisational talents, King played a vital role in the demise of Jim Crow in the South. Although little more than a figurehead for the Montgomery bus boycott, it gained him national prominence. Protesters recognised his value in terms of inspiration and publicity, and King was willing to be led as well as to be leader. While A. Philip Randolph masterminded the March on Washington (see page 123), King's unforgettable speech was its highlight. He successfully orchestrated Birmingham (see page 122), which played a big part in encouraging the Kennedy administration to support what became the 1964 Civil Rights Act. King also masterminded Selma (see page 127), which was key in the passage of the Voting Rights Act. His manipulation of white violence and belief in the effectiveness of mass protest were essential in changing the focus of black activism from litigation. NAACP's litigation strategy had probably gone as far as it could go and it took mass action to make a reality of the anti-segregation principles enshrined in *Brown*.

King did not achieve the crucial legislation of 1964–5 by himself. Black protesters, the NAACP, CORE, SNCC, churches, local community organisations and thousands of unsung field workers also played an important part. The federal government, especially the Supreme Court and President Lyndon Johnson, played a vital role, as did changing white opinion and white extremists (President Kennedy joked that 'Bull' Connor was a civil rights movement hero). Perhaps historian Steven Lawson (1998) summed it up best when he said, 'The federal government made racial reform possible, but Blacks in the South made it necessary.'

King failed in Chicago, but ghetto problems were great and long-standing. After his death and after the rise of the Black Power movement, the federal government continued in the direction signposted by Presidents Kennedy and Johnson and supported affirmative action. It could be argued that King (and the civil rights and Black Power movements) played a crucial role in the introduction of that policy.

Summary diagram: King, the ghettos and black divisions

1966	–	Watts	–	Mock 'de great lawd'
	–	Chicago	–	Failure
	–	Meredith March	=	Black divisions exposed
1967	–	*Where Do We Go From Here?*		
	–	Black Power		
1968	–	Assassination	→	Riots

7 Black Power

▶ *Why and with what results did Black Power emerge in the 1960s?*

The influence of Malcolm X (see page 132), ghetto problems (see page 134) and the experiences of SNCC and CORE (many of whose members were Northerners) in Mississippi (see page 124) all contributed to the rise of Black Power. Some considered the ghetto riots of 1964–8 a result and/or demonstration of Black Power.

Black Power and ghetto riots

In July 1964, Malcolm X predicted that America in that summer 'will see a bloodbath'. Days later, Harlem rioted. During the five so-called 'long hot summers' of 1964–8, there were 238 other race riots in over 200 cities. The first major race riot was in Watts (see page 134) in 1965. Virtually every large city outside the South had a race riot. There was certainly a 'copycat' element: sixteen cities experienced serious riots in 1964, 64 in 1968. These riots led to over 250 deaths (mostly the result of the police shooting rioters), 10,000 serious injuries, 60,000 arrests and a great deal of damage to ghetto businesses.

Newark riots, 1967

The two major uprisings of summer 1967 took place in Newark and Detroit. While 2700 US Army troops used 201 rounds of ammunition as they tried to restore order in Detroit, National Guardsmen and state police expended 13,326 rounds in three days in Newark, New Jersey.

The underlying cause of the revolt in Newark was poverty and deprivation. Significantly, the riots broke out the day after plans for the Second Annual Black Power Conference in Newark were announced. They were triggered

Definitions of Black Power

The words 'black power' first came to prominence during the Meredith March (see page 139). The older generation of civil rights leaders were hostile. NAACP leader Roy Wilkins considered Black Power advocates racists and no better than the Ku Klux Klan.

'Nobody knows what the phrase "black power" really means,' said the *New York Times*. SNCC's Cleveland Sellers said, 'There was a deliberate attempt to make it ambiguous ... [so that] it meant everything to everybody.' In 1968, Elijah Muhammad (see page 129) said, 'Black power means the black people will rule the white people on earth as the white people have ruled the black people for the past six thousand years.' Martin Luther King Jr called Black Power 'a slogan without a program'. He disliked the words: 'It sounds like you are trying to say black domination'. When people persisted in talking of 'Black Power', King tried to give it more positive connotations:

The Negro is in dire need of a sense of dignity and a sense of pride, and I think black power is an attempt to develop pride. And there is no doubt about the need for power – he can't get into the mainstream of society without it ... Black power means instilling within the Negro a sense of belonging and appreciation of heritage, a racial pride ... We must never be ashamed of being black.

SNCC's Floyd McKissick also attempted a positive definition:

Black Power is not hatred ... [It] 'did not mean black supremacy, did not mean exclusion of whites from the Negro revolution, and did not mean advocacy of violence and riots ... [but] political power, economic power, and a new self-image for Negroes.

Republican Nathan Wright was one of those who emphasised 'economic power'. His campaign for a Black Power capitalist movement won support from SCLC and from Republican presidential candidate Richard Nixon, who said in 1968 that Black Power meant, 'more black ownership, for from this can flow the rest – black pride, black jobs, black opportunity and yes, black power'. In contrast, black car workers in Detroit, Michigan, thought Black Power meant a black working-class revolution.

Black Power supporters invariably emphasised black pride and black culture. Many adopted Afro hairstyles and African garb, and black students successfully agitated for the introduction of black studies programmes.

by police brutality against a local black cab driver, and were the worst since Watts in 1965. Snipers fired at law enforcement officers, guns were stolen from a department store, and families stole clothes, toys, electrical appliances and liquor from ruined stores. The authorities called in the National Guard, which in combination with state troopers engaged in what black citizens considered to be indiscriminate shooting of suspected looters. Over twenty died and hundreds were injured.

The NAACP denounced the Newark rioters, but blamed local officials for their inaction over Newark's high poverty rate and awful slums. The *New York Times* agreed, criticising Governor Richard Hughes for describing the riots as 'plain and simple crime'. The newspaper said the term 'rebellion' was more appropriate.

Over 1000 people attended the Black Power Conference, which met after the riot. The participants included community organisers, businessmen, and Black Power activists. Black nationalist writer LeRoi Jones told the press, 'We are over 60 percent of the population of Newark, New Jersey, and we will govern ourselves or no one will govern Newark, New Jersey.' In 1970, Kenneth Gibson was elected Mayor of Newark – the first black leader of a major Northeastern city. However, 'white flight' (see page 101) had eroded Newark's tax base, so ghetto conditions did not improve.

The white response to the riots

The most famous of the many city, state and federal government investigations into the urban riots was the National Advisory Commission on Civil Disorders (commonly known as the Kerner Commission) set up by President Johnson. Like the other reports, the Kerner Report, released in February 1968, emphasised the social and economic deprivation in ghettos (see page 134). The reports also noted that the violence was frequently triggered by what were perceived as oppressive police policies and indifferent white political machines. The reports invariably recommended increased expenditure on the ghettos, but most whites were unwilling to finance improvements, particularly after the Vietnam War led to tax rises (as Table 7.1 shows, the Vietnam War cost far more than Johnson's Great Society, but many taxpayers focused on the latter as the source of their woes). While blacks increasingly perceived whites as uninterested and unsympathetic, whites increasingly perceived blacks as seeking 'handouts'. A 1965 poll showed 88 per cent of whites advocated black self-improvement, more education and harder work, rather than government help. A 1966 poll showed 90 per cent opposed new civil rights legislation. In a 1967 poll, 52 per cent said Johnson was going 'too fast' on integration, and only 10 per cent said 'not fast enough'.

Table 7.1 Federal government expenditure

| Great Society, 1963–9 | $15.5 billion |
| Vietnam War, 1965–73 | $120 billion |

Ghetto rejection of the older civil rights organisations

The civil rights organisations tried to respond to ghetto frustration, for example, King's Chicago campaign. However, many ghetto inhabitants and younger black activists considered that Martin Luther King Jr's emphases on the South, the 'white man's' Christian religion, and non-violence, were unhelpful to black ghetto progress. They were inspired by the success of civil rights activism in the South, but looked to new leaders such as Malcolm X and Stokely Carmichael, whose 'by any means necessary' philosophy seemed a more appropriate response to white oppression than King's 'love thine enemy'.

The expulsion of whites from SNCC and CORE

In 1966, the Meredith March demonstrated the radicalisation of SNCC and CORE and their alienation from the older organisations. By 1964, CORE was more active in the ghettos (it established 'Freedom Houses' to provide information and advice on education, employment, health and housing) and more impatient with black inequality. When James Farmer resigned as leader of

CORE in December 1965, the radical Floyd McKissick was elected in his place. In 1966, CORE, endorsed Black Power, and declared non-violence inappropriate if black people needed to defend themselves. In 1967, the word 'multiracial' was excised from CORE's constitution. By 1968, whites were excluded from CORE membership.

SNCC members were equally impatient with the slow progress toward equality and disillusioned by the lack of federal protection in the Mississippi Freedom Summer (see page 124) and by the Democratic Party's unwillingness to seat black delegates at the Democratic **National Convention** at Atlantic City in 1964. So, SNCC elected the more militant Stokely Carmichael to replace John Lewis as leader in 1966, and voted to expel whites. In 1967, Carmichael was replaced by the even more militant Henry 'Rap' Brown ('violence is as American as cherry pie'). Brown advocated armed self-defence. After he urged a black audience in Cambridge, Maryland, to take over white-owned stores in the ghettos through violence if necessary, a race riot erupted. In February 1968, SNCC merged with the Black Panthers, the most radical of all black organisations.

> **KEY TERM**
>
> **National Convention**
> Before the presidential election, the Republicans and Democrats hold conferences in which each party selects or confirms its candidate for the presidency.

John Lewis 1940–

When studying in Nashville for the ministry, Alabama-born John Lewis participated in the 1960 sit-ins. His parents were 'shocked and ashamed' when he was jailed: 'My mother made no distinction between being jailed for drunkenness and being jailed for demonstrating for civil rights.' It was years before she forgave him. In 1961, he participated in the Freedom Rides. In 1963, he was elected chairman of SNCC. A staunch advocate of non-violence, he was the youngest speaker at the 1963 March on Washington (see page 123), where other black leaders dissuaded him from criticising the civil rights bill ('What is in the bill that will protect the homeless and starving?'). He co-ordinated SNCC's Mississippi Freedom Summer in 1964 and led marches in Selma in 1965, where 'Sheriff Clark's temper played right into our hands' (see page 127). The only former civil rights leader to be elected to Congress, he represented Georgia's fifth Congressional district from 1988. When Barack Obama was elected President in 2008, Lewis said:

> *If someone had told me this would be happening now, I would have told them they were crazy, out of their mind, they did not know what they were talking about … I just wish the others were around to see this day … To the people who were beaten, put in jail, were asked questions they could never answer to register to vote, it's amazing.*

He was on the stage during President Obama's inauguration in 2009, the only surviving speaker of the March on Washington. The President signed a photograph for Lewis with: 'Because of you, John. Barack Obama.'

The Black Panthers

The Black Panthers were founded in 1966 in Oakland, California, by Huey P. Newton and Bobby Seale. Newton said he chose the panther as a symbol because it 'never attacks. But if anyone attacks him or backs him into a corner the panther comes up to wipe the aggressor or that attacker out.' The Black Panthers declared themselves 'the heirs of Malcolm X'. Their ten-point platform included full employment, decent housing, 'education that teaches us our true [black] history', worldwide working-class struggle, **reparations**, **self-determination**, an end to police brutality, and ghetto improvements.

Despite having only around 5000 members in 30 loosely affiliated urban chapters in cities such as Oakland, Boston, New Orleans, Chicago and Kansas City, the Black Panthers had a considerable impact. Their newsletter had a circulation of around 250,000 by 1969, and they impressed many ghetto residents with their practical help. They had over 40 clinics advising on health, welfare and legal rights. They provided free breakfasts for thousands of black schoolchildren: in 1970, the Southern California chapter of the Free Breakfast programme served up over 1700 meals weekly. The Black Panthers raised awareness of sickle cell anaemia, a disease that disproportionately affected black people, and in 1969 they set up their first 'liberation school', a summer school for black children in Berkeley. Its curriculum was designed to generate knowledge of and pride in black culture and history. Other schools followed in cities such as Philadelphia and New York.

KEY TERMS

Reparations Federal government payment of compensation for slavery to black Americans.

Self-determination The ability of black Americans to choose their own destiny.

? Looking at Huey Newton's pose in Source I, what point was he trying to make?

SOURCE I

The iconic photograph of Huey Newton in 1967.

The Black Panthers appeared strong and fearless to many black Americans. They stockpiled weapons for self-defence and tailed the police in the hope of exposing their brutality. That led to many violent shootouts. In 1967, armed Black Panthers surrounded and entered the California state legislature to protest repressive legislation. They particularly impressed black youths with their paramilitary uniforms (predominantly black with berets and leather jackets) and militant rhetoric (Seale would cry, 'Power to the People … The revolution has come … time to pick up the gun' at rallies). Unsurprisingly, the Black Panthers were targeted by the police and **FBI**, which, along with their internal divisions, served to dramatically decrease their influence and dynamism by the early 1970s.

People have always been fascinated by the Black Panthers, who had ample media coverage. Indeed, Newton's biographer Hugh Pearson (1995) considered them 'little more than a temporary media phenomenon'. While whites usually reviled them, polls indicated that a majority of black Americans sympathised with them and with other black nationalists. In contrast, while 80 per cent of black Americans approved of the NAACP in 1963, only 20 per cent did so by 1969.

> ## KEY TERM
>
> **FBI** The Federal Bureau of Investigation was set up in 1924 to help deal with crime.

Case study: Fred Hampton – successful or unsuccessful?

Opinions of the Black Panthers and their achievements vary, as demonstrated by reactions to Fred Hampton (1948–68). Born in a Chicago suburb, he was an NAACP activist who joined the Black Panthers. The FBI monitored him closely from 1967 and he was shot in 1968 during a 4.45a.m. police raid on his flat. NAACP leader Roy Wilkins declared the killing illegal. Hampton's family brought a case against the city, state and federal governments, and years later were awarded $1.85 million in damages. In 1991 and 2004, Chicago City Council approved the celebration of a 'Fred Hampton Day'. In 2006, Chicago police officers voiced objections to a proposal that a Chicago street be named after him. Hampton's life is celebrated in rap music and hip-hop. Some see him as a hero who among other things calmed Chicago's warring gangs, others as a troublemaker.

The significance of Black Power

Suggested reasons for the decline of the Black Power movement by the early 1970s include that it was:

- always relatively ill-defined and poorly organised
- unrealistic in thinking America was ripe for revolution
- sexist and alienated its female supporters
- targeted by the white authorities.

However, the movement had a lasting impact. It contributed to growing black pride (a 1970 poll revealed that 64 per cent of black Americans took pride in the Black Panthers). The movement raised black American morale, especially by encouraging college courses on black history and culture. It failed to solve ghetto problems, but they were probably insoluble while white taxpayers remained unwilling to fund improvements.

There is disagreement over the impact of Black Power in relation to violence. What most black Americans considered to be self-defence, most white Americans perceived as violence. Some suggest that self-defence and/or violence alienated whites and stopped a previously effective civil rights movement achieving more after 1965. Some respond by arguing that ghetto problems were insoluble. Others argue that the Black Power movement played a part in encouraging some white support for affirmative action (see page 140).

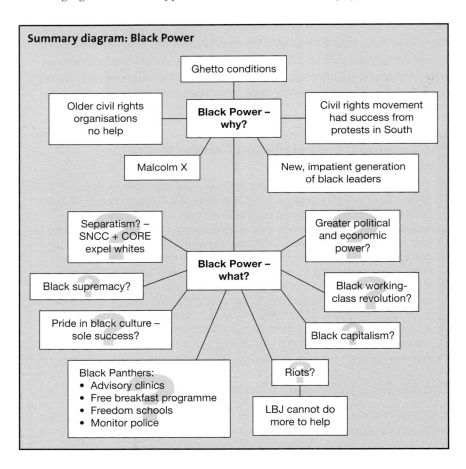

Summary diagram: Black Power

- Ghetto conditions
- Older civil rights organisations no help
- **Black Power – why?**
- Civil rights movement had success from protests in South
- Malcolm X
- New, impatient generation of black leaders

- Separatism? – SNCC + CORE expel whites
- Black supremacy?
- Pride in black culture – sole success?
- Black Panthers:
  - Advisory clinics
  - Free breakfast programme
  - Freedom schools
  - Monitor police
- **Black Power – what?**
- Greater political and economic power?
- Black working-class revolution?
- Black capitalism?
- Riots?
- LBJ cannot do more to help

Chapter summary

Prior to the 1960s, the NAACP was the organisation most successful in eliciting a helpful federal government response. From the 1930s, NAACP litigation focused upon education, culminating in the *Brown* ruling against segregated schools. *Brown* was a moral triumph, but not all Southern schools were desegregated. The NAACP bore considerable responsibility for the successful Montgomery bus boycott (1956), which brought Martin Luther King Jr to prominence and suggested the potential of mass black activism.

Civil rights activists and organisations used a variety of tactics. The bus boycott and NAACP litigation led to the desegregation of Montgomery's buses. From 1960, student sit-ins led to the desegregation of lunch counters across the South. CORE's Freedom Rides of 1961 prompted federal government support for integrated interstate transport. Marches in Birmingham and the March on Washington in 1963 helped shame the Kennedy administration into promoting a civil rights bill.

The black organisations were plagued by inter-organisational rivalry. The NAACP favoured litigation and resented newcomers, SCLC and CORE favoured demonstrations, while SNCC disliked the leader worship they associated with King and SCLC, and focused upon empowering black Americans at grassroots level, as in their Mississippi campaign of 1961–4.

The combination of President Johnson, black activists and changing white opinion led to the 1964 Civil Rights Act, which ended *de jure* segregation in the South, and to the 1965 Voting Rights Act, which facilitated black voting. Many individuals, organisations and the federal government played an important part in such successes, but King was a uniquely inspirational leader who orchestrated productive campaigns in Birmingham and Selma. After successfully focusing upon the South, King turned to ghetto problems, but achieved little. White voters did not want their economic well-being threatened by higher taxation to finance ghetto improvements or by black Americans moving into their neighbourhoods.

Black divisions became public when militants called for Black Power during the Meredith March (1966). Black Power emerged from a long tradition of black nationalism and separatism, demonstrated in the Nation of Islam (NOI), whose most famous minister was Malcolm X. Malcolm's bitter attacks on white America won him a great ghetto following. The Black Power movement owed much to Malcolm's teachings, ghetto problems, the lack of federal protection for activists, and the slow pace of progress. Black Power meant different things to different people – it could mean a ghetto riot, black pride, black economic self-sufficiency, black political power, or black supremacy. The most famous Black Power group was the Black Panthers, who aided the ghetto poor and aimed to expose police brutality. That, coupled with participation in crime, encouraged the white authorities to oppose and destroy them. The Black Power movement raised black morale and helped create a legacy of black studies in educational institutions, but was in decline by 1970 because of its vague aims, internal divisions, and the opposition of white authorities. Some claimed it irreparably damaged the civil rights movement, others that the civil rights movement had done all it could do when it revolutionised the South. Further progress would have cost white America too much.

Refresher questions

1 What tactics did the NAACP use between 1909 and 1954?

2 What did the three significant Supreme Court rulings on segregation in 1950 say?

3 In what ways was the *Brown* ruling significant?

4 Why did the Supreme Court rule as it did in the *Brown* ruling?

5 What were the causes and consequences of the Montgomery bus boycott?

6 Why and with what results did SCLC campaign in Birmingham in 1963?

7 How, why and with what results were the 1964 Civil Rights Act and the 1965 Voting Rights Act passed?

8 How did Malcolm X's aims, methods and support differ from those of Martin Luther King Jr?

9 What was the significance of the Meredith March?

10 Which groups criticised Martin Luther King Jr and why?

11 Why were whites reluctant to deal with ghetto problems?

12 Why did many ghetto residents reject the older civil rights organisations?

13 How did definitions of Black Power differ?

14 What were the aims, methods and importance of the Black Panthers?

15 Why did Black Power decline?

 Question practice

SOURCE ANALYSIS QUESTIONS

1 Assess the value of Source B (page 110) for revealing the extent of the federal government's commitment to racial equality in the early 1950s and the reasons why the Supreme Court made the *Brown* ruling. Explain your answer, using the source, the information given about its origin and your own knowledge about the historical context.

2 Assess the value of Source H (page 137) for revealing Martin Luther King Jr's opinion of the success of the civil rights movement and the relationship of black Americans with white Americans in the late 1960s. Explain your answer, using the source, the information given about its origin and your own knowledge about the historical context.

ESSAY QUESTIONS

1 'It was the Supreme Court that was responsible for the improved position of black Americans in the Southern states in the period 1950–63.' How far do you agree with this statement?

2 To what extent was President Johnson responsible for the passage of the 1964 Civil Rights Act and the 1965 Voting Rights Act?

CHAPTER 8

Changing portrayals of civil rights issues in fiction, film and television

Many consider popular culture a barometer of social change, but while the literary and visual depiction of black Americans certainly changed between 1850 and 2009, the extent to which popular culture reflected and shaped changing attitudes is hard to measure. After a long history of both sympathetic and unsympathetic portrayals of black characters in literature and the visual arts (both portrayals sometimes coexisted within the same work), sympathetic portrayals became more frequent and more favourable as the twentieth century progressed. However, they often generated criticism for perpetuating demeaning or unrealistic stereotypes. Changing portrayals of race relations between 1850 and 2009 reflected the tensions in American race relations and some changes in attitudes, and perhaps helped shape the debate over the issues.

This chapter covers those changing portrayals and attitudes in sections on

★ Nineteenth-century literary and visual representations of black Americans

★ *Birth of a Nation*

★ *Gone With the Wind*

★ Fiction after *Gone With the Wind*

★ Film, 1940–92

★ Television

Key dates

1852	*Uncle Tom's Cabin* published	1967	*Guess Who's Coming to Dinner*; *In the Heat of the Night*
1885	*Adventures of Huckleberry Finn* published		Early 1970s' Blaxploitation movies era
1915	Box-office triumph of *Birth of a Nation*	1977	*Roots* televised
1936	*Gone With the Wind* published (filmed 1939)	1987	*Beloved* published (filmed 1998)
		1988	*Mississippi Burning*
1957	*Island in the Sun*	1992	*Malcolm X*
1960	*To Kill a Mockingbird* published (filmed 1962)	2002–8	*The Wire*
		2009	*The Help* published (filmed 2011)

Nineteenth-century literary and visual representations of black Americans

▶ *Did art and literature shape and reflect nineteenth-century perceptions of race relations?*

Slavery and its abolition had a significant impact upon nineteenth-century portrayals of black Americans.

Visual representations

Prior to the Civil War, there were several categories of visual representations of black Americans. One was demeaning. Examples could be found in *Harper's Weekly*, the most popular contemporary periodical, and in advertisements for the popular minstrel shows that had white people in blackface portraying black

SOURCE A

Why do you suppose that the abolitionists frequently reproduced the image in Source A?

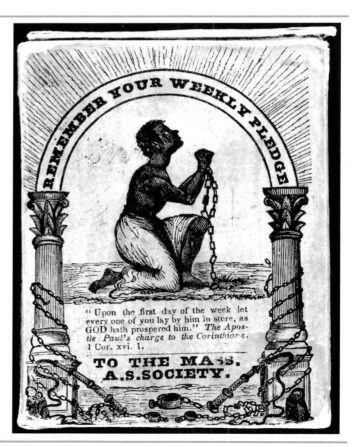

A popular and much-reproduced image of a slave, in this instance on the collection box of the Massachusetts Anti-Slavery Society, c.1850.

SOURCE B

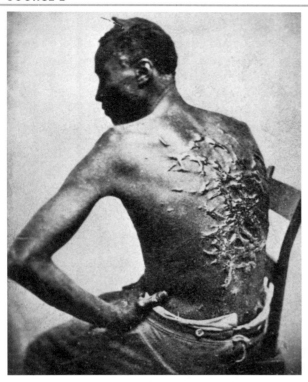

Photography was a new medium in the mid-nineteenth century, but a considerable number of photographs of black Americans were taken during the Civil War. This photograph of the scarred back of a Louisiana slave who had been beaten by his owner was published in *Harper's Weekly* in July 1863. It was taken by itinerant photographers after the slave arrived in a Union camp.

It was expensive to take and publish photographs, so how would you account for Source B?

people as unintelligent, idle, superstitious and carefree. The minstrel shows were criticised by white Southerners, who resented their sympathetic attitude toward runaway slaves, but also by abolitionists, who disliked their depiction of happy slaves. A second category was abolitionist portrayals designed to arouse sympathy for the cause. These invariably showed desperate slaves, deprived of all agency. A third category of visual representation was visual depictions commissioned by black Americans to demonstrate black respectability and similarity to white people. This category is well illustrated in the famous photograph of black anti-slavery campaign Sojourner Truth, which showed her dressed in middle-class fashion.

The Civil War introduced a new category, photographs of black soldiers in Union uniform. Photography was a new medium, and the novel sight of empowered black Americans served to fascinate photographers and those who bought copies of photographs.

After the Civil War, visual portrayals were predominantly demeaning, as shown in political posters (see page 20), in the illustrations for the various presentations of *Uncle Tom's Cabin* (see page 156), and in the illustrations for the *Adventures of Huckleberry Finn* (see page 158).

Uncle Tom's Cabin – the novel

Harriet Beecher Stowe was born into a deeply religious and well-educated family in Connecticut. In 1832, the family moved to Cincinnati, Ohio, where she met and married academic and abolitionist Calvin Ellis Stowe. The couple frequently sheltered slaves who had escaped from the South, and from June 1851 to April 1852, Mrs Stowe's 40-instalment story of *Uncle Tom's Cabin* was published in the anti-slavery newspaper, *The National Era*, then published in book form in 1852. Within a year, a record 300,000 copies were sold. In 1855, a contemporary described it as 'the most popular novel of our day'.

The story told of how the deeply religious slave Tom was separated from his wife and children and sold by a Kentucky plantation owner. A shared love of the Bible resulted in a close relationship between Tom and Eva, the daughter of his next master. When Eva and her father died, Tom was sold to the evil Simon Legree, who beat Tom to death because he hated Tom's religiosity.

SOURCE C

From Harriet Beecher Stowe, *Uncle Tom's Cabin*, John P. Jewett, 1852, p. 80.

If it were your Harry, mother, or your Willie, that were going to be torn from you by a brutal [slave] trader, to-morrow morning, – if you had seen the man, and heard that the papers were signed and delivered, and you had only from twelve o'clock till morning to make good your escape, – how fast could you walk? How many miles could you make in those few brief hours, with the darling at your bosom, – the little sleepyhead on your shoulder, – the small, soft arms trustingly holding onto your neck?

? What did Source C aim to do and how effectively does it do it?

It is difficult to assess the impact of novels, but few contemporaries doubted that *Uncle Tom's Cabin* generated Northern sympathy for slaves and increased the North–South hostility that culminated in the Civil War. When Stowe met President Lincoln, he supposedly said, 'So you are the little woman who wrote the book that started this great war.' The book's effectiveness was attested in the Southern literary response: *Uncle Tom's Cabin* provoked over twenty novels in which Southerners portrayed slavery as a benign institution, for example, *Aunt Phillis's Cabin* (1852), by Mary Henderson Eastman.

The historian James McPherson described *Uncle Tom's Cabin* as 'the most influential indictment of slavery of all time' (1988), attributing its influence to its emphasis upon the break-up of the family, which touched readers' hearts. While the words of Harriet Beecher Stowe were obviously influential, some historians have argued that the illustrations in the various editions of the book and the stage performances of the play had an even greater impact.

Uncle Tom's Cabin – the plays

Uncle Tom's Cabin was frequently performed as a play, acquainting millions more with its anti-slavery message. Professor of English Eric Lott (1993) estimated that

SOURCE D

One of the six engravings done by Hammatt Billings for the first edition of *Uncle Tom's Cabin* (1852), this one shows Tom and Eva studying the Bible in the garden. It was revolutionary to depict an adult black male and a young white female in such close proximity, especially at a time when slaves were forbidden to read.

> Looking closely at Source D, what can you see that might particularly anger a white racist?

around 3 million people saw the plays, which first appeared in 1852. Some were true to Stowe's book, such as George L. Aiken's version, which Stowe herself saw performed. However, as time went on, some versions were less anti-slavery or even pro-slavery and many portrayed black people in demeaning fashion. These plays were still being performed in the early twentieth century.

Uncle Tom's Cabin – the illustrations

When *Uncle Tom's Cabin* was published in 1852, it was unusual in that it had illustrations. Drawn by Hammatt Billings, they emphasised Tom's Christianity and his close relationship with Eva. For example, in a second edition, in 1853, Billings portrayed Eva sitting on her father's lap – and, in a virtually identical pose, in Uncle Tom's lap. The Christian images were given further emphasis by a cover picture of Jesus Christ.

Black Americans controlled by enslavement were unthreatening, but after Emancipation and Reconstruction (see Chapter 2), many white Americans grew uneasy about the potential activities of black American males. This was reflected in changing visual depictions of Uncle Tom. Art historian Jo-Ann Morgan (2007) traced the countless visual depictions of the characters in *Uncle Tom's Cabin*, whether in illustrations for the book, advertisements for stage plays, paintings, prints or sheet music (the book inspired many songs). Morgan argued that the subversive nature of Stowe's book was itself subsequently subverted. While Billings emulated images from anti-slavery works and used Christian iconography, subsequent images reflected different perceptions. Morgan saw this change as exceptionally well demonstrated in the fate of Billings' depiction of Eva sitting alongside a youngish, manly Tom, as they read the Bible together in an arbour. Eva has her hand on his knee. Stowe described Tom as 'a large, broad chested, powerfully made man', but artists who drew that scene after Emancipation invariably made Tom far older (usually white-haired), Eva more dominant, and Tom more dependent. For example, while Stowe had made much of their joint Bible reading, an illustration by W.L. Burford (*c*.1900) was captioned, 'Tom tries to write a letter with Eva's assistance.' Furthermore, post-Emancipation depictions of Tom are markedly less Christ-like than the Tom depicted by Stowe and Billings. According to Morgan, Tom's fate in subsequent depictions 'tells us just how revolutionary *Uncle Tom's Cabin* was'. It also tells us that visual depictions of Tom reflected changing and less sympathetic white attitudes.

SOURCE E

? How would you account for the different portrayals of Uncle Tom in Sources D and E?

🔑 KEY TERM

Lithograph A type of print.

Colourful **lithographs** were printed between the 1880s and the 1920s to advertise 'Tom Shows'. Like so many of these advertisements, this one is undated, but serves as an excellent example of the development of Tom from Harriet Beecher Stowe's dynamic and youngish student of the Bible into a non-threatening white-haired old man. In the later nineteenth century, lithographs increasingly depicted black Americans in a stereotypical and demeaning fashion, for example, thick-lipped and grinning inanely.

Black reactions to Uncle Tom

Black reactions to *Uncle Tom's Cabin* changed over the years. Upon first publication, the famous abolitionist Frederick Douglass praised it, but by 1865, he noted how the black role in the Civil War had swept away the 'delusion' that black people would just let themselves be whipped as Uncle Tom had. When black Americans became more assertive during the twentieth century, the name 'Uncle Tom' was contemptuously given to those deemed to be excessively subservient to whites and willing to accept suffering. With the rise of black assertiveness after the Second World War (see Chapter 7), some editions of the book contained illustrations that showed Tom as heroic once again.

Literary portrayals after the Civil War

Enslavement continued to inspire literature after the Civil War. Rose-tinted recollections of slavery characterised the so-called 'plantation tales' written by white Southerners and popular across the United States in the 1880s. These tales usually featured ex-slaves who referred to the enslavement years, as in Thomas Nelson Page's *Marse Chan* (1884), as 'good ole times'. Possibly, the popularity of these stories reflected both Northern and Southern white fears of a new order in which black Americans did not know their place. In contrast to the 'plantation tales', the even more popular *Adventures of Huckleberry Finn* (1885) was unsympathetic towards slavery.

Adventures of Huckleberry Finn

In **Mark Twain**'s novel, *Adventures of Huckleberry Finn*, Huck Finn is adopted by the kindly Widow Douglas. His drunken bum father 'Pap' kidnaps him and treats him like a slave, locking him up and beating him. Huck escapes and meets Jim, a slave belonging to Miss Watson, the sister-in-law of Widow Douglas. Jim escaped because he heard Miss Watson talk about selling him and separating him from his family. Although Huck doubts whether it is right to help a runaway slave because a slave is someone's property, he tries to help Jim go North to a free state. Huck helps Jim avoid capture until two unscrupulous white men capture him and sell him to relations of Huck's friend, Tom Sawyer. Huck and Tom free Jim, but then Jim sacrifices his freedom to help Tom after Tom gets shot. Somewhat belatedly, Tom reveals that the recently deceased Miss Watson had freed Jim in her will.

Twain wrote after the abolition of slavery but set the novel during the pre-Civil War period. In 1870, he had married into an abolitionist family, and slavery and race relations are central themes in *Adventures of Huckleberry Finn*. Huck finds a world in which the 'good' white people such as Miss Watson and Tom's relations accept slavery unquestioningly. Huck is ambivalent about Jim. On the one hand, he is willing to 'go to hell' for helping Jim, suggesting a black life is of equal worth to a white life. On the other hand, when Tom's relation asks Huck if anyone has been hurt in an explosion on the steamboat, he answers, 'No'm.

 KEY FIGURE

Mark Twain (1835–1910)

Samuel Langhorne Clemens was born to a slave-owning Missouri family. After working as a printer and on Mississippi river boats, he joined the Confederate cavalry during the Civil War, deserted along with the rest of his division, then went West and tried silver mining and journalism. He wrote under the name of 'Mark Twain', the words called out on a riverboat to signal that the water depth was safe for passage. Mark Twain's novels sold well, especially *The Adventures of Tom Sawyer* (1876) and its sequel, *Adventures of Huckleberry Finn* (1885). He had a great contemporary reputation.

Killed a nigger.' She responds, 'Well, it's lucky; because sometimes people do get hurt.' There, both seem to take it for granted that the loss of a black life means nothing. At this time, Huck is pretending to be Tom, so he might be trying to fit in with the traditional white role here, although it may be that he has failed to complete his journey away from racism. Toward the end of the book, Huck and Tom toy with Jim, prolonging and accentuating his enslavement. The knockabout comedy of this section was, the author acknowledged, the most successful part of the book: possibly Mark Twain was simply out to entertain rather than to preach a consistent philosophy in these last chapters. In the end though, Huck goes West, saying he does not want to be 'sivilized' by the Widow Douglas and a slave-owning culture.

Huckleberry Finn – reflecting and shaping contemporary perceptions

The fact that the most popular section of *Adventures of Huckleberry Finn* was that in which Jim is horribly teased by his friend Huck might seem to suggest that if the novel shaped contemporary perceptions of race relations, it would not have been for the better. Perhaps in his apparent ambivalence about how to depict black characters, Mark Twain reflected that while there was considerable consensus outside the white South that slavery was wrong, there was a reluctance and/or inability on the part of white Americans to see black Americans as their equals.

The *Adventures of Huckleberry Finn* was an immediate bestseller, much admired by many contemporaries. However, some Southerners resented its criticisms of the South and slavery. Furthermore, the book was banned by several libraries, including that of Concord, Massachusetts, which described it as 'trash and suitable only for the slums'. Such bans were invariably based on grounds of the book's crudity. In 1905, the Brooklyn Public Library banned the book because Huck frequently lied, 'not only itched, but scratched', was dirty, had poor grammar, said 'sweat' instead of 'perspiration', and was a poor role model for children.

The history of the illustrations of the slave Jim in successive editions of Twain's novel reflected changing perceptions. The first illustrator, E.W. Kemble, frequently depicted Jim in a stereotypical and demeaning fashion, saying, 'My coons caught the public fancy'. Interestingly, Kemble's representations of black people outside the United States were much more sympathetic, reminding us that artists and writers can be constrained by audience prejudices and expectations. As one might expect, the illustrations of Jim became more dignified as the twentieth century progressed.

Adventures of Huckleberry Finn in the twentieth century

From the mid-twentieth century, as sensitivity about perceived racism grew ever more pronounced, the *Adventures of Huckleberry Finn* was criticised as racist. In 1957, the National Association for the Advancement of Colored People (see page 48) said it included 'racial slurs' and 'belittling racial designations'. Academic Stephen Railton (1987) said it portrayed black people stereotypically, using comedy in the style of the minstrel shows that were popular during the nineteenth century and characterised by scenes containing happy-go-lucky, dim-witted slaves on plantations in the Old South. In the last two decades of the twentieth century, *Adventures of Huckleberry Finn* became a highly controversial aspect of the school curriculum. The novel was taught in the majority of schools in the United States, but it made some people uneasy. Liberals disliked the use of the word 'nigger', and some felt that Jim's superstition and ignorance were demeaning. This suggests that literature was perceived as shaping and/or reflecting perceptions. From 1982, former school administrator John Wallace of Virginia began a crusade against the book, which he called the 'most grotesque example of racism I've ever seen in my life'. In a controversy in Cherry Hill, New Jersey, some black American families claimed studying the book in class embarrassed black students. However, in 1998, the Ninth Circuit Court of Appeals ruled against Kathy Monteiro's claim that black children suffered psychological damage when the novel was on the school's required reading list. She claimed that her black daughter suffered more racial taunts from white students after they had read the book. The three judges said that they found it difficult to believe that the taunts were a result of having read the book, believing that while literature reflected and perhaps shaped ideas at the time of writing, it no longer retained that power when read subsequently, because readers would recognise that a book is a product of the beliefs of a particular time.

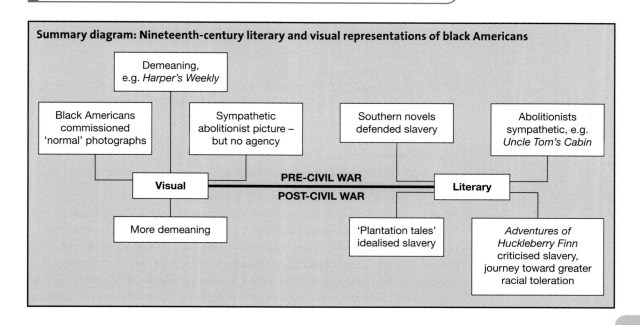

Summary diagram: Nineteenth-century literary and visual representations of black Americans

Birth of a Nation

▶ *How can the influence of* Birth of a Nation *be measured?*

In 1915, every American town with a population over 5000 had at least one movie theatre. In 1920, 50 million Americans went to the movies – roughly half the population. Many people believe this new and incredibly popular medium of entertainment reflected and shaped changes in American society. The most famous and influential of silent movies ('talkies' were not developed until the late 1920s) was based on a Thomas Dixon (1864–1946) novel. Dixon came from a slave-owning North Carolina family. He opposed slavery but favoured segregation. Horrified by the portrayal of the South that he saw in an 'Uncle Tom' play (see page 154), he sought to correct it in bestselling novels such as *The Clansman* (1905), a romanticised history of the Ku Klux Klan that inspired the movie *Birth of a Nation* (1915).

Birth of a Nation was directed by D.W. Griffith, whose father had fought in the Confederate army. The three-hour movie told of Confederate war hero Ben Cameron, who is sharply contrasted with immoral and dangerous black men (played by white actors in blackface). In the movie's depiction of Reconstruction (see page 22), Republican legislators are lazy and stupid, while armed black men try to stop white men voting, and a black soldier tries to rape Cameron's younger sister. As a result, Cameron establishes the Ku Klux Klan, who lynch the black soldier and restore white control, at which point Jesus Christ appears in the sky to signal his approbation.

Contemporary reactions to *Birth of a Nation*

Birth of a Nation was a phenomenal box-office success. White crowds flocked to see it – 1 million in New York City in its first year alone. It had a powerful impact upon many viewers. 'Every man who comes out of one of our theaters is a Southern partisan for life', said Thomas Dixon. In his autobiography, Catholic priest and Professor of Dramatics Father Daniel Lord recalled that the movie had overwhelmed him as a boy and that he had left the movie theatre convinced that he had witnessed a medium sufficiently powerful to 'change our whole attitude toward life, civilization, and established customs.' *Birth of a Nation* inspired the re-establishment of the Ku Klux Klan. Clearly, this was a movie that reflected contemporary Southern white perceptions of the past and that some whites saw as shaping the attitudes of others.

Black commentators agreed that the movie impacted upon perceptions and behaviour. Black intellectual W.E.B. Du Bois and the NAACP blamed it for an upsurge in lynching and called for a boycott. Black riots stopped screenings in several cities – 1000 black Philadelphians tried to force their way into the premiere, but were stopped by the police. In contrast, Booker T. Washington (see page 45) criticised the massive black demonstrations against the movie, claiming that they gave it free publicity. The director, D.W. Griffith, denied that he was a racist, saying black people 'were our children, whom we loved and cared for'.

The revitalisation of the Ku Klux Klan

After its early successes, the Ku Klux Klan virtually collapsed, due to federal government action and the successful reassertion of white supremacy after Reconstruction (see page 28). *Birth of a Nation* revitalised the Klan, which claimed 4 million members by the mid-1920s. The Klan now opposed Catholics, Jews and immigrants as much as black people, and was national rather than Southern: Michigan had more members than any other American state, demonstrating how the Great Migration (see page 56) had spread American racial tensions to the North and Midwest. However, the Klan collapsed again in the 1930s, because of leadership scandals, laws outlawing the wearing of masks in public, and a $10 membership fee that was very expensive in the Depression (see page 67).

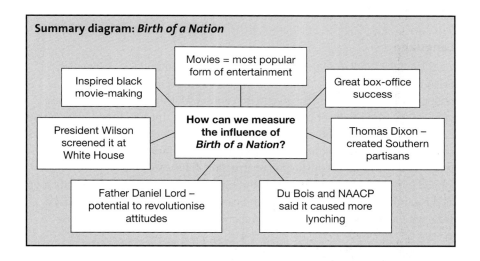

Summary diagram: *Birth of a Nation*

3 *Gone With the Wind*

▶ Did *Gone With the Wind* *reflect and/or shape changing perceptions of race relations?*

Born in Atlanta, Georgia, Margaret Mitchell (1900–49) grew up listening to her grandmother's tales of life in the South during the Civil War and Reconstruction. Mitchell's novel *Gone With the Wind* (1936) told of the O'Hara family of Tara plantation in Georgia. Gerald's charismatic, wilful daughter Scarlett pines for genteel Ashley Wilkes, but he marries Melanie Hamilton. Scarlett marries Melanie's brother Charles, who dies of pneumonia. Scarlett attracts but rejects roguish Rhett Butler. The Civil War devastates Atlanta and Scarlett's beloved Tara. Scarlett marries her sister's dull beau, Frank Kennedy, in order to keep Tara. When Scarlett is attacked by a black man as she drives through the black Shantytown, the local Ku Klux Klan go to seek revenge and Frank is killed. Scarlett finally marries Rhett but the marriage is tempestuous. Rhett leaves her, but Scarlett is a survivor and does not lose hope: 'I'll think about it tomorrow. Tomorrow is another day.'

The popular and critical reception

Gone With the Wind topped the fiction bestseller lists in the United States in 1936 and 1937 and won the 1937 Pulitzer Prize for fiction. Initially, the book was criticised by a few white liberals and many black Americans. As racial sensibilities changed over the years and the book remained popular (a 2014 Harris poll found it to be the second favourite book of American readers), the criticisms increased.

Criticisms have invariably focused upon the language and the depictions of slavery, the Ku Klux Klan and Reconstruction.

Language

Gone With the Wind used the language of the Civil War and Reconstruction period, but words such as 'darky' and 'nigger' were increasingly perceived as politically incorrect during the twentieth century. Within a year of the novel's publication, film producer David Selznick was deeply uneasy about the impact of the word 'nigger' on contemporary movie audiences (see page 164). Mitchell was criticised for her animal imagery: for example, when Tara field hand Big Sam is reunited with Scarlett during Reconstruction, 'His water-melon pink tongue lopped out, his whole body wiggled, and his joyful contortions were as ludicrous as the gambollings of a mastiff.' When Scarlett's **Mammy** looks at the ruined Tara, her face is 'sad with the uncomprehending sadness of a monkey's face'.

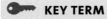

KEY TERM

Mammy A black nursemaid or nanny in charge of white children.

Slavery as a benevolent institution

The O'Hara family of *Gone With the Wind* is one that treats its slaves well. The house servants, Mammy, Pork, Prissy and Uncle Peter, remain loyally with their white masters even after slavery is abolished. Mitchell was criticised for depicting slaves as docile and happy, but to be fair, some house slaves were doubtless treated well, and she did touch upon white mistreatment of slaves when Gerald O'Hara scolds his daughter for being hard on them. Furthermore, options for uneducated freed domestics were invariably limited. Mitchell was probably correct in the depiction of the relationship between house slaves and whites in some families during the Civil War and Reconstruction.

Mitchell was also criticised for stereotypical black characters: Prissy is foolish and unreliable; Uncle Peter is an Uncle Tom (see page 157); Mammy seems to have no existence other than as part of the O'Hara family. However, Mitchell's

Mammy was an assertive character, so much so that contemporary white Southerners criticised her familiarity with Scarlett, whose behaviour she frequently criticises.

The favourable depiction of the Ku Klux Klan

Mitchell was criticised for romanticising the Ku Klux Klan, but she indicated some disapproval of some Klan activities. For example, Ashley Wilkes supports it but is 'against violence of any sort', and he and Rhett Butler convince other Georgians that it is unproductive and should be disbanded.

The unfavourable depiction of freedmen during Reconstruction

Mitchell's grandmother convinced her that congressional Reconstruction (see page 22) was awful for Southern whites. Mitchell describes former field hands during the early days of Reconstruction as 'creatures of small intelligence … Like monkeys or small children turned loose among treasured objects whose value is beyond their comprehension, they ran wild.' The novel attributed the hardships suffered by the freed men to their inability to care for themselves as their owners once had. Mitchell repeatedly reflects traditional Southern white fears of the sexually aggressive black male lusting after white women. In Shantytown, while a white man grabs her horse's bridle, Scarlett is attacked by 'a squat black negro with shoulders, chest like a gorilla … so close that she could smell the rank odour of him … [as he ripped at her bodice and] fumbled between her breasts'.

Mitchell's attitude toward slavery and Reconstruction reflected that of her family and of historians whom contemporaries considered reputable. Her perceptions reflected those of Southerners of her time. As for whether or not her book shaped attitudes – the history of the movie of *Gone With the Wind* is particularly illuminating on this issue, revealing that some people thought that it might.

The movie

David Selznick's film of *Gone With the Wind* (1939) was one of the most popular movies ever. It received a rapturous reception from the public from the first and has been repeatedly rereleased ever since. It remains the highest rated film ever shown on television – 65 per cent of American viewers saw its first airings during 1976.

Making the movie

When Selznick set about making the movie of *Gone With the Wind*, a considerable amount of his correspondence was preoccupied with race. By spring 1937, he had received many letters from black organisations: a Pittsburgh group wrote, 'We consider this work to be a glorification of the old rotten system of slavery, propaganda for race-hatreds and bigotry, and incitement of lynching.' Selznick was Jewish, and a Jewish organisation told him that the novel contained latent 'anti-Negro antipathy'. Selznick assured his black correspondents that no movie company 'intends to offer to the public material that is offensive or conducive to race prejudice'. Regardless of his own racial sensibilities, Selznick did not want to offend black Americans. After all, they might attend his movie, which would be lucrative, or boycott it, which would not.

Selznick's correspondence with screenwriter Sidney Howard revealed much about contemporary racial sensitivities and suggests that perceptions of race were changing during the 1930s and that controversies over *Gone With the Wind* had helped precipitate change. While Mitchell might be considered typical of many white Southerners, there was obviously much in the book that worried other whites. Many black and white individuals asked Selznick to cut out the word 'nigger', and he did. He insisted upon the reversal of the race roles in the rape scene: in the film, the attacker becomes a white man and Selznick ordered that 'the Negro [should be] little more than a spectator'. As a Jew, Selznick particularly disliked the contemporary reincarnation of the Ku Klux Klan, which opposed Jews and Catholics as well as black Americans. He wanted to 'cut out the Klan entirely', and told Howard,

> *I for one, have no desire to produce any anti-Negro film … In our picture I think we have to be awfully careful that the Negroes come out decidedly on the right side of the ledger … Another great problem is going to be to get the background in unobtrusively while we concentrate on the 'personal story' … The picture must not emerge as anything offensive to Negroes … [nor cast] too bad a light on even the Negroes of the Reconstruction period.*

The movie's reception

During the three-day celebration of the premiere in Atlanta, thousands of Confederate flags were waved in the streets. Although some disapproved of Mammy (played by Hattie McDaniel) as too familiar with the O'Hara family, the vast majority of white Southerners were delighted by the film. Black cast members were reminded of contemporary nationwide racism when they could not attend the premiere in the Southern city of Atlanta because they could not sit with the white cast members and when Hattie McDaniel was segregated from her co-stars and had to sit at a table at the back of the room in the Academy Awards (Oscars) ceremony in the Western city of Los Angeles.

Contemporary white audiences and film critics had no problem with the film's portrayal of black people, but some contemporary black critics such as black dramatist Carlton Moss did. He criticised the film as a 'nostalgic plea for sympathy for a still living cause of Southern reaction', with stereotypical characters: 'shiftless and dull-witted Pork', 'indolent and thoroughly irresponsible Prissy' and a Mammy 'doting on every wish of Scarlett'. Big Sam's 'radiant acceptance of slavery' nauseated Moss. Some black Americans demonstrated against the movie in several cities, but others crossed picket lines and considered the film a fine showcase for black actors.

SOURCE F

From a 1939 article written by Susan Myrick, a reporter for a Southern newspaper, the *Macon Telegraph*, and a technical adviser on *Gone With the Wind* (available at: http://xroads.virginia.edu/~ma99/diller/mammy/gone/myrick. html).

Oscar Polk, who is playing Pork, the servant of Gerald O'Hara, in GWTW [Gone With the Wind], brought me a copy of the Chicago Defender, *Negro newspaper of Chicago, so I might read his admirable defense of the picture. There had been some criticism of the play by members of his race and Oscar Polk's defence is intelligent and worthwhile. I quote a part of it: 'I am from the South and am as familiar with Southern traditions as any member of my race. The characters that appear in the picture, Pork, Mammy, Prissy, Uncle Peter, Big Sam and Geems, are all true to life – all of them could, in fact, have lived. As a race we should be proud that we have risen so far above the status of our enslaved ancestors and be glad to portray ourselves as we once were because in no other way can we so strikingly demonstrate how far we have come in so few years.'*

How does Source F defend *Gone With the Wind*'s portrayal of black characters?

Polk was not the only black actor to be criticised by the black community. Butterfly McQueen was criticised then and since for her Prissy. Malcolm X (see page 131) subsequently recorded being the sole black American in the movie theatre when it was shown and, 'When Butterfly McQueen went into her act, I felt like crawling under the rug.' Hattie McDaniel won an Oscar for her Mammy, but NAACP Secretary Walter White criticised her for repeatedly accepting Uncle Tom roles. Her response was realistic: 'Why should I complain about making seven thousand dollars a week playing a maid? If I didn't, I'd be making seven dollars a week actually being one.' White was not a particularly perceptive film critic: McDaniel ensured her characters were never subservient.

Reflecting and shaping changing perceptions of race relations

The great popularity of both book and film might suggest that *Gone With the Wind* reflected contemporary and unfavourable white perceptions of black Americans. Writing in the *Atlantic Monthly* in December 1999, Leonard J. Leff said *Gone With the Wind* was 'a barometer of race relations in the 1930s and 1940s'. Its continued popularity might suggest that it perpetuated and failed to change unfavourable perceptions, but there were many reasons for *Gone With the Wind*'s popularity that had little to do with any view on race relations. The 1930s was a decade dominated by uncertainty, both economic and international. *Gone With the Wind*'s message of loss and change would have resonated with many readers and moviegoers. Scarlett's insistence that tomorrow is another day could offer them hope. No doubt some of those who read the book and/or went to see the movie hankered for the Old South, but for others, the Old South was simply the necessary background against which the lives of two particularly fascinating characters (played on screen by two particularly charismatic performers, Clark Gable and Vivien Leigh) developed.

Like *Birth of a Nation*, *Gone With the Wind* served to stimulate debate about race relations. While it reflected Southern white perceptions, Selznick's anxieties about the presentation of black characters in *Gone With the Wind* reflected greater contemporary racial sensitivity on the part of some whites, while black protests against the movie illustrated their growing assertiveness.

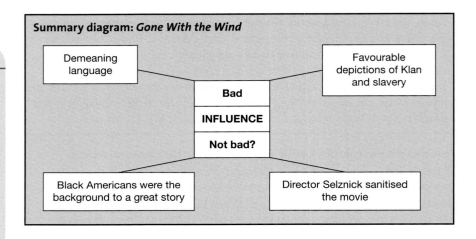

Summary diagram: *Gone With the Wind*

🔑 **KEY FIGURES**

Harper Lee (1926–2016)

Born in Monroeville, Alabama, Lee never wrote another novel after her first, *To Kill a Mockingbird*, was a surprise bestseller. When old and in poor health, she supposedly assented to the publication of *Go Set a Watchman* (2015), an early draft of what developed into *To Kill a Mockingbird*.

Oprah Winfrey (1954–)

Born in Mississippi, the 'Queen of all Media' was frequently described as the world's most influential woman as well as the richest black American of the twentieth century. Her exceptionally successful television talk-show ran from 1986 to 2011. She was also a film producer, occasional actress and philanthropist.

🔑 **KEY TERM**

White trash Poor white people, especially those living in the South.

④ Fiction after *Gone With the Wind*

▶ *Has fiction reflected and/or shaped racial attitudes since 1936?*

By 1960, there was far greater awareness and activity in relation to racial inequality, and this was reflected in **Harper Lee**'s novel *To Kill a Mockingbird*.

To Kill a Mockingbird

To Kill a Mockingbird (1960) was a Pulitzer Prize winner and remains much loved and much studied in American schools. **Oprah Winfrey** called it 'our national novel'. It tells of widower and lawyer Atticus Finch and his son Jem and daughter Scout, who live in the fictional town of Maycomb, Alabama. When Atticus agrees to defend Tom Robinson, a black man accused of raping '**white trash**' Mayella Ewell, the townspeople criticise him as a 'nigger-lover'. Atticus, his children and their friend Dill save Tom from a lynching. Although Atticus discredits the testimonies of Mayella and her father Bob Ewell, the all-white jury finds Tom guilty. He tries to escape and is shot and killed. The mysterious Boo saves Jem and Scout from Bob Ewell's vengeful attack.

Although set in the 1930s, the book illustrates the preoccupations of the 1950s and some critics believe it reflected Harper Lee's thoughts on the developing civil rights movement.

To Kill a Mockingbird and race relations

Some consider race relations the main theme of the book, which has received much praise for its advocacy of tolerance. Most of the adult white residents of Maycomb are racist, with the exception of Atticus (who calls racism 'Maycomb's usual disease') and Miss Maudie, who has pride in 'those people in this town who say that fair play is not marked WHITE ONLY.' The children Jem and Scout are free of racial (and class) prejudice: Jem says, 'It ain't right!' for an all-white jury to convict a man just because he is black; Scout cannot understand how her teacher can oppose Hitler but support the 'Guilty' verdict – 'It is not right to persecute anybody, is it?' As in *Huckleberry Finn* (see page 157), racial injustice is viewed and exposed through the eyes of innocent children.

However, some have criticised Harper Lee's portrayal of Tom Robinson as typical of a patronising white Southern writer: for example, Tom needs a white man to save him. Others have criticised Atticus for not challenging the legal *status quo*. Such criticisms rather miss the point. Whatever more modern and liberal sensibilities might have wanted, the outcry when Atticus agrees to do his duty and defend Tom indicates that he and his children would have been in danger had they sought to combat racism in any other way. Furthermore, it is unlikely that there would have been any black lawyers to defend Tom in a small Southern town in the 1930s.

The book has been a consistent but controversial choice for use in American classrooms since 1963. Criticisms have usually reflected contemporary preoccupations. Many early Southern white complaints focused on the white Mayella's attraction to Tom. That was the main source of anxiety of a Richmond, Virginia, school board that tried to ban the book as 'immoral literature'. However, by the 1970s, black and (liberal) white criticism often focused on the book's lack of sufficient condemnation for racism in Maycomb, and on its stereotyping and marginalisation of black characters. In contrast, some people have claimed that the book helped the civil rights movement. For example, literature professor Joseph Flora (2006) said it 'arrived at the right moment to help the South and the nation grapple with the racial tensions' that resulted from 'the accelerating civil rights movement'. Martin Luther King Jr's close associate Andrew Young said the book 'inspires hope in the midst of chaos and confusion' (2010). Young rejected criticisms of Lee's repeated use of the word 'nigger' because that was contemporary usage. Diane McWhorter (2010) praised Harper Lee: 'For a white person from the South to write a book like this in the late 1950s was really unusual – by its very existence an act of protest.'

Maycomb/Monroeville

Accounts of the reception of *To Kill a Mockingbird* in Monroeville and in the South in 1960 vary. In a 1961 *Life* magazine interview, Lee said, 'I'm not like Thomas Wolfe [unwelcome in the Southern town he wrote about]. I can go home again.' Jane Ellen Clark, director of the Monroe County Heritage Museum, asked Monroeville residents what they thought of the book when it first came out. 'Most people said they didn't pay it any mind ... When the movie rights were sold and Gregory Peck [the actor who played Atticus Finch] came to Monroeville, that is when they sat up and took notice.' However, black teacher Mary Tucker, who said that she was one of Monroeville's few black residents who read the book in 1960, recalled that white people 'resented' the fact that many of the characters were based upon real people and that Atticus defended a black man.

In a 1963 interview, Harper Lee was asked about the movie:

REPORTER: *What's going to happen when it's shown in the South?*

MISS LEE: *I don't know. But I wondered the same thing when the book was published. But the publisher said not to worry, because no one can read down there.*

Just how much the book was Lee's 'act of protest' is disputed, because Lee's editor Tay Hohoff, a Northern white liberal, coached and cajoled the author through dramatic revisions between 1957 and 1960 – 'I was a first-time writer so I did as I was told.' Amidst much controversy, Lee's first version of *To Kill a Mockingbird*, entitled *Go Set a Watchman*, was published in July 2015 and in it Atticus says, 'Do you want Negroes by the carload in our schools and churches and theaters?'

Overall, when published in 1960, *To Kill a Mockingbird* reflected the state of flux in contemporary views of race relations. It continued to reflect current and changing perspectives in the next few decades. From the first, it was widely read, and the 1962 movie version was a big hit. Atticus was a hero to generations of readers and moviegoers. That might suggest that Harper Lee managed to shape views on race in a positive fashion, although such shaping is difficult to quantify.

SOURCE G

From Mary McDonagh Murphy, editor, *Scout, Atticus and Boo*, Penguin, 2010, pp. 58, 78–9, 112, 142, 152, 177–9, which explores the positive impact of *To Kill a Mockingbird* upon lovers of the book.

[Lee Smith, novelist, teacher, born Virginia, 1944] This novel ... changed the way I thought about race, class and discrimination ... students are reading it today with the same responses we all had in the sixties ... It still has a galvanizing effect on the younger reader.

[Mark Childress, novelist, born Monroeville, Alabama, 1957] It was published before the biggest explosions of the civil rights movements, and helped bring it along ... To Kill a Mockingbird was one of the most influential novels ... the

? To what extent does Source G constitute good evidence that *To Kill a Mockingbird* reflected and changed perceptions of race relations?

book really helped [white Southerners] come to understand what was wrong with the system … It also helped the white Southerner because there was distance between the South she was writing about and the present day when it was published. That allowed them to feel, 'Well, we've moved a little beyond that.' And because she was a white Southerner, there was something that allowed them to hear what she was trying to say.

[Rick Bragg, author, teacher, born Alabama, 1959] You hear that over and over again, especially from young men that have been forced to read it, young men who grew up on the wrong side of the issue that dominates this book. They start reading it, and the next thing you know, it's not just held their interest, it's changed their views … that's almost impossible, but it happens.

[Diane McWhorter, historian, born Alabama, c.1950] Every Southern child has an episode of cognitive dissonance having to do with race, when the beliefs that you've held are suddenly called into question … For me, it was seeing To Kill a Mockingbird.

[Wally Lamb, teacher and novelist, born Connecticut, 1950] I taught high school for twenty-five years, and just about every year, I did To Kill a Mockingbird *with students. It was a book they read because they wanted to, not because they had to … I think, in its own way,* To Kill a Mockingbird *– and I don't mean to overstate this – sort of triggers the beginning of change and certainly puts on to the stage the questions of racial equality and bigotry in the way, a century earlier, Harriet Beecher Stowe's* Uncle Tom's Cabin *sort of stirred things up and got people riled up enough and motivated to change things.*

[Allison Moorer, singer, songwriter, born Alabama, 1972, Monroeville resident 1986 onwards] There was a black side of town, and there was a white side of town, and there still is.

Beloved

Most contemporary critics lavished praise upon **Toni Morrison**'s *Beloved* (1987), which won the Pulitzer Prize and contributed to her Nobel Prize for literature (1993). In 2008, the *New York Times* declared *Beloved* the best novel of the past 25 years. *Beloved* focused upon the black community's struggle with the memory and crippling legacy of slavery, which the novel suggests also damages the white population. There is no direct reference to the hopelessness of late twentieth-century ghetto life, but it is possible to find themes and explanations that relate to it echoing throughout the book.

Plot

Beloved tells of Sethe, a devoted mother who kills one of her children rather than see her taken into slavery. The novel is set during Reconstruction (see Chapter 2), but the characters look back to Africa, enslavement and the Civil

KEY FIGURE

Toni Morrison (1931–)
Perhaps America's most successful black author, Morrison was born in Ohio to a family that had joined the Great Migration (see page 56) in order to escape Southern racism. Educated at Howard University (1949–53) and then Cornell, she variously worked as editor, novelist and professor. Her novels explore the black American experience. Some consider *Beloved* her best work.

War period. The malevolent spirit of the murdered daughter haunts Sethe's family home and causes her two sons to run away and her other daughter, Denver, to become an anxious recluse. When a girl who seems to be the dead daughter, Beloved, returns home, she leeches the life out of Sethe until the black community finally rallies around and exorcises her.

Although many critics thought highly of the novel *Beloved*, there were reservations, for example, over the 'ghost' elements of the story.

SOURCE H

From the assessment of *Beloved* by Ted Gioia, a music historian (available at: www.thenewcanon.com/beloved.html).

… if the Nobel judges love Morrison, college professors love her more … I can't imagine another novel of recent years assigned by more teachers in more classrooms … Beloved is that rarity among contemporary novels: it was selling by the bucketload even before Oprah gave it her stamp of approval … In the final analysis, the importance of this book is no longer a matter of good or bad writing, and perhaps never was. For twenty-somethings and thirty-somethings, this is the book that spurred them into dialogues on race and gender and other thorny issues that still haunt our national debate.

> ? According to Source H, what is the significance of the novel *Beloved*?

The movie

Oprah Winfrey (see page 166) produced and starred in the movie *Beloved* in 1998. Critics loved it but it was a box-office disaster. Winfrey declared it to be the worst moment of her otherwise successful career, and recalled eating 30 pounds of macaroni cheese in a vain attempt to avert acute depression. In 2013, she asked, 'Was it a mistake to not try and make [*Beloved*] a more commercial film? … But at the time, I was pleased with the film that we did because it represented to me the essence of the *Beloved* book.'

The movie's box-office failure raises the question as to why a popular book was an unpopular movie, despite a faithful adaptation. Perhaps the audiences differed. Perhaps readers were more educated and consequently more liberal than regular cinema audiences. Perhaps ordinary white American moviegoers simply do not want to see a film with views on the impact of slavery that they do not share or perhaps care about. Or perhaps they simply wanted to avoid a deeply depressing movie.

The Help

The Help (2009) was the first novel of white writer Kathryn Stockett (1969–), who was born in Jackson, Mississippi. It quickly became a bestseller and was made into a movie (2011).

The story tells of white college graduate Skeeter, who has a different view of race relations from her segregationist family and friends in Jackson, Mississippi, in the early 1960s. Desperate to be a writer, Skeeter persuades a number of local black domestics to recount how they bring up and love affectionate white children, but then watch them growing up into racists like their parents. Their collaborative book, published in New York, is a bestseller. Skeeter has to leave Mississippi because of her **integrationist** beliefs and the book. The domestics are saved from employer retribution because the leading racist amongst Jackson's upper-class white women does not want to be recognised as the employer who greedily ate a chocolate pie cooked by her sacked maid Minny, in which Minny put her own excrement. The maid Aibileen writes so well that she gets Skeeter's old job on the local newspaper. Minny has a 'good' white employer, the white trash Celia, who has married the scion of a notable local family.

Popularity and significance

The book and the movie adaptation were both highly successful. Most critics liked both, although some criticised the story as saccharine – a 'big ole slab of honey-glazed hokum', said the *New York Times*. In comparison to the book, the film sweetened the story of Skeeter's rejection by Jackson white society. The story is not particularly believable: few black domestics would have risked job loss and intimidation, but in 2009–11, it suited white Americans to think that there were sympathetic whites such as Skeeter and that domestics had a happy ending (in this case, plentiful book royalties).

SOURCE I

From 'An Open Statement to the Fans of *The Help*', published in August 2011 by the Association of Black Women Historians (available at: http://newamericamedia.org/2011/08/association-of-black-women-historians-open-letter-to-fans-of-the-help.php).

On behalf of the Association of Black Women Historians (ABWH), this statement provides historical context to address widespread stereotyping presented in both the film and novel version of The Help. *The book has sold over 3 million copies, and heavy promotion of the movie will ensure its success at the box office. Despite efforts to market the book and the film as a progressive story of triumph over racial injustice,* The Help *distorts, ignores, and trivialises the experiences of black domestic workers. We are specifically concerned about the representations of black life and the lack of attention given to sexual harassment and civil rights activism …*

The Help's *representation of these women is a disappointing resurrection of Mammy – a mythical stereotype of black women who were compelled, either by slavery or segregation, to serve white families …*

Both versions of The Help *also misrepresent African-American speech and culture. Set in the South, the appropriate regional accent gives way to a child-like, over-exaggerated 'black' dialect. In the film, for example, the primary character, Aibileen, reassures a young white child that 'You is smat*

KEY TERM

Integrationist Desirous to participate in the 'American dream' without separation of the races.

To what extent do you suppose Source I reflects contemporary black and white reactions to *The Help*? **?**

[smart], you is kind, you is important.' … We do not recognize the black community described in The Help *where most of the black male characters are depicted as drunkards, abusive, or absent. Such distorted images are misleading and do not represent the historical realities of black masculinity and manhood.*

Furthermore, African-American domestic workers often suffered sexual harassment as well as physical and verbal abuse in the homes of white employers. For example, a recently discovered letter written by Civil Rights activist Rosa Parks indicates that she, like many black domestic workers, lived under the threat and sometimes reality of sexual assault. The film, on the other hand, makes light of black women's fears and vulnerabilities turning them into moments of comic relief.

Summary diagram: Fiction after *Gone With the Wind*

1960	*To Kill a Mockingbird*	Promoted liberalism BUT Tom demeaned?
1987	*Beloved*	Prompted thought about slavery's legacy BUT moviegoers rejected?
2009	*The Help*	Liberal heroine BUT back to servants?

 # Film, 1940–92

▶ *Has film reflected and/or shaped changing racial attitudes since 1940?*

As the twentieth century progressed, film drew wider audiences than literature, suggesting that it probably better reflected attitudes to race and was more influential than literature in shaping those attitudes.

In the 1930s, Walter White of the NAACP complained of the ubiquitous movie depictions of black Americans as servants. The Second World War brought change: the contemporary emphasis upon national unity resulted in the depiction of heroic black soldiers in several wartime movies. Female characters were more problematic: actress and singer Lena Horne arrived in Hollywood during the war and complained: 'They didn't make me into a maid, but they didn't make me into anything else either. I became a butterfly pinned to a column singing away in Movieland.' Horne was confined mostly to nightclub singer interludes. Such black entertainer interludes were common in Hollywood movies of the 1940s, because it was easy to cut them for Southern white audiences. However, there was also a slowly growing 'Negro problem' genre. Southern white reactions to this genre varied. The black soldier hero of *Home of the Brave* (1949) cracks under the pressure of racism during the fight against Japan, telling his psychiatrist, 'I learned that if you're colored, you stink … You're something strange, different … Well, you make us different, you rats.' Rather unrealistically, he lives happily ever after, invited into a business partnership with a white soldier. The film was very successful, even in the South, perhaps because, as the *Memphis Commercial Appeal* noted, it warned any 'smug section of the nation' that the black problem was not 'exclusively the South's baby'. Several movies dealt with interracial romances, but until 1956, Hollywood's Motion Picture Code forbade showing interracial marriages. The mixed-race heroine of *Pinky* (1949) has to give up her white fiancé when her true colour is revealed. It was 1957 before the first interracial movie embrace in *Island in the Sun* (1957).

Island in the Sun (1957)

In *Island in the Sun*, Hollywood explored the problems facing interracial relationships on a British West Indian island. It was obviously less controversial to explore such relationships when the characters were Britons rather than Americans. Advertisements for, and showings of, the movie demonstrated American difficulties with race. In a carnival scene, a black islander character dances in a 'primitive savage' style totally removed from the nature of her character in other scenes. Significantly, Hollywood used that image for the movie posters. Black American singer Harry Belafonte played an aspiring politician who eventually spurns the wealthy, white, upper-class woman, played by Joan Fontaine, who wants to marry him, so that he can focus upon helping his island. This black–white romance totally lacked passion. Much to the fury of Belafonte, the studio cut most of the scenes in which he and Fontaine touched each other.

At a time when 298 American counties still banned mixed-race marriages, the film generated an outcry. Some Southern movie theatres boycotted it. It was banned in Memphis and the South Carolina legislature threatened to fine any theatre that showed it. There were widespread protests in the Northern state of Minnesota, where parents feared the film would encourage mixed-race parties. Fontaine received hate mail from all across the United States and feared for her career, while a white supremacist group based in California, the American Nationalist group, published a flyer calling upon people to boycott the movie because of its interracial themes. Despite or perhaps because of such controversies, *Island in the Sun* was the third highest grossing film of 1957.

Hollywood's increased interest in race

By the 1960s, movies were beginning to challenge racial stereotypes and attitudes. For example, in the critically acclaimed *The Defiant Ones* (1958), black and white convicts chained together needed to cooperate to survive. In the end, the black convict gives up his freedom for the white man. Some

SOURCE J

? Why do you suppose the poster shown in Source J uses this unrepresentative image from *Island in the Sun?*

This poster advertising *Island in the Sun* shows an island celebration. The black characters in all the other scenes always dressed in Western-style clothes.

Southern movie theatres refused to show the film, but black audiences jeered the final scene as reminiscent of the stereotypical devoted slave. Hollywood was gaining confidence in opposing prejudice, but moviemaking was a business, and Hollywood had to be careful. The musical *South Pacific* (1958) was about interracial romances. Although a big box-office hit in most of the United States, it was unpopular in the South and nearly caused a race riot on Long Island in New York State.

In 1961, a Los Angeles NAACP leader complained that, 'Any time [movies] have a crap game [gambling with two dice] they show plenty of Negroes. But when do you see a Negro doctor or lawyer? … They will show you a scene with a baseball crowd and … not a single Negro. This is ridiculous.' The great change in black attitudes and assertiveness in the 1960s encouraged Hollywood to respond to the NAACP's insistence that 'more Negroes should be used in movies'. According to *New York Times* columnist Murray Schumach, the 1963 March on Washington was crucial in bringing about change: Hollywood had 'decided to rejoin the nation after nearly 16 years of spiritual secession'. This new Hollywood was reflected in the career of **Sidney Poitier**, the biggest black movie star of the decade.

Some of Poitier's movie characters were edgy. The movie of Lorraine Hansberry's play *A Raisin in the Sun* (1961) told of one black family's dream of escaping the ghetto for the integrated suburbs. Poitier portrayed a dissatisfied character: 'I open and close car doors all day long, I drive a white man around in his limousine and I say, "Yes, sir". Mama, that ain't no kind of a job.' Hollywood clearly anticipated an interested and sympathetic white audience response to such despair and the movie did well at the box office. Significantly, Poitier found himself unable to rent a house in a desirable white Los Angeles neighbourhood while making the film.

Most of Poitier's roles in the 1960s were blandly integrationist. He received an Academy Award nomination for *The Defiant Ones* (1958), then won the award for *Lilies of the Field* (1963). Both films lauded integration. 'I was still the only one', recalled Poitier, and because he was Hollywood's sole black leading man, the media was fascinated. He grew exasperated: 'Why don't you ask me human questions? Why is it everything you ask refers to the Negroness of my life and not to my acting?' Of Poitier's *A Patch of Blue* (1965), the *Film Quarterly* review said, 'The implicit moral is that affection between a Negro man and a white girl is all right so long as the girl is blind, ignorant, underdeveloped and 18 years old.' *New Yorker* critic Brendan Gill decried the 'caricature of the Negro as a … sort of Christian saint, selfless and well-groomed' as 'becoming a movie cliche nearly as tiresome and, at bottom, nearly as patronizing as the cretinous figure that Stepin Fetchit [a popular actor in the 1930s] used to play.' In contrast, the Ku Klux Klan picketed a Memphis movie theatre showing *A Patch of Blue*, because it was 'ungodly' and had 'the nigger's name above the white woman's on the marquee'.

Poitier had several big hits at the end of the decade: *Guess Who's Coming to Dinner* (1967), about a interracial romance, and *In the Heat of the Night* (1967), about a black police officer facing discrimination in the South, were among the five nominations for the Academy Awards' Best Picture in 1968 – a 'snapshot … of the American psyche as reflected in its popular culture', according to film historian Mark Harris (2008).

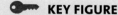

KEY FIGURE

Sidney Poitier (1927–)

Born to a Bahamian family in Miami, Poitier worked as a dishwasher in New York City, where he learned to read at the age of seventeen. After serving in the US Army, he became an actor. In the late 1960s, he was a big box-office star. Several of his films dealt with race relations, and he was the first black American male to win an Oscar (Academy Award).

Sidney and sex

Many black Americans despaired of the de-sexing of Sidney Poitier in movies such as in *Guess Who's Coming to Dinner*, in which he refused to sleep with his white fiancée, and there was but one chaste kiss between them.

White liberals and black critics were perhaps out of touch with contemporary reality, as demonstrated by the nationwide headlines when Secretary of State Dean Rusk's daughter married a black student in September 1967. Rusk offered President Johnson his resignation, lest it embarrass the administration. Johnson refused his offer, but the State Department received hundreds of angry communications and many members of Rusk's family refused to attend the wedding.

Liberal critics expected *Guess Who's Coming to Dinner* to flop, but audiences flocked to see it, even in the South, where audiences ignored Ku Klux Klan protests. Of course, there were many who went to see it to bid farewell to a legendary screen pairing: Spencer Tracy and Katharine Hepburn played the bride's parents (Tracy died three weeks after he finished filming).

SOURCE K

From the reports of the weekly American entertainment magazine, *Variety*, on reactions to the 1967 movie *Guess Who's Coming to Dinner* in early 1968 in the Southern city of Atlanta, Georgia, and the Northern city of Cincinnati, Ohio.

When [the movie studio] Columbia chose to have Atlanta … [hold the premiere] of 'Guess Who's Coming to Dinner?' at the northside Capri Cinema rather than at a downtown house, it meant that hordes of Negroes plus hippies of both races flocked into the community of Buckshead to see the record-breaking … film on miscegenation.

Undoubtedly many residents were shocked by this unusual influx, and last week their anger was expressed by Lamar Q. Ball, the segregationist editor of the North Side News. 'Never in your life have you Northsiders ever seen such a crowd in Buckshead. For three nights in one incomprehensible row!' he said in a front-page editorial, 'Blacks and mulattos [mixed race] in part of the line outnumbered whites. This was anything but the usual North side Sunday night crowd … Black escorts for dun-coloured girls could be seen enviously eyeing the blonde and brunet[te] dates of white college students … The subject of the picture is what attracted these hordes, many of whom have become contemptuous of their elders for denouncing those who are willing to destroy the white race just by encouraging moron Negroes to vote.'

In questioning the offbeat booking, he asked, 'Why wasn't this movie presented … [downtown, where] no one would have noticed the race-mixing … '

And he approvingly quoted … [a woman who said,] 'Here is a subject that's fit only for secret discussion … This is nothing to be brought out in the open

? Does Source K suggest that perceptions of race relations were changing across the United States?

> *for sound-minded people to view in a theater, shoulder to shoulder with perverts.'*
>
> *Ball's viewpoint is obviously a minority one. Reviews in the general press were favorable in Atlanta, which has long been considered one of the South's most liberal cities. And, as implied above, business at the Capri has been outstanding …*
>
> *Columbia's 'Guess Who's Coming to Dinner?' with Sidney Poitier got a record-making and rock-throwing reception in southern Ohio cities 26 miles apart.*
>
> *In Cincinnati – which had riots last summer – the picture is jamming the 3000-seat Albee with mixed race audiences setting record grosses for the Negro-engaged-to-white-gal tale.*
>
> *In Hamilton, robed Klansmen picketed the Court Theaters, Wednesday night. Next came counter-picketing in window smashing of nearby stores and a filling station …*

In the Heat of the Night (1967)

The 1967 movie *In the Heat of the Night* was based on John Ball's novel, written in 1960 and published in 1965. In the novel, the black hero was not an angry young man, but since Ball had written it, there had been many race riots (see page 142), so the movie sharpened the racial antagonisms.

The movie tells of the murder of a Chicago businessman who planned to build a factory in Sparta, Mississippi. A black Northerner, Virgil Tibbs (played by Sidney Poitier), happens to be passing through the town and is found at the train station with a wallet full of money. Racist white police chief Bill Gillespie assumes Tibbs is the murderer, then discovers that Tibbs is a Philadelphia homicide detective. Tibbs is keen to show his professional superiority and keen to prove that an arrogant, rich white supremacist is the murderer. The victim's widow is impressed by Tibbs which, coupled with Tibbs' experience in homicide, forces Gillespie to accept his assistance. Tibbs meets racism in his investigations, but Gillespie grows to admire him. The murderer turns out to be the man at the diner who refused to serve Tibbs.

The film studio that made the movie recognised that it could be produced so cheaply that it could survive without Southern white audiences. Director Norman Jewison's determination to film on location proved problematic. Poitier refused to film in the South, because he had recently been frightened by the burning of a white cross (the Ku Klux Klan signature) on the lawn of his New York home after his wife had organised a fundraiser for James Meredith (see page 139), and so most of the filming was done in three Illinois locations. However, a few days were spent in Tennessee in order to film alongside a cotton field. The crew checked into a Holiday Inn motel: 'There was no other place we could find that accepted black people', Jewison recalled. 'The Holiday Inn only did because it was a national chain that had an integrated policy by then.' When the local population found out that the film was about a black detective, they grew hostile and threatening.

In one scene, there is a disparity between the book and the film. In the book, Tibbs is questioning a racist who then slaps him; Tibbs fails to react. In the movie, Tibbs returns the slap: the first major motion pictures scene in which a black man defends himself. In an interesting example of how one can become more of an activist in hindsight, Poitier claimed that,

> [The slapping scene] was almost not there. I said, 'I'll tell you what, I'll make this movie for you if you give me your absolute guarantee when he slaps me I slap him right back and you guarantee that it will play in every version of this movie.' I try not to do things that are against nature.

However, there are doubts about the veracity of his claims: copies of the original screenplays suggest that Tibbs was *always* going to return the slap, which is confirmed by the Canadian director Norman Jewison and the screenwriter.

The significance of *In the Heat of the Night*

In the Heat of the Night was one of the most popular pictures of 1967, and, along with *Guess Who's Coming to Dinner*, was nominated for an Oscar for Best Picture. At the Academy Awards ceremony, postponed for two days out of respect for the assassinated Martin Luther King Jr, Academy President Gregory Peck said, 'Society has always been reflected in its art, and one measure of Dr. King's influence on the society we live in is that of the five films nominated for Best Picture of the Year, two dealt with the subject of understanding between the races.' *In the Heat of the Night* won.

In the Heat of the Night is one of several 1960s' movies that reflected the influence of white liberals and black performers in Hollywood. Most critics were positive. Bosley Crowther's review said, 'the hot surge of racial hate and tension as it has been displayed in many communities this year … is put forth with realism and point'. Many critics approved the way that the Sidney Poitier character also needed to learn a racial tolerance lesson, and, like *Life* magazine, saw the movie as 'a fine demonstration that races can work together'. However, a minority, such as Andrew Sarris, thought it a 'fantasy of racial reconciliation'. The *Village Voice* dismissed it as 'liberal propaganda'.

The success of *In the Heat of the Night* might seem to suggest that liberal views of race relations must have been accepted by considerable numbers of cinema audiences. Rod Steiger, who played Gillespie, recalled watching multiple New York audiences reacting to the slapping scene: 'You could hear the black people say, "Go get them Sidney!" and the white people saying "Oh!".' The scene drew cheers in many movie theatres. However, that was New York City, where audiences and film critics were generally more liberal than in much of the rest of the country. The movie was popular elsewhere, but the popularity of a film does not necessarily prove that it reflects the attitudes of the audiences who flocked to see it. Motives for going to see a movie vary and several questions need to be asked:

- Is it the only movie that is available for the viewer to see at a particular time?
- Does the viewer want to see a particular star?
- Is the viewer influenced by the fact that the movie has won an Academy Award?
- Does the viewer hold opposing views of the movie and want to see exactly what its unacceptable message is?

There is a similar problem when considering whether a movie shapes perceptions of race relations. Although Tibbs and Gillespie got on well in the movie, opposition to desegregated schools continued.

> ### Sidney Poitier's explanation of his success
>
> In a 1992 interview, Sidney Poitier tried to explain his stardom. He said that he was in Hollywood at just the right time, when anti-racist sentiments were 'in vogue'. He felt that he suited Hollywood's needs, because he was 'a pretty good actor' and an integrationist. 'I was selected almost by history itself.'

Blaxploitation films

In his 1980 autobiography, Sidney Poitier recalled how black criticism of some of his late 1960s' movie roles such as that in *Guess Who's Coming to Dinner* upset him. One black critic referred to him as a 'clean cut eunuch in the white world', while some white critics also felt it was time for some realism: in a February 1967 *Los Angeles Times* article, Bert Prelutsky wrote:

> *Where is the Negro American life depicted in movies as it's lived by American Negroes? Where's the child desertion and illegitimacy, the policy games and the bag women? Do you think for a moment that you will ever go to a movie and see Sidney Poitier fathering an illegitimate child, live off his wife's earnings or mug an old Jew on the subway? … the pendulum [has swung too far and Sidney Poitier just plays a] Negro in white face.*

Such criticisms were perhaps unrealistic. White audiences were probably not ready to sympathise with ghetto conditions (see page 137), and prejudices remained great.

Slowly, some movies began reflecting contemporary, angry black radicalism. Between 1969 and 1974, independent black filmmakers and studios made what became known as Blaxploitation films, with black casts and action-packed adventures in the ghettos. Blaxploitation movies were a result of:

- the black reaction against bland black characters in mainstream movies
- the recognition that black people constituted 30 per cent of the audience in city cinemas
- the greater black awareness generated by Black Power (see page 142)
- Hollywood's desperate search for any movies that made money.

Blaxploitation movies featured black heroes overcoming corrupt whites, along with black and white women as sex objects (commentators attributed this to feelings of emasculation in the ghettos). These films aimed to please black audiences. The most significant was the independently produced *Sweet Sweetback's Baadasssss Song* (1971), in which a black stud kills two white police officers who had hurt an innocent black youth. Black inner-city audiences loved the film, as did some young whites. White critics disliked it. One found it 'almost psychotic' in its hatred of white people. In the same year, a major studio produced *Shaft* (1971), an even bigger hit. It was a relatively conventional detective story, except in that the detective was black. The movie was a massive hit and famously helped save the studio MGM from bankruptcy. It showed that white audiences were now willing to accept and enjoy films with virtually all-black casts.

Blaxploitation movies aroused tensions within the black community. Some middle-class black critics rejected the violence, drug dealing and gangsters of the 60 or so Blaxploitation films. They claimed that the smash hit *Super Fly* (1972) glorified a Harlem cocaine dealer and contributed to a dramatic increase in cocaine use amongst ghetto youths and that this glamorisation of ghetto life distracted blacks from the collective political struggle. The head of the Hollywood NAACP branch protested, 'We must insist that our children are not constantly exposed to a steady diet of so-called black movies that glorify black males as pimps, dope pushers, gangsters and super males.' Supporters claimed these films drew attention to a corrupt, racist society, but one wonders if they simply reinforced white perceptions of black sexuality.

Movies invariably reflected contemporary preoccupations, and the growth of the feminist movements in the mid-1970s encouraged the appearance of black superwomen, such as *Foxy Brown* (1974). Foxy was typical of such characters in that she cleaned up the ghettos. She arranges for the castration of a corrupt white man who killed her lover and brother, then takes his severed appendages to his equally evil white girlfriend.

SOURCE L

From Alvin F. Poussaint, 'Blaxploitation Movies: Cheap Thrills That Degrade Blacks', *Psychology Today*, Volume 7, Number 9, February 1974, p. 26. Poussaint was a psychiatrist. He participated in the civil rights movement.

Black youth in Brooklyn dramatically increased their use of cocaine after the movie Super Fly *glamorized the narcotic … These films, especially 'blaxploitation' films, have their heaviest impact on black youths …*

These movies glorify criminal life and encourage in black youth misguided feelings of machismo that are destructive to the community as a whole …

Negative black stereotypes are more subtle and neatly camouflaged than they were in the films of yesteryear, but the same insidious message is there: blacks are violent, criminal, sexy savages who imitate the white man's ways as best they can from their disadvantaged sanctuary in the ghetto.

Many [black] cast members try to dismiss the possibility that blaxploitation films have a negative effect on audiences. They assert that movies … have no lasting effect on theatergoers …. but … movies of any type are seldom mere entertainment because they teach cultural values and influence behavior …

Movies have lied to us before. The movies were at least partially responsible for teaching blacks and whites that Africans were savages, and that their Afro-American descendants were lazy, happy-go-lucky, thieving, sexually promiscuous, and mentally inferior …

Some blacks and whites argue that such [blaxploitation] films are psychologically beneficial to the black viewer. They reason that these films show the black man or woman as a hero … youthful black audiences seem to support [this argument] …

> **?** Is Source L good evidence to prove the contention that movies shape and/or reflect changing perceptions?

By the end of the 1970s, the pure black movie was out of fashion and crossover films that starred blacks and whites became common in the 1980s. Several black–white buddy movies were very popular in the 1980s, for example, *Lethal Weapon* (1987).

The Color Purple

The most talked about 1980s' film about black Americans was *The Color Purple* (1985). The NAACP criticised its depiction of brutal black males, but some critics and audiences loved it. In an interesting example of how Hollywood is careful not to offend audiences, the movie of *The Color Purple* touched only lightly upon the lesbian relationship between the Whoopi Goldberg character and another woman. Whether Hollywood had a problem with lesbians or simply with black lesbians is difficult to ascertain. Goldberg certainly found it difficult to have a screen sex life: West Coast preview audiences demanded that a love scene between her and white Sam Elliot be cut from *Fatal Beauty* (1987), a reminder that interracial romance remained a problem.

Mississippi Burning

It is perhaps significant that Hollywood rarely explored the dramatic struggles of the early 1960s' civil rights movement. Director Alan Parker's *Mississippi Burning* (1988) touched upon it. Based somewhat loosely upon the FBI investigation into the murder of three white civil rights activists in Philadelphia, Mississippi, during the Freedom Summer of 1964 (see page 124), the film focuses on the eventually successful efforts of two white FBI agents to find the murderers and obtain their conviction, in the face of the uncooperative local law enforcement officials and townspeople. The agents finally manipulate a confession out of a Ku Klux Klan member. The movie was made on location in Neshoba County, Mississippi, where the three civil rights activists had been murdered in 1964.

? Judging from Sources M and N, had there been 'progress in race relations' in Mississippi by 1989?

SOURCE M

From Stanley Kauffman, writing in *The New Republic*, 9 January 1989 (available at: http://law2.umkc.edu/faculty/projects/ftrials/price&bowers/movie.html).

[The] biggest surprise in the film is that the states of Mississippi and Alabama cooperated in the making of Mississippi Burning. *of [sic] course the production put money in the pockets of residents in the area – many of them are seen in the film* – but I doubt that this would have been decisive 24 years ago. Perhaps the clearest sign of progress in race relations down there is that the location shooting was done where it was.*

*Several sources claim that Klan members were amongst the extras.

SOURCE N

From Hal Lipper, *St Petersburg Times*, 22 January 1989 (available at: http://law2.umkc.edu/faculty/projects/ftrials/price&bowers/movie.html).

The racial violence that erupted in this lumber-milling community 24 years ago is like a festering wound that refuses to heal …

'They [the film makers] just want to stir up trouble between the races. It's all out of proportion,' declares Lawrence Rainey, the former Neshoba County sheriff who was exonerated of conspiracy charges in connection with the murders.

Disagreeing is the 1964 president of the Neshoba County chapter of the National Association for the Advancement of Colored People. Jessie Gary considers the picture an important reminder of the mistreatment blacks endured.

Audience and critical reception

Many critics were positive. Roger Ebert of the *New York Daily News* wrote, 'More than any other film I've seen, this one gets inside the passion of race relations in America … *Mississippi Burning* is the best American film of 1988'. However, black activists such as Coretta Scott King criticised the movie as a distortion of history. She had not seen the movie, but wanted one that focused on the heroism of black activists rather than white FBI agents. The *Washington Post* agreed. While some critics felt the violence in the movie accurately reflected life in the South in 1964, it irritated others, including one black critic who resented the way the black characters were passive recipients of violence at a time when civil rights activists were putting their lives on the line during their campaigns in the South.

The critical reception indicated that the depiction of race relations was a minefield, which no doubt helps explain why Hollywood hesitated to undertake frequent explorations. Furthermore, the film was not a massive hit: it was number 33 in the list of biggest grossing movies of 1988. The contrasting popularity of the Poitier films of 1967 with that of *Mississippi Burning* might have reflected the revival of racial conservatism in the 1980s. Perhaps white audiences were tired of black victims, whether in the South of 1964 or in the ghettos of the 1980s.

Still, Hollywood remained content to depict black heroes, in movies such as *Bird* (1988), the story of black jazz musician Charlie Parker (and his white buddy), and *Glory* (1989), the story of a black regiment (and its white officer) in the Civil War. New Yorker Denzel Washington played a rebellious soldier in *Glory*, and became a big star in the 1990s, a decade rich in black American filmmakers, directors and actors in Hollywood. In 1991, two movies made by and starring black Americans, *New Jack City* and *Boyz N the Hood*, generated outbreaks of violence in movie theatres, raising the question as to whether movies shaped as well as reflected attitudes. White audiences particularly liked *Boyz N the Hood*, perhaps because it did not focus on white racism.

The most famous and controversial black director was Spike Lee, who gained notoriety with *Do the Right Thing* (1989). It depicted a day in the life of black residents of Brooklyn's Bedford Stuyvesant district, culminating in a race riot. Some white critics feared that it would provoke a real race riot, but it never did. Even more controversial was Lee's *Malcolm X*.

Malcolm X

Spike Lee's movie *Malcolm X* (1992) was based upon *The Autobiography of Malcolm X* (1969), the result of a collaboration between Malcolm and the writer Alex Haley. The autobiography is basically as Malcolm would have wanted it told – father murdered by white supremacist, mother's mental illness, criminal career (greatly exaggerated according to Manning Marable's acclaimed biography) as 'Detroit Red', conversion to the Nation of Islam in jail, advocacy of the doctrine of separatism, then conversion to a more racially tolerant version of Islam, which led to his assassination.

Preparations for the film were controversial:

- Lee criticised the initial choice of Norman Jewison to direct the film, because Jewison was white. Lee had much black support and Jewison, who did not like the script, gladly backed down.
- The choice of Lee worried some black nationalists: the poet Amiri Baraka said, 'We will not let Malcolm X's life be trashed to make middle-class Negroes sleep easier.'
- Lee ran over budget, but prominent black Americans such as Bill Cosby and Oprah Winfrey rescued him.
- Lee pointedly asked to be interviewed by black journalists because they had 'more insight' into Malcolm, and because he sought to support black journalism.

Inevitably, there were those (black and white) who felt the film failed to reflect the Malcolm that they thought they knew. For example, Nell Irvin Painter wrote in the *American Historical Review* in April 1994 that the movie 'glosses over the weirder themes in Elijah Muhammad's doctrine' and was 'an artifact of this time rather than of the 1960s', as in its emphasis upon Malcolm's clash with the police (police brutality against black Americans had preoccupied Los Angeles during the furore over the Los Angeles Police Department's treatment of Rodney King, between March 1991 and April 1992).

Critics loved the film and Denzel Washington's portrayal of Malcolm, but it had only moderate success at the box office. The film came 32nd in the list of top-grossing films of 1992, taking $48 million. It was no box-office smash – the year's top grosser, *Aladdin*, took $217 million, and each of the next ten movies in the list took over $100 million. Given that black Americans probably constituted the majority of the audiences, it is unlikely to have shaped the attitudes of many whites toward Malcolm and race relations. However, as *New York Times* film critic Vincent Canby wrote in November 1992, 'The real triumph of *Malcolm X* is that Mr Lee was able to make it at all'. The making of a film about a man who most white Americans traditionally disliked might seem to suggest that Hollywood and white opinion now looked upon black militancy more favourably. However, in February 2015, Ashley Clark wrote in the British newspaper *The Guardian* that he doubted that Hollywood would ever make a movie 'as unapologetically supportive of a radical, controversial black figure … on such a grand scale again'. Overall, it seems that the movie's history reflected black confidence and assertiveness (especially Spike Lee's) but also white ambivalence.

Summary diagram: Film, 1940–92

Date	Movie	Portrayals	Impact
1915	*Birth of a Nation*	Evil blacks in Reconstruction	Popular with whites
1949	*Home of the Brave*	Heroic black soldier nearly destroyed by racism but happy integrationist ending	Successful – audiences liked happy integration
1957	*Island in the Sun*	Blacks human – romantic leads – interracial	Big audiences but much hostility
1958	*The Defiant Ones*	Black and white need to cooperate	Popular – but blacks mocked it
1967	*Guess Who's Coming to Dinner*	Interracial romance	Popular – but white opposition in some places
1967	*In the Heat of the Night*	Brilliant black detective wins white racist cop's respect but also learns not to let his prejudices affect his judgement	Audiences liked races cooperating and both learning lessons. Meanwhile, real-life race riots across USA
1970s	Blaxploitation movies	Black studs defeat whites, ghettos glorified	Young whites and blacks liked; black middle class feared confirmation of stereotypes, glorified bad ghetto behaviour
1980s	Buddy movies	Integration nice – it works	Popular but in real-life, schools re-segregated
1988	*Mississippi Burning*	Black victims, white heroes	Wrong heroes?
1992	*Malcolm X*	Black hero	Reasonably popular but big black audience turnout – and 'never again' (*The Guardian*)

6 Television

▶ *Has television shaped and/or reflected changing perceptions of race relations?*

During the 1950s, television became the most popular form of entertainment in the United States. While black entertainers were frequently visible, the NAACP argued that the few black characters on display in other programmes were stereotypical. It organised a boycott of the brewery that sponsored the popular comedy *Amos 'n' Andy*, because it demeaned black Americans as lazy, stupid and cunning. The American network CBS stopped production of the show in 1952, but other stations showed reruns.

The problem was that television programmes depended upon advertising and were therefore designed for maximum mass appeal. This impacted upon the presence of black performers on television. Southern white audiences were a particular problem. For example, the first major network to have a leading black character in a drama series was CBS with *East Side/West Side* (1963), but it was cancelled after one season because Southern stations refused to show it.

Prior to the mid-1960s, television viewers were unaccustomed to seeing black performers, apart from comic stereotypes and entertainers. Then a few characters emerged that went beyond the stereotypes. When in 1968 the Kerner Commission reported on the 'Civil Disorders', it concluded that 'our nation is moving toward two societies, one black, one white – separate and unequal', and advocated that television 'must hire Negroes, it must show Negroes on the air, it must schedule programmes relevant to the black ghetto'.

During the 1970s, CBS began showing 'social consciousness' programmes such as *All in the Family*. Its central character was Second World War veteran and blue-collar worker Archie Bunker, who ranted at blacks, feminists, homosexuals and hippies. His liberal creators intended Archie to be a rather ridiculous bigot, but **Middle America** liked and agreed with him. The show ran from 1971 to 1979, topping the ratings from 1971 to 1976. Archie probably reflected racist attitudes rather than positively contributing to changing perceptions. ABC's mini-series *Roots* (1977) had greater potential as a catalyst for change.

Roots

Roots explored the origins of America's racial tensions. The series dramatised African-American writer Alex Haley's fictionalised (some said plagiarised) story of the enslavement of his ancestors.

Roots tells of Kunta Kinte, born to a Mandinka warrior in eighteenth-century West Africa. Captured by black collaborators and white slave traders, he is sent to Maryland and sold as a slave. He repeatedly tries but fails to escape and is whipped into accepting his American name. Kunta Kinte and his descendants have to deal with a great many unpleasant whites, including slave traders, slave owners, an overseer who whips Kunta Kinte, slave-catchers who chop off his foot, white rapists, a Ku Klux Klan group, and a senator who exploits sharecroppers. The black characters are invariably 'good guys' – one slave family takes in a starving white couple during the Civil War. By the end of the series, Kunta Kinte's descendants are free from slavery and farming their own hard-won land.

Broadcaster ABC was not very confident about the reception that *Roots* would receive amongst white audiences. After all, this was a narrative of white atrocities perpetrated upon innocent black victims. However, a record-breaking 100 million viewers tuned in for the last episode – nearly half the American population. 'Never had so many white viewers watched anything black in the

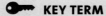
KEY TERM

Middle America A term invented by the media to describe ordinary, patriotic, middle-income white Americans.

history of television', said historian Henry Louis Gates (1992). White viewers liked *Roots* because it:

- had an extremely talented black cast
- contained many familiar white actors, chosen to reassure audiences – they featured prominently in previews
- was an 'American dream' story of immigrant progress (from slavery to freedom) that focused upon family life, which made it easier for whites to relate to the characters
- had a slave captain with a conscience inserted by the writers in the first episode, in order to make white audiences feel better about their role in the slave trade.

Roots received great critical acclaim and countless awards. Sociologist Herman Gray (1992) argued that *Roots* opened up a whole new era of black American representation on television. It helped to accustom white viewers to watching programmes dominated by black performers, which could be interpreted as reflecting increasingly sympathetic white attitudes. Whites certainly admired and enjoyed watching black television performers, which could be considered to have influenced race relations for the better. On the air from 1985, the chat show *The Oprah Winfrey Show* became a phenomenal success, and *The Cosby Show*, about a black doctor and his model family, was the top-rated sitcom for most of the late 1980s. However, by the early twenty-first century, a predominantly black cast in a drama series remained a rarity. That was one of the features that made the television drama *The Wire* exceptional.

The Wire

Created by white Baltimore journalist David Simon, *The Wire* was a television drama that explored life in the decayed, industrial seaport city of Baltimore, Maryland. It ran for five seasons (2002–8) on the expensive cable channel HBO, which had a reputation for quality programmes.

Each of the five series focused on an aspect of life in majority-black Baltimore, Maryland (or 'Bodymore, Murdaland' as the graffiti on the show christened it):

- Series 1: the drug trade amongst the black residents of the decaying projects.
- Series 2: corruption in the white-dominated unions of the decaying seaport. Simon described this series as 'a meditation on the death of work and the betrayal of the American working class'.
- Series 3: the predominantly black and corrupt city government. Simon said this series 'reflects on the nature of reform and reformers, and whether there is any possibility that political processes, long calcified, can mitigate against the forces currently arraigned against individuals'.
- Series 4: the crumbling school system, failing to serve the black ghetto children.
- Series 5: the corrupted, declining white-dominated newspaper industry.

> ## Truth or fiction?
>
> Sheila Dixon, Mayor of Baltimore from 2007 to 2010, publicly criticised *The Wire* for being 'overly negative'. In January 2009, she was indicted on charges of theft and misconduct in office. She was found guilty on one count of misappropriation of gift cards.

Within each series, the Baltimore Police Department played an equal or dominant role in the story, but Simon insisted the city was the real star of the show, the theme of which was 'how institutions have an effect on individuals'. He listed the institutions as the Baltimore Police Department, the drug-trafficking operations, the stevedores' union, City Hall, the Baltimore public school system, and the *Baltimore Sun*. He said *The Wire* was 'not designed purely as an entertainment. It is, I'm afraid, a somewhat angry show'.

Both black and white characters are flawed in varying degrees. Most of the crimes are perpetrated by black characters, many of whom are vicious killers, but Baltimore is a majority-black city, and *The Wire* makes it clear that most of these characters are trapped in their drug-dominated existence by their environment, their peers, and even their own relations, and that opportunities to escape are pretty rare. The series barely touched upon the topic of black-and-white hostility, which might suggest a **post-racial society** – or recognition that the demonisation of whites totally alienated white audiences. The almost total absence of the issue of white police brutality against black Americans was unrealistic. A prominent interracial romance might be taken to suggest that the entertainment industry had at last come to terms with that issue – or that *The Wire* was defiantly integrationist. Most critics considered *The Wire* to be concerned with class rather than race, but some insisted that it reinforced stereotypes of the urban poor as welfare dependent, lazy, criminal and immoral. Significantly, the series always placed a few prominent whites amongst the drug addicts.

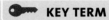

KEY TERM

Post-racial society
One free of racism and discrimination.

Reception

The Wire's ratings were average and it never won any major television awards, but many critics judged it one of the greatest ever television dramas. Simon attributed the poor ratings for the first series to the

- plot complexities
- timeslot at which it was shown
- street language that many viewers found incomprehensible
- predominantly black cast.

He might have added that subscriptions to HBO were expensive. Viewing figures remained poor by the time of the third series, and there was talk of cancellation. Simon joked about an 'audience of seventeen on a Sunday night'

(Season 4 averaged only 1.6 million viewers per episode), but was happy to hear that bootleg copies were circulating in West Baltimore's ghetto. Critics blamed the low viewing figures on the complex plotting.

San Francisco Chronicle writer Tim Goodman said *The Wire*

> tackled the drug war in this country as it simultaneously explores race, poverty and the 'death of the American working class', the failure of political systems to help the people they serve and the tyranny of lost hope. Few series in the history of television have explored the plight of inner-city African-Americans and none – not one, has done it as well.

It is probably there, rather than in plot complexities, that the main explanation for *The Wire*'s lack of popularity with audiences lay. President Barack Obama said it was his favourite television series, and this was not surprising, because *The Wire* was a thoughtful exploration of much that many considered in need of reform in American society, and particularly in the black inner-city ghettos. As *Variety* pointed out, *The Wire* was 'a series of such ambition that it is, perhaps inevitably, savoured only by the appreciative few.' As *Beloved* had shown, white audiences were not particularly interested in being educated on black problems. Significantly, several universities, including Harvard, offered classes on *The Wire* in courses ranging from law to sociology to film studies. It seems fair to conclude that the media can reflect slowly changing attitudes, and, all other things being equal, occasionally shape them. *The Wire* aimed to shape attitudes. It was a plea for a better America, particularly for black ghetto residents. It was deliberately aimed at a select audience: 'Fuck the average viewer', Simon said in a 2008 interview with BBC 2's *Culture Show*. He knew that, just as in the 1960s (see page 144), most Americans would not want to listen. There perhaps lies the conclusive proof that media can only shape attitudes to a very limited extent.

Summary diagram: Television

1950s	Demeaning *Amos 'n' Andy*, not much else
1968	Kerner Commission – show black lives
1970s	Bigot *Bunker* popular BUT *Roots* very popular – does not mean attitudes changed
2002–8	*The Wire* – no depiction of racism, just the state of the race in the ghettos

Chapter summary

Literary and visual representations of black Americans often reflected changing attitudes. Prior to the Civil War, there was much sympathetic abolitionist visual and literary propaganda. *Uncle Tom's Cabin* was a highly influential anti-slavery novel, but the fate of Uncle Tom in subsequent plays and illustrations showed the developing fear of and hostility toward freed black males. Slavery continued to inspire writers after its abolition. White Southerners wrote nostalgic 'plantation tales' that idealised slavery, but Mark Twain's popular *Adventures of Huckleberry Finn* was unsympathetic to enslavement. Demeaning depictions were nothing new but they dominated the post-Civil War period, perhaps due to white fears over the loss of the old system of race control. There, as so often, the depictions certainly reflected and probably shaped contemporary perceptions.

The late nineteenth- and early twentieth-century triumph of white supremacy was reflected in and encouraged by the movie *Birth of a Nation*, which inspired the rebirth of the Ku Klux Klan. The novel *Gone With the Wind* also depicted the supposed evils of Reconstruction, but Hollywood toned them down in the movie, suggesting that attitudes were changing. As the twentieth century wore on, increased racial sensitivities would lead to a gradual decrease in unflattering representations.

Beginning with *To Kill a Mockingbird*, later twentieth-century fiction often promoted liberal ideas, but film audiences seemed less ready than readers to accept thought-provoking material reflecting the black experience, as demonstrated in the fate of the film of the novel *Beloved*. Movies continued to become more liberal after *Gone With the Wind*, but there were some dramatically unfavourable reactions to interracial screen romances in *Island in the Sun* and *Guess Who's Coming to Dinner* – although the intensity of the white opposition had decreased by the time of the latter. By 1992, some whites were willing to watch the young *Malcolm X* have a white girlfriend.

Television was slow to include black characters, and as so often, Southern white audiences were crucial there. However, *Roots* and *The Wire* had predominantly black casts. Whites were the bad guys in *Roots*, but in *The Wire*, the city depicted seemed to have gone beyond racism. If that reflected some change in attitudes, it also reflected the continuing white refusal to do anything about ghetto poverty. Although media treatment of black Americans might reflect greater racial tolerance, it did not seem that there had been any 'shaping' of views about helping struggling black Americans.

Refresher questions

1 What evidence do we have to confirm the contemporary effectiveness of Harriet Beecher Stowe's anti-slavery novel?

2 How did *Uncle Tom's Cabin* plays reflect changing white attitudes?

3 Why did late nineteenth-century lithographs grow increasingly hostile in their portrayal of black Americans?

4 With regard to the *Adventures of Huckleberry Finn*, what are the arguments that support and oppose the idea that literature reflected and shaped perceptions?

5 Which nineteenth-century visual genres generally demeaned black Americans?

6 Which, if any, nineteenth-century visual genres depicted black Americans as regular Americans?

7 How can it be argued that the movie *Birth of a Nation* reflected and shaped perceptions of black Americans?

8 What do the differences between the book *Gone With the Wind* and the movie of the same name suggest?

9 How did Hattie McDaniel defend herself against accusations that she always played Uncle Tom roles?

10 What arguments could be used to say that *To Kill a Mockingbird* was not a force for change?

11 What might the differing receptions for the book and movie versions of *Beloved* suggest?

12 In what ways did some black Americans find *The Help* offensive?

13 Why was the slapping scene in *In the Heat of the Night* significant?

14 How could it be argued that *Mississippi Burning* reflected changing attitudes?

15 Did *The Wire* prove that the United States was a post-racial society by the twenty-first century?

 Question practice

ESSAY QUESTIONS

1 To what extent were film and television important in shaping white attitudes to black Americans in the period 1900–2009?

2 To what extent was literature responsible for changing the attitudes of white Americans to black Americans in the years 1852–2009?

CHAPTER 9

After the 1960s: Barack Obama and black Americans 1968–2009

After 1968, all black Americans could vote and *de jure* segregation had ended. Between 1968 and 2009, the number of middle-class black Americans grew, many of them were integrated within white society, and more black politicians were elected to office. However, the political, economic and social status of many black Americans remained inferior to that of white Americans. Arguably, the positives outweighed the negatives. Amongst the positives were the improved situation in the South and the election of black American Illinois Senator Barack Obama as President in 2008. Some thought that Obama's election signalled that the United States had at last become a 'colour-blind' society, but voting statistics, comments during the campaign and continuing controversies over race during Obama's presidency suggest otherwise.

These issues are covered in sections on

★ Migration back to the South in the late twentieth century

★ The status of black Americans, 1968–2009

★ Barack Obama – life and career to 2006

★ The Democrat presidential nomination race in 2008

★ Obama's victory in the 2008 presidential election

★ The significance of Obama's victory

Key dates

1970s	Demographers noted black migration to the South	2004		Barack Obama elected to the US Senate
	Federal government promoted affirmative action	2008	June	Obama defeated Hillary Clinton for the Democrat presidential nomination
1980s	School integration peaked		Nov.	Obama defeated Republican John McCain in the presidential election
1992	Rodney King scandal			

Migration back to the South in the late twentieth century

▶ *What explains black American migration to the South after 1970?*

From the 1970s, demographers and the media took notice of a new and pronounced migratory trend: black Americans were returning to the South in great numbers and fewer black Americans were leaving it. In the period 1965–70, only one 'border' Southern state, Maryland, was among the top ten black migration gainers, but by the period 1975 and 1980, seven Southern states ranked amongst the top ten black migration gainers and black Americans migrated back to the South at twice the rate of white Americans.

The states that attracted the most black migrants were Florida, Georgia, North Carolina and Texas. While New York, Chicago, Los Angeles and San Francisco experienced a great out-migration, the most attractive metropolitan magnet for black Americans was Atlanta, Georgia. Other metropolitan magnets for migrants were Washington DC, Dallas and Houston (Texas), Charlotte and Raleigh (North Carolina), and Orlando and Miami (Florida). Over half of these black migrants had college degrees. By 2010, 57 per cent of black Americans lived in the South, the highest percentage in 50 years (60 per cent had lived in the South in 1960). Overall, the black population of the South increased by almost 3.6 million during the 1990s. The main underlying reason for the return was that the South had changed dramatically since the original Great Migration: Martin Luther King Jr's friend Bayard Rustin found the South transformed by 1980, 'from a reactionary bastion into a region moderate in racial outlook and more enlightened in social and economic policy'.

The 'pull' factors for the mass black migration back to the South included:

- quality of life
- economic prospects
- 'call to home'
- climate and geography.

Quality of life

In many ways, the Great Migration to the North had proved disappointing. In the North and Midwest, black Americans were concentrated in ghettos with ever-decreasing economic opportunities, poor housing and schools, high crime levels, and urban congestion. In the '**New South**', *de facto* segregation was less pronounced than in other American regions, racial violence was no longer a common instrument of social control, there was less crime, and more black Americans held office in the South than in any other region (Atlanta Mayor Shirley Franklin and Houston Mayor Lee Brown were migrants).

 **KEY TERM**

New South Some people consider that the South was totally transformed after the Civil Rights Act of 1964 and the Voting Rights Act of 1965, legislation that helped bring about greater racial equality.

Desegregation in the South after 1970

One reason behind the return of black Americans to the South was that the South was a less *de facto* segregated society in housing and in schools. During the presidency of Richard Nixon (1969–74) the percentage of Southern black American children in segregated schools fell from 68 per cent to 8 per cent. That statistic owed much to the Supreme Court's *Swann v. Charlotte-Mecklenburg* ruling of 1971, which said that it was time for the full implementation of school desegregation. Southern school desegregation peaked in 1988, when 43 per cent of black schoolchildren attended schools that were more than 50 per cent white. In an interesting contrast, Boston's public schools contained 45,000 white children in 1974 but only 16,000 in 1989. However, Southern schools slowly began re-segregating after 1988.

The explanations of black Americans for their migration South

As early as the 1970s, the media was taking notice of the new black migration. Interviews with black Americans explaining why they had migrated to the South became commonplace.

1. Quotations from *Ebony* magazine, 1971 (available at: www.inmotionaame.org/print. cfm;jsessionid=f8301686751443062090644?migration=11&bhcp=1).

Earnest Smith hated the discrimination, segregation and violence of Mississippi, and moved to Chicago in 1944. However, he moved back to Mississippi in 1970:

For the first 20 years, life in Chicago was real nice ... But the last five years was when I come to gettin' scared. They killed King and the people started tearin' up the place. Crime in Chicago got so bad that I got scared and started carryin' a gun ... Everybody's been wonderful [back here in Mississippi] ... White folks always used to always hurry you up or curse at you when I left. Now they stop you on the street to say 'Hello' and some of them call you 'Sir.' And they say 'yes ma'am' and 'no ma'am' to my wife and call her 'Miss Smith.' Things changed so much, one guy come here from Chicago and brought his white wife.

Elijah Davis moved back to Jackson, Mississippi, in 1970, after 20 years in Gary, Indiana:

Before I left here years ago, there were places you couldn't go, places you couldn't eat at, and you couldn't make a decent living. But I can live in peace here. I can walk anywhere in town without fear.

John Ash said, 'The high cost of land and high property taxes in California made Atlanta very attractive to us ... It just seemed as if we could get more from money by settling here.' Dentist Dr Terry Reynolds liked Atlanta because 'Blacks are in businesses here that you would not conceive of them being in anywhere else.' His business associate Dr Walker B. Moore said, 'Atlanta is alive ... Other cities are dying.' By the 1990s, some black Americans referred to Atlanta as 'the Harlem of the 90s'.

2. Quotations from *Christian Science Monitor* magazine, 16 March 2014 (available at: www. csmonitor.com/USA/Society/2014/0316/Why-African-Americans-are-moving-back-to-the-South).

Charlie Cox's family left rural West Point, Mississippi, when he was nine years old. After 35 years working at General Motors in Chicago, he and his family retired to West Point: 'It's quiet here. You can relax more down here. I don't worry about my car when I park out here in the yard ... The cost of living is cheaper, the property taxes – all that is cheaper. I just wanted to relax.'

Betsy Hurt grew up in Columbus, Mississippi, but migrated to Chicago in 1953 in search of work. When the Great Recession began in 2007, her quiet Chicago neighbourhood was transformed after factory closures, layoffs and foreclosures. Gangs moved in, selling drugs and stripping homes of aluminium. Mrs Hurt's neighbours began to move out and renters took their places. In 2011, a gunfight broke out in front of her house, and a few days later, gang members tried to shoot her grandson. 'That was the final straw. My children said, "You're going to leave there," so I let my house go into foreclosure and closed the door on 30 years of memories.' Many of her friends had retired and returned South, so she settled in Raleigh, North Carolina, where her daughter lived. Mrs Hurt moved into a senior citizen apartment complex and found that many of the new neighbours were also from the North. 'When I first got here, it just looked magical. I never would have thought I would end up here, but it's just awesome. It's a very, very nice, safe place.'

Lorrin Woods was born and raised in Philadelphia, but felt the city had become too dangerous, so she moved to Alabama, where her family had roots. 'Alabama is one of those states that have bad reputations, but those times have passed. It's not 1854 any more. Alabama is a new frontier and a wonderful place for opportunities'

Aretha Frison was born in Detroit, but her ancestors were slaves in Tuscaloosa. As a child, she visited family in Tuscaloosa and became fascinated by the South. In 2006, she moved to New Orleans: 'My roots are here in the South, even though they went north for a while.'

3. Quotations from *USA Today* (available at: http://usatoday30.usatoday.com/news/nation/census/2011-06-30-black-south-census-migration_n.htm).

In June 2011, the newspaper USA Today asked a group of black Americans in Palm Coast, Florida, why they had migrated there. Mike Morton said he had moved from New York in 2006: 'It's like living on a vacation. When I visit New York now, it's culture shock. I don't hear car horns down here. As soon as you get to New York, you're hearing thousands of them.' Linda Sharpe Haywood and her retired New York City police detective husband moved from New York in 1999: 'There was very little crime. People were very friendly. It was also an economic decision. We were able to buy a house here that we wouldn't have been able to afford in New York.' Edmund Pinto arrived from New York in 2001: 'My mother has a friend who lives here. I came to visit my mother's friend 15 or 16 years ago. I fell in love with the place upon my visit. I just couldn't believe how lovely the neighborhoods were … The climate was a big factor. The cost of living was lower.' Another retired New Yorker, James Sims, said, 'We're all like family here'.

Economic prospects

A major factor behind the Great Migration to the North was the perceived opportunity for economic betterment. While the South was a region with an impoverished rural economy, the North and Midwest were booming industrialised areas with plentiful unskilled and semiskilled work available. However, in the later twentieth century, manufacturing industries struggled in the old industrial centres of what became known as the 'Rust Belt'. Great manufacturing cities such as predominantly black Detroit, the centre of the American automobile industry, decayed dramatically. The number of jobs available was more than halved between 1945 and 1977 (see Table 9.1).

Table 9.1 The decline of Detroit

Year	Detroit manufacturing firms	Numbers employed by manufacturing firms
1947	3272	338,400
1977	1954	153,300

While economic opportunities in the North and Midwest decreased, they increased in the South (see Table 9.2). Companies preferred to invest in the South because the unions were less powerful, regulations were lighter, land was cheaper, and national and local government offered tax breaks. Employment opportunities in the 'Sun Belt' became greater than those in the 'Rust Belt'.

Table 9.2 The growth of manufacturing in the South

Year	Percentage of US manufacturing output in Michigan and Illinois	Percentage of US manufacturing output in South
1963	30%	21%
1989	16%	29%

Along with more job opportunities, the South offered lower taxes and cheaper property. The 2010 median family home price in Northeastern metropolitan areas was $243,900, compared with $153,700 in metropolitan areas in the South. Groceries, utility bills and healthcare also cost less in the South. The appeal of an area where the cost of living was lower was great, especially for those who had experienced the exceptionally high cost of living in California, a state that began to experience great economic problems in the 1990s.

'Call to home'

Anthropologist Carol Stack considered the 'call to home' a major factor in migration. Many of those who had participated in the Great Migration, along with their children or grandchildren, felt an affinity with the culture of the South – the migrants had brought their language, music and food from the South, so returning there felt like going home. This was especially so when there were still relations living in the South.

A 1973 survey of returning migrants to Birmingham, Alabama, noted that more than half of the respondents had moved back for family reasons. Some were returning to take care of ageing relatives. Atlanta businessman Jesse B. Blayton explained, 'Grandma is here … Most American blacks have roots in the South. The liberation thinking is here. Blacks are more together. With the doors opening wider, this area is the Mecca.'

Author and poet Maya Angelou wrote an article, 'Why Blacks Are Returning to Their Southern Roots' in *Ebony*, in April 1990:

> *The answer to the question 'Why are so many young Black people moving South today?' is that the American South sings a siren song to all Black Americans. The melody may be ignored, despised or ridiculed, but we all hear it … They return and find or make their places in the land of their foreparents. They find and make friends under the shade of trees their ancestors left decades earlier. Many find themselves happy, without being able to explain the emotion. I think it is simply that they feel … that they can come home again.*

Actor Morgan Freeman was born in Tennessee and grew up in Mississippi. His family moved North during the Great Migration. He explained why he returned to the South:

> *This is home. This is where my roots are … [We] built the South, and we know it. What I own in the South isn't because I went and bought it. What I own is my place here, because my mother, my father, my grandmother, my grandfather, my great-grandmother … all the way back to my great-great-great-grandmother, who happens to be a Virginian – that's where they had the farms.*

The phenomenon of 'heirs' property' encouraged migration to the South. It was possible to build a home near family members on land that had been deeded to multiple family members as long ago as the Reconstruction era.

Climate and geography

While the North and Midwest suffer harsh winters, the South has a temperate climate and many so-called 'snowbirds' (especially retirees) sought to escape freezing winters. Younger migrants such as Aretha Frison (see page 195) liked the beaches.

This is not to say that the situation of all black Americans in the South was totally transformed. Some continued to face poverty and social and institutional prejudice. Nevertheless, by the early twenty-first century, life in the South was very different for black Americans from what it had been between 1850 and 1965.

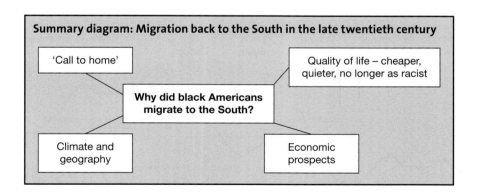

Summary diagram: Migration back to the South in the late twentieth century

'Call to home'

Quality of life – cheaper, quieter, no longer as racist

Why did black Americans migrate to the South?

Climate and geography

Economic prospects

The status of black Americans, 1968–2009

▶ *How far had the black American situation improved since 1968?*

The late twentieth century was a period of progress for some black Americans, but economic, social, legal and political inequality remained an issue.

Economic status

Statistics for the last decades of the twentieth century demonstrated continued black inferiority:

- One-third of black Americans and one half of black children lived below the poverty line.
- One-third of black Americans had low-status, low-skilled jobs in low-wage occupations, their average earnings half those of whites.
- Black unemployment was twice that of whites.

On the positive side, the federal government promoted affirmative action, as demonstrated when the Supreme Court ruled in *Griggs v. Duke Power Company* (1971) that the company's hiring tests discriminated against black employees. Affirmative action helped make one-third of African Americans middle class by the year 2000 (see Figure 9.1), but a white backlash developed and by the early twenty-first century an increasingly conservative Supreme Court threatened its continued existence.

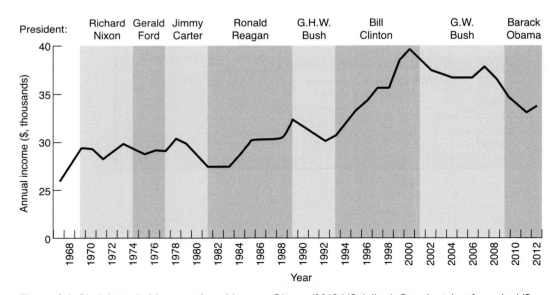

Figure 9.1 Black household income from Nixon to Obama (2012 US dollars). Based on data from the US Census Bureau, Current Population Survey and Annual Social and Economic Supplements.

Social status

White opposition to integrated education demonstrated continuing black social inequality. In 1971 the Supreme Court ruled it time for the full implementation of school desegregation (*Swann v. Charlotte-Mecklenburg*), specifying the **busing** of black and white children to each other's schools as the way to achieve it. The percentage of black students in the South in integrated schools peaked during the 1970s and 1980s, but *de facto* segregation proved harder to combat in the North, which experienced a great white backlash against busing. The nationwide opposition to integrated schools caused private school numbers to rise and 'white flight' to accelerate. The federal government became less supportive and schools across the nation grew increasingly segregated in the later twentieth century. However, black educational prospects improved (see Table 9.3), partly as a result of affirmative action.

KEY TERM

Busing Transporting white or black children to schools in an area other than that in which they live, to ensure integrated schools in that area.

Table 9.3 Percentage of black adults aged 25–29 who completed college between 1970 and 1990

Year	Black females	Black males
1970	6%	6%
1980	12%	11%
1990	15%	10%

Trends in housing were more encouraging. By 1992, half the black population lived in neighbourhoods over 50 per cent white, and the number of interracial marriages and cohabitants rose – slowly. However, around one-third of black Americans continued to live in segregated, overcrowded and impoverished inner-city ghettos where life expectancy was lower (see Table 9.4) and schools remained poorly funded and segregated.

Table 9.4 Black and white American life expectancy 1960–90

Year	Average age at death for black Americans	Average age at death for white Americans
1960	63.6	70.6
1970	64.1	71.7
1980	68.1	74.4
1990	69.1	76.1

Status in the legal system

By 1992, black Americans were quite well represented in police departments, but racism in law enforcement and the legal system continued. For example, after a high-speed car chase in Los Angeles in 1991, white police caught up with black suspect Rodney King and were filmed beating him up. Riots erupted in Los Angeles after an all-white jury found the police innocent: 55 died, 2300 were injured and riots followed in Atlanta, Birmingham and Chicago. In 1992, in statistical proportions common across the United States, it was found that the Sheriff's Department of Volusia County, Florida, stopped a disproportionate number of black American drivers on the portion of the interstate highway that ran through the county: although black Americans constituted only 5 per cent of the drivers on that portion of the road, they constituted 70 per cent of those stopped by the police, and were stopped for far longer periods than white drivers. Equally disproportionate was the number of black males in jail. Black Americans constituted around 12 per cent of the country's population, but over half of the prison population. The black viewpoint was that this denoted unequal black status and that the police unfairly victimised black Americans. White conservatives insisted that black Americans were more likely to commit crime, while white liberals pointed out that poor education and a high unemployment rate contributed to black involvement in crime, drugs and gang turf wars.

Political status

The number of elected black officials rocketed in the late twentieth century. During the 1970s, some states helped ensure the election of black officials by drawing congressional districts in which black American voters were grouped together, although by the early twenty-first century, the Supreme Court was less inclined to protect black voters.

The number of black Americans elected mayors of major cities increased dramatically. During the 1970s and 1980s, many major cities elected black mayors – Detroit (1973), Los Angeles (1973), Washington DC (1974), Birmingham (1979), Chicago (1984) and Philadelphia (1988). Black mayors of major cities became unexceptional.

A growing number of black Americans were elected to the US House of Representatives. Congressional re-districting increased the number of black congressmen from 45 in 1990 to 69 in 1992. However, black candidates rarely won nationwide contests in which white votes were crucial. As a result, black US senators were rare. Barack Obama was the sole black senator when he ran for the presidency in 2008. On the other hand, in 1988, Jesse Jackson made a serious run for the Democratic nomination for the presidency and was the frontrunner until controversy erupted over his anti-Semitic remarks.

Clearly, the status of many black Americans had improved after 1968, but considerable inequality remained. This was illustrated in the life, work and career of Barack Obama.

Summary diagram: The status of black Americans, 1968–2009

	Improved?	No better?
Economic	• Growing middle class • Affirmative action	Many impoverished
Social	Half lived in neighbourhoods over 50% white	• Many *de facto* segregated schools across USA • One-third in ghettos
Legal	Many black police officers	• Racial profiling • White police brutality (perceived)
Political	• Far more elected officials • Black mayors of major cities • Nation elected black president	• Rarely won statewide elections • Supreme Court less keen to protect Voting Rights Act

---

Barack Obama – life and career to 2006

▶ *What was the importance of the political career of Barack Obama to 2006?*

Barack Obama was born in 1961 in Hawaii to a Kansas-born white mother, whose ancestors had owned slaves, and a black Kenyan student father who had another wife back home. Race relations in Hawaii were often cited as a model for the rest of the United States, but it was uncommon for blacks and whites to date in Hawaii, let alone marry. In 1963, Barack Obama's father left to study at Harvard. He could not afford to take his wife and two-year-old son with him. 'How can I refuse the best education?' he said. The only other time Barack saw his father was during a one-month visit when he was ten years old.

Barack Obama's childhood was not a typical black American experience. His father was black, but not an American. Although young Barack spent his first six years in Hawaii, his mother then married an Indonesian student and the family moved to Indonesia. In his first book, *Dreams From My Father* (1995), Obama recalled an idyllic childhood in Indonesia, but his contemporaries told reporters differently. After his mother's marriage got into difficulties, she sent him back to Hawaii in 1971 and he lived with his white grandparents and attended an elite private school. He wrote of feeling that he did not belong (a black scholarship student in a rich white school), but rejected his mother's suggestion that he return to Indonesia. He watched black dancers and comedians on television and read Malcolm X's autobiography.

Barack Obama

1961	Born in Hawaii
1967	Moved to Indonesia
1971	Lived with grandparents in Hawaii
1985	Community organiser in Chicago
1988–91	Harvard Law School
1995	*Dreams From My Father* published
1996	Elected to the Illinois Senate
2004	Elected to the US Senate
2006	*The Audacity of Hope* published
2008	Defeated Hillary Clinton for the Democrat presidential nomination
	Defeated Republican John McCain in presidential election

Although Barack Obama's background was not typically black American, he frequently strove to present himself as such in his published works and speeches.

After very limited political experience for a presidential candidate, his 'American dream' life story, personality, rhetorical abilities and skilled campaigning, coupled with his opponents' weaknesses, led to his election as President of the United States in 2008. This was seen by contemporaries as a great milestone in the history of American race relations.

In *Dreams*, Obama wrote of his struggle to establish his identity, although a friend recalled his 'biggest struggles were his feelings of abandonment … missing his parents'. Although other black Americans such as Malcolm X experienced an identity crisis, Barack Obama's was exacerbated by a foreign father, having lived outside the United States, and an upbringing dominated by a white mother and white grandparents. They gave him conflicting stories as to why they had left Texas: his grandfather told him it was because of racism, his grandmother said it was because her husband had been offered a better job. Obama subsequently admitted that his white grandmother made racist comments that upset him. Although his contemporaries remember him as a happy high school student in Hawaii, Obama recalled that he drank alcohol, smoked pot, and even used cocaine: 'Junkie. Pothead. That's where I'd been headed: the final, fatal role of the young, would-be black man.' It appears that he was trying to establish himself as experiencing typically black American struggles. As he admitted in his introduction to *Dreams From My Father*, autobiography tempts an author to have 'selective lapses of memory'. He wrote his autobiography while working with Chicago's black community and seems to have looked back on a more 'black' childhood than he actually had.

Black community organiser

After somewhat half-hearted study at a Los Angeles college, Barack Obama attended prestigious Columbia University, New York. From 1985, he worked as a community organiser in a black Chicago neighbourhood adversely affected by a steel plant closure. His task was to mobilise the neighbourhood to lobby political leaders for better schools and job training. Despite being half white, he had aligned himself with black America. He found a religious identity in Reverend Jeremiah Wright's socially activist black church. One of Reverend Wright's sermons was entitled 'The Audacity of Hope', a title Obama borrowed for his second book.

During 1988–91, Obama studied at Harvard Law School. As he was the first black editor of the *Harvard Law Review*, the *New York Times* profiled him and a publishing company commissioned him to write his autobiography. He worked at a Chicago law office during the summer vacation. There he met Michelle Robinson, a Harvard graduate who had grown up in Chicago's black South Side ghetto and then attended two top universities, Princeton and Harvard.

SOURCE A

The *New York Times* quoted Obama on race on 5 February 1990 (available at: www.nytimes.com/1990/02/06/us/first-black-elected-to-head-harvard-s-law-review. html).

The fact that I've been elected [editor of the Harvard Law Review*] shows a lot of progress. It's encouraging. But is important that stories like mine aren't used to say that everything is okay for blacks. You have to remember that for every one of me, there are hundreds or thousands of black students with at least equal talent who don't get a chance.*

SOURCE B

Extract from Barack Obama, *The Audacity of Hope*, Random House, 2006, p. 365.

I have witnessed a profound shift in race relations in my lifetime. I have felt it as surely as one feels a change in the temperature. When I hear some in the black community deny those changes, I think it not only dishonors those who struggled on our behalf but also robs us of our agency to complete the work they began. But as much as I insist that things have gotten better, I am mindful of this truth as well: Better isn't good enough.

After Harvard, Obama returned to Chicago, worked on a black voter drive that registered over 100,000 voters, and learned political lessons about grassroots organising that helped him defeat Hillary Clinton in the race for the Democratic nomination in 2008. In 1992, he married Michelle and in 1995, he published his autobiography, *Dreams From My Father*. He chose to work for a small law firm that specialised in civil rights and housing discrimination cases for low-income clients.

In 1996, he ran successfully for the Illinois Senate, defeating the former incumbent, an African American woman, on a legal technicality. This made him unpopular with some black senators, who called him the 'white man in black face'. They would taunt him, 'You figured out whether you are white or black yet, Barack, or still searching?'

> **?** How far do Sources A and B suggest black Americans had attained greater equality during Barack Obama's lifetime?

The importance of the political career of Barack Obama

Obama served in the Illinois Senate from 1997 to 2004, focusing on issues of particular interest to black Americans. Amongst these were welfare legislation, tax credits for low-income families, reform of the capital punishment system, job and housing discrimination, a universal healthcare system, and **racial profiling** in traffic stops (see page 200) across the state. He won conservative support for a new law against racial profiling, by saying that the law would protect Illinois from potentially costly lawsuits over racial discrimination.

In 2000, he ran for the US Congress, but was defeated by the incumbent, ex-Black Panther Bobby Rush, who served eight successive terms in the House of Representatives. Rush used the 'not black enough' argument against the half-white Obama, whose father was not a black American.

In 2004, he ran for the US Senate, speaking out against the war in Iraq. At first, no one thought he would win in a strong field for the Democratic nomination, but polls showed voters were attracted by his 'American dream' life story.

> ### The war in Iraq
>
> An 11 September 2001 terrorist attack on the United States led President George W. Bush (2001–9) to declare a 'war on terror'. In 2003, Bush ordered the invasion of Iraq in order to overthrow the government of Saddam Hussein, which supposedly held weapons of mass destruction and supported anti-American terrorists. Saddam Hussein's overthrow was accomplished speedily, but a US occupation force remained there until 2011 in an unsuccessful attempt to establish stable government. The American public increasingly opposed the involvement.

Election to the US Senate, 2004

In 2004, Obama won the Democratic nomination for the Illinois Senate seat. Desperate to regain the seat from the Republicans and to have an African American senator, the national Democratic Party was very supportive. When the Republican candidate suffered a divorce scandal, the Republicans struggled to field another candidate. Meanwhile, the media concentrated on Obama, aware of the historic significance of his campaign: there had been but two black members of the Senate since Reconstruction. The Democratic presidential candidate John Kerry invited Obama to give the keynote address in the 2004 Democratic National Convention, which put Obama in the national spotlight.

Rhetorical abilities

In his 2004 Convention speech, entitled 'The Audacity of Hope', Obama urged voters to associate Americanism with the Democratic Party. His oratory was comparable to that of Martin Luther King Jr when it tapped into the belief in the 'American dream' that Obama himself had lived.

SOURCE C

From Barack Obama's speech to the Democrat National Convention, 27 July 2004 (available at: www.washingtonpost.com/wp-dyn/articles/A19751-2004Jul27. html).

... let me express my deep gratitude for the privilege of addressing this convention. Tonight is a particular honor for me because, let's face it, my presence on this stage is pretty unlikely. My father was a foreign student, born and raised in a small village in Kenya. He grew up herding goats, went to school in a tin-roof shack. His father, my grandfather, was a cook, a domestic servant to the British. But my grandfather had larger dreams for his son. Through hard work and perseverance my father got a scholarship to study in a magical place, America, that's shown as a beacon of freedom and opportunity to so many who had come before him.

While studying here my father met my mother. She was born in a town on the other side of the world, in Kansas. Her father worked on oil rigs and farms through most of the Depression. The day after Pearl Harbor, my grandfather signed up for duty, joined Patton's army, marched across Europe. Back home my grandmother raised a baby and went to work on a bomber assembly line. After the war, they studied on the GI Bill, bought a house through FHA [see page 104] and later moved west, all the way to Hawaii, in search of opportunity. And they too had big dreams for their daughter, a common dream born of two continents.

My parents shared not only an improbable love; they shared an abiding faith in the possibilities of this nation. They would give me an African name, Barack, or 'blessed,' believing that in a tolerant America, your name is no barrier to success. They imagined me going to the best schools in the land, even though they weren't rich, because in a generous America you don't have to be rich to achieve your potential.

And I stand here today grateful for the diversity of my heritage, aware that my parents' dreams live on in my two precious daughters. I stand here knowing that my story is part of the larger American story, that I owe a debt to all of those who came before me, and that in no other country on Earth is my story even possible.

> What might white American voters have found appealing in Source C? **?**

Obama was quickly talked about as a future Democratic presidential candidate and three months after that speech was elected to the US Senate with 70 per cent of the Illinois vote. He defeated conservative black Republican Alan Keyes, who claimed that a white mother and a Kenyan father made Obama 'not black enough'. Keyes was a significant choice: he had served in the Reagan administration, but lived in faraway Maryland. Clearly, the Republican Party believed that being black was politically vital in this particular election, but could not find a suitable candidate amongst Illinois Republicans.

Obama in the US Senate

In the US Senate, Obama followed the typical Democratic Party line. He voted against the nomination of John Roberts as chief justice of the Supreme Court, expressing concerns about his record on civil rights and abortion (African Americans were usually supportive of abortion because of awareness of the difficulties of bringing up children in poverty). He opposed the proposal that required photo ID for voting, because it could prevent poorer citizens (amongst whom were many black Americans) who lacked a driver's licence or a passport from voting. He gained publicity as the sole black senator, as when he toured New Orleans, devastated after Hurricane Katrina, with ex-presidents George H.W. Bush and Bill Clinton.

Long before Obama declared he planned to run for the presidency, an internet-based 'draft Obama' movement began. Obama announced his candidacy in February 2007, on the Illinois site where Lincoln delivered his famous 'House Divided' speech in 1858 ('I believe this government cannot endure, permanently half slave and half free'). He presented himself as all-American, in the tradition of Abraham Lincoln who had, like Obama, served in the Illinois state legislature. Obama's oratory, like that of Martin Luther King Jr, pressed the right white buttons.

The importance of Barack Obama's political career prior to his election as President lay in that

- it showed the important role that black voters and candidates played in the Democratic Party
- he was only the third black US senator since Reconstruction, which suggested that there might be a greater white willingness to vote for a black candidate.

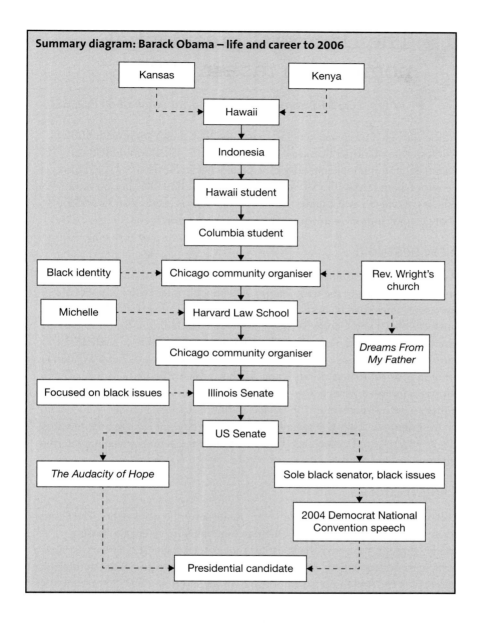

Summary diagram: Barack Obama – life and career to 2006

4 The Democrat presidential nomination race in 2008

▶ *Why did Barack Obama win the Democrat nomination in 2008?*

At the start of 2008, it was generally assumed that New York senator Hillary Clinton, wife of former President Bill Clinton (1993–2001), would win the Democrat nomination to stand for the presidency in November 2008. However, Senator Obama from Illinois won. There was little difference between the policies of Obama and Clinton, but voters felt he was exciting and stood for change, and Clinton's campaign was surprisingly error-prone.

New beats old

Barack Obama was a novelty, a black American candidate with a dramatic life story, and this caught the imagination of Democrat voters wary of political dynasties. There had been two Bushes in the White House, George H.W. Bush (1989–93) and George W. Bush (2001–9). Now Hillary Clinton sought to emulate her husband. Governor Bill Richardson of New Mexico said, 'What hurt her was her sense of entitlement, that the presidency was hers.' While the Clintons overestimated Hillary's appeal, they underestimated Obama's. Dick Morris, a former adviser to President Bill Clinton, grew increasingly critical of Hillary Clinton's campaign. 'She made an initial strategic blunder by focusing on experience … They don't want experience. They want change and newness. That's why they're Democrats.' Polls confirmed that Democrat voters preferred 'change' to 'experience'.

Clinton errors

Hillary Clinton and her campaign team made several crucial errors. The Clinton team was far less effective than Obama's in mobilising voters and raising money through the use of the latest technology (see page 212). Hillary Clinton's campaign was modelled on Bill Clinton's 1992 campaign and failed to recognise and exploit the contemporary importance of the internet. The Clinton campaign raised less money than the Obama team. Clinton was still raising money in the old-fashioned way, through one-time big money donors. The Obama campaign added money raised through the internet, through which Obama supporters gave small sums but gave them repeatedly.

Campaign manager Patti Solis Doyle and chief strategist Mark Penn were old friends of Hillary Clinton, but others on the campaign staff considered them very poor organisers. By the time Clinton steeled herself to fire Solis Doyle, the damage was irreparable. The campaign staff were dismayed that Mark Penn was the campaign's only pollster, whereas the Obama campaign had four pollsters tracking public opinion. Penn had run Bill Clinton's campaign in 1996, but its success owed much to the fact that Clinton was an incumbent and his opponent was an uninspired Republican choice. Peter Baker of the *New York Times* wrote in June 2008 that Hillary Clinton 'did little to stop the in-fighting back home among advisers who nursed grudges from their White House days … [and were] distracted from battling Senator Obama while they hurled expletives at one another, stormed out of meetings and schemed to get one another fired'.

The Clinton team tried to portray Obama as un-American, but the tactic backfired. The Obama team accused Clinton's staff of dirty tricks when they circulated a picture of him in African dress, including a turban. The picture was taken on his 2006 visit to Kenya, and the Obama team pointed out that it is only polite to wear the traditional clothing of a country one visits. These Clinton tactics probably alienated some black voters and white liberals. For some, the alienation was increased when Bill Clinton claimed that Obama was only winning support because he was black.

SOURCE D

During the 2008 Democrat primaries, Hillary Clinton's chief strategist Mark Penn urged her to pose as the 'American' candidate (available at: http://edition. cnn.com/2008/POLITICS/08/12/atlantic.clinton.staff/).

All of these articles about his boyhood in Indonesia and his life in Hawaii are geared toward showing his background is diverse, multicultural … Save it for 2050. It exposes a strong weakness for him – his roots to basic American values and culture are at best limited. I cannot imagine America electing a president during a time of war [see page 204] who is not at his center fundamentally American in his thinking and in his values.

In their study of the 2008 campaign, John Heilemann and Mark Halperin (2010), found some who believed that Hillary Clinton's camp saw Bill as a loose cannon but that she felt unable to talk to him about it. 'Bill's behavior that started off in Iowa, carried on in New Hampshire, and culminated in South Carolina really was the beginning of the end. Unfortunately, for whatever reason, he just kind of imploded. I think, if I had to look back on it, it became more about him than about her. It really was destructive', according to a Clinton campaign staffer. *Newsweek* magazine said the former President had 'morphed from statesman into attack dog'. Another Clinton team insider said, 'The issue became, "If she can't control her husband in the campaign, who the hell is going to run this White House?" ' Heilemann and Halperin also suggested that Clinton continued to focus upon being a valuable member of the US Senate, while Obama, who cared less about his Senate seat, gave 100 per cent of his time and energy to the presidential race.

The *New York Observer* offered their interpretation of Obama's victory in a headline article on 23 May 2008, 'Clinton's Fate Was Sealed by the Calendar'. The article argued that if the Democrat Party rules had been different, for example, if important and pro-Clinton states such as Florida and Michigan had held their primaries a few weeks earlier, she would have won.

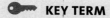 **KEY TERM**

Primaries Elections to choose a party's candidate for elective office.

To what extent was Source D correct in arguing that there was much that was un-American about Barack Obama?

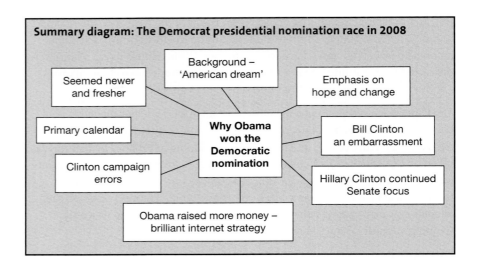

Summary diagram: The Democrat presidential nomination race in 2008

5 Obama's victory in the 2008 presidential election

▶ *Why did Obama win the 2008 presidential election?*

Barack Obama's victory over the Republican candidate John McCain in the 2008 presidential election was due to factors in Obama's favour and to McCain's errors.

The 'Bush effect'

Many commentators believed the main reason for Obama's victory was the unpopularity of Republican President George W. Bush: the American people feared that another Republican President would simply continue Bush's unpopular policies. People were tired of Bush's war in Iraq, and disillusioned by Republican Party scandals. Polls showed that economic problems were the main concern of 63 per cent of voters. In September 2008 the giant bank Lehman Brothers declared bankruptcy and triggered the near collapse of the financial sector. That crisis was widely blamed on Republican 'light touch' regulation policies, which had left the financial sector unmonitored. McCain lost his lead in the polls the day after the Lehman Brothers collapse and never regained it. Obama's response to the financial disasters seemed far more measured and reassuring than that of McCain, who appeared to panic. Some have argued that any Democratic candidate would have won the presidency in 2008.

Obama's personality and rhetorical abilities

Obama's positives were demonstrated during his struggle with Hillary Clinton for the Democrat nomination. In his battle against McCain, the polls continued to show his 'American dream' life story attracting voters. His charismatic personality and rhetorical abilities made him an outstanding campaigner. Back in January 2008, Hillary Clinton had attacked Obama's undoubted rhetorical abilities, arguing, 'Making change is not about what you believe; it's not about a speech you make.' She was right about the limitations of rhetorical ability once in power, but the importance of campaign rhetoric was indisputable. Obama rightly responded, 'The truth is, actually, words do inspire. Words do help people get involved.' He came across as more likeable than both Clinton and McCain. He came across as intelligent, highly motivated, self-confident, and possessed of an inner calm. In contrast, McCain sometimes appeared to be a grumpy old man (he was over 70). Most viewers adjudged Obama the clear winner in their televised debates.

Young voters found the age difference significant, and many voters felt McCain's age made his choice of running mate especially important. While Obama countered accusations of his own youth and inexperience with long-serving Senator Joe Biden, McCain's choice of Alaska governor Sarah Palin was the worst of his many campaign errors.

Sarah Palin

Initially, McCain's selection of Sarah Palin seemed to energise the Republican Party. Her greater conservatism reassured the Republican right, and she was photogenic and had a folksy 'hockey mom' appeal. However, her inexperience and lack of knowledge turned many voters against her and against the ticket. Voters worried about McCain's age and poor health record and it was rumoured that his own staff feared for the nation if he won and she became President.

Palin made several campaign gaffes that made some consider her unfit for high office. She seemed unable to answer a 'soft' interviewer's questions on what newspapers she read and which Supreme Court cases she considered particularly significant. She said Africa was a country. When 73 million viewers watched the televised debate between Palin and the Democratic vice presidential candidate, Joe Biden, they were particularly unimpressed with her response to questions on the financial crisis:

> Biden: *If you notice, Gwen [the debate moderator], the Governor did not answer the question [on the financial crisis].*

> Palin: *I may not answer the questions that either the moderator or you want to hear, but I'm going to talk straight to the American people.*

Palin's repeated assertions that only Republicans were patriotic alienated independent voters.

Finance

Obama raised far more money than McCain, primarily due to an astute tactical decision. All previous major party presidential candidates had accepted federal funds that matched the funds that they had raised, but Obama was the first to reject this option during the general election campaign. McCain took the federal funds, which then limited the amount that he could spend from his own campaign funds. This left Obama with a massive financial advantage. He was able to pay for far more advertisements, and one commentator likened McCain 'to someone trying to have a conversation with a man with a megaphone'.

New election strategies

The Obama campaign out-spent, out-advertised and out-organised the Republicans, and its extensive use of the internet was revolutionary. Obama's website encouraged visitors to register their interest. Those who registered were regularly emailed and encouraged to establish links with other Obama supporters. This network inspired more voter registration than McCain's campaign and proved important in fundraising. A significant proportion of Obama's smaller donations and his many grassroots volunteers owed much to this network. When media attacks were made on Obama's pastor, Obama's response was put on YouTube, received 5.2 million viewers, and helped counter the attacks.

Policies

Contemporary voters' main preoccupations were the country's economic problems and the Iraq War. Obama's policies on a speedy exit from Iraq, US energy independence, and more freely available healthcare all emphasised hope and change, themes that always resonated with the electorate. The positivity of Obama's campaign was also in evidence in the candidates' advertising. By 61 per cent to 31 per cent, voters perceived Obama's advertisements as far more positive and more focused on policies (see Table 9.5) than McCain's, which tended to concentrate upon attacks on Obama and the Democrats.

The role of race in the election

Race was an issue in the campaign, although rarely out in the open. When Sarah Palin told a Florida audience, 'This is not a man who sees America the way you and I see America', she seemed to be referring to Obama's race. When *Newsweek* asked Obama if the US was ready for an African American candidate, he answered:

> *I absolutely think America is ready … Stereotypes and prejudices still exist in American society, and for the highest office in the land a female or African American candidate would, at the outset, confront some additional hurdles to show that they were qualified and competent. But what I've found is that the American people – once they get to know you – are going to judge you on your individual character.*

Table 9.5 Obama's and McCain's policy differences

Issue	Obama's position	McCain's position
Bailout of struggling financial institutions	In favour of bailout, but also emphasised ending tax cuts for the wealthy	In favour of bailout
Iraq War	Emphasised getting out as quickly as possible	Would clearly have stayed there longer in order to finish what the USA had started
Free trade and **NAFTA**	Less enthusiastic, wanted Canada and Mexico on 'a level playing field' with the USA with regard to stricter labour and environmental standards	Enthusiastically pro-free trade
Environment	Emphasised it more than McCain	Had a reasonably good record for a Republican
Same-sex marriage and abortion	More liberal	More conservative
Gun control	Advocated far greater regulation	Far less keen on greater regulation
Energy independence	Greatly emphasised	Less emphasis
Healthcare	Greatly emphasised reform of the healthcare system to make it available for a larger number of Americans	Less emphasis

The statistical history was discouraging. Only two African Americans had been elected state governor since Reconstruction, Douglas Wilder of Virginia and Deval Patrick of Massachusetts. Obama was the sole black American in the United States Senate – and there had only been two others before him.

There was considerable debate over whether Obama won despite or because of his blackness, and both viewpoints had persuasive advocates.

Victory in spite of race

A considerable number of Americans, including labour leader Richard Trumka, believed that 'there are a lot of white folks out there' who would not vote for a black person. In January 2008, Robert Ford, a black state senator from South Carolina, supported Hillary Clinton in the Democratic primary because he feared Obama could not beat the Republican candidate. He pointed out that of around 8000 black elected officials in the United States, 99 per cent represented districts with a 50 per cent or more black population. He believed black politicians did not get elected outside black areas.

Obama certainly lost the white vote quite heavily in the South (see Figure 9.2). In Louisiana, the Democrat presidential candidate John Kerry won 24 per cent of the white vote in 2004, but Obama only got 14 per cent. In several states, whites who voted for a Democratic governor did not vote for Obama. In Virginia, Obama beat McCain by 51 per cent to 47 per cent, but the Democratic gubernatorial candidate won by 64 per cent to 34 per cent.

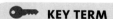

KEY TERM

NAFTA North American Free Trade Association, established during Bill Clinton's presidency to encourage trade between the United States, Mexico and Canada.

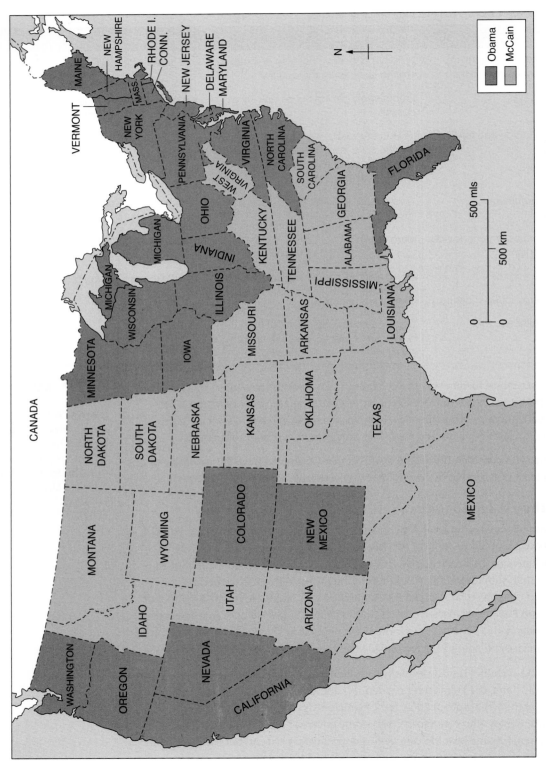

Figure 9.2 The respective states won by the Democrat Barack Obama and the Republican John McCain in the 2008 presidential election.

While Obama played down his race, the **shock jocks** made much of his name, associating Obama with terrorist leader Osama bin Laden, and intimating that Obama's middle name, Hussein, should make Americans highly suspicious after the Muslim terrorist attacks of 9/11 (see page 204). Many Americans were suspicious, as demonstrated by the continuing controversies over Obama's name (see page 220) during his presidency.

Victory because of race

Former vice presidential candidate and keen Hillary Clinton supporter Geraldine Ferraro said Obama was only successful because he was black:

> If Obama was a white man, he would not be in this position, and if he was a woman [black or white] he would not be in this position. He happens to be very lucky who he is. And the country is caught up in the concept.

Some commentators thought Obama won because of the minority vote. He certainly did well amongst minorities, but Democrats always did. He got 95 per cent of the black vote, compared to 88 per cent for John Kerry in 2004. More black Americans turned out in 2008, no doubt because of Obama's candidacy: they constituted 11 per cent of the electorate in 2004, but 13 per cent in 2008. That was over 2 million more voters. Obama also did better than Kerry with the Latino vote. Obama had particular appeal to minorities, but also won a little more of the white vote than previous Democrat presidential candidates (43 per cent, compared to Kerry's 41 per cent and Al Gore's 42 per cent in 2000). Obama won 8 per cent more of the independent vote than McCain, which owed much to his being an energising candidate. The conviction that his would be a historic victory appealed to many voters.

Sometimes, the voting patterns were surprising: Pennsylvania voted for Barack Obama in November 2008, even though the state was described as 'male and pale' in terms of representation and Obama was perceived to have offended Pennsylvania's white working class by seeming to describe them as losers. Pennsylvania had been one of the states most reluctant to elect African Americans. Pennsylvania's Governor Ed Rendell favoured Hillary Clinton for the Democratic nomination, and claimed that some conservative whites in Pennsylvania were not ready to vote for an African American candidate. Obama's victory in Pennsylvania could be seen as a triumph against racism, or it could be interpreted as due to other factors, such as President Bush's unpopularity.

North Carolina produced another surprising result: Obama was the first Democrat presidential candidate to win it in 32 years. As North Carolina had sent the racist Jesse Helms to the Senate for 30 years, this was a considerable achievement. Obama won only 35 per cent of the white North Carolina vote, although that was up 8 per cent on John Kerry in 2004. That 8 per cent, along

🔑 **KEY TERM**

Shock jocks Right-wing radio commentators, such as Rush Limbaugh.

with the surge in African American turnout and North Carolina's changing demography (more minority and youthful voters), helped explain Obama's victory in North Carolina.

Problems in Obama's campaign

1 How Obama's pastor nearly cost him the election

During the presidential election campaign, Obama's twenty-year-long association with his black nationalist pastor Jeremiah Wright became an issue with right-wingers, who made much of the pastor's controversial statements. In March 2008, Obama said he could no more disown Jeremiah Wright than he could his racist white grandmother, but then he publicly disowned him a few weeks later, which upset left-wingers.

The Wright words

- 'The government gives African Americans the drugs, builds bigger prisons, passes the **three-strikes law** and then wants us to sing God Bless America. No, no, no. Goddamn America, that's in the Bible for killing innocent people. Goddamn America for treating our citizens as less than human. Goddamn America for as long as she acts like she is God and she is supreme.'

- 'The government invented the HIV virus as a means of genocide against people of color.'

- 'Bill Clinton did the same thing to us [African Americans] that he did to Monica Lewinsky' (translation: he screwed us).

- 'Hillary [Clinton] never had a cab whizz past her because her skin was the wrong colour. Hillary never had to worry about being pulled over in her car as a black man driving in the wrong ... I am sick of Negroes who just do not get it. Hillary was not a black boy raised in a single parent home, Barack was.'

- 'We have supported state terrorism against the Palestinians [by supporting Israel] and black South Africans [by supporting the white racist regime prior to the ending of apartheid] and now we are indignant because the stuff we have done overseas is now brought right back into our own front yard [9/11]. America's chickens are coming home to roost.'

2 How Michelle Obama might have cost her husband the election

Many considered Michelle Obama to be a big plus in her husband's presidential campaign. The couple seemed to have the glamour of John and Jackie Kennedy. Part of the appeal of both couples lay in two beautiful children.

However, Mrs Obama, elegant, articulate and well educated, nearly 'blew it': as her husband gained popularity, she said, 'For the first time in my adult lifetime, I am really proud of my country.' Mrs Cindy McCain quickly responded that she was *always* proud of her country. Many felt Michelle Obama was referring to American racism, but her husband claimed that she meant that it was the increased popular interest in the political process that made her 'really proud of my country'.

KEY TERM

Three-strikes law After three convictions, for whatever minor offences, a person would be imprisoned for life.

SOURCE E

Michelle Obama campaigning for her husband Barack Obama at the University of Virginia, Charlottesville, in September 2008.

Overall, Obama failed to transcend race in the election, and it would be the same in his presidency. The United States was not a post-racial or colour-blind society as yet.

Why did Americans find the slogan shown in Source E appealing?

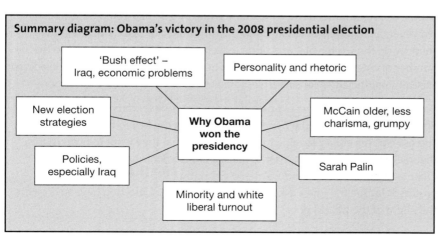

Summary diagram: Obama's victory in the 2008 presidential election

- 'Bush effect' – Iraq, economic problems
- Personality and rhetoric
- New election strategies
- McCain older, less charisma, grumpy
- **Why Obama won the presidency**
- Policies, especially Iraq
- Sarah Palin
- Minority and white liberal turnout

The significance of Obama's victory

▶ *In what ways was Obama's election significant?*

Barack Obama's victory inspired black Americans and liberally inclined whites, and led many Americans to conclude that theirs was now a colour-blind society.

The black American response

Barack Obama was not universally and uncritically beloved by black Americans. During the election campaign, some felt he was not 'one of them' because his father was Kenyan. However, Michelle Obama compensated somewhat: her descent from American slaves made her a 'real' African American. Black class divisions also emerged during the election campaign, during which Obama criticised absentee black fathers. That led leading black spokesman Jesse Jackson to criticise him, and the criticism was picked up by a microphone: 'See, Barack's been talking down to black people … I want to cut his nuts off.' Jackson, whose son was a great Obama supporter, made a public apology.

However, most black Americans were enthusiastic supporters of his candidacy, including high-profile celebrities such as Oprah Winfrey. Once Obama was elected, there was universal black rejoicing for the historic significance of American acceptance of a black President.

A colour-blind America?

The November 2008 triumph of a black American was widely regarded as a historic event, but was interpreted negatively as well as positively.

In what many considered to be an indication of racial equality, a black American had been elected President of the United States only 40 years after all black people were guaranteed the vote. Many white people had voted for him. However, he had relied heavily upon the minority vote (McCain beat him soundly on the white vote) and upon a decline in voting numbers due to the number of older white voters who stayed at home (some Republicans considered McCain insufficiently conservative, some feared Sarah Palin).

Some black commentators expressed scepticism. Conservative black intellectual Shelby Smith argued in the *Los Angeles Times* that the key to Barack Obama's success was his ability to tell white Americans what they want to hear, that is, that racism is no longer a barrier to black advancement. According to Smith, Obama offered redemption for America's original sin of slavery. History professor Jacqueline Jones asked, 'What does Obama's election have to do with the plight of the [black] poor?'

SOURCE F

Extract from the *New York Times* article of 4 November 2008, headlined 'Obama Elected President as Racial Barrier Falls'.

Barack Hussein Obama was elected the 44th president of the United States on Tuesday, sweeping away the last racial barrier in American politics with ease as the country chose him as its first black chief executive.

The election of Mr. Obama amounted to a national catharsis — a repudiation of a historically unpopular Republican president and his economic and foreign policies, and an embrace of Mr. Obama's call for a change in the direction and the tone of the country.

But it was just as much a strikingly symbolic moment in the evolution of the nation's fraught racial history, a breakthrough that would have seemed unthinkable just two years ago …

'This is a historic election, and I recognize the significance it has for African-Americans and for the special pride that must be theirs tonight,' Mr. McCain said [in his concession speech], adding, 'We both realize that we have come a long way from the injustices that once stained our nation's reputation.'

Some expressed the hope that the nation had now entered a post-racial phase. Harvard philosopher Tommie Shelby said,

> *Many whites are weary of black claims of grievance. They think that black political solidarity is no longer necessary. For some whites, that is the significance of Obama's victory – it puts the last nail in the coffin of black identity politics.*

In the first few months of Obama's presidency his approval ratings were exceptionally high, suggesting that his race was not an issue. A Gallup poll revealed that over 70 per cent of Americans said Obama's election would improve race relations and was a massive milestone. However, the director of the Southern Poverty Law Centre, which monitored hate groups, said, 'We know that immediately after Barack Obama's election the computer servers of several major white supremacist web sites collapsed because they got such a huge amount of traffic.' In March 2009, a reporter asked President Obama whether his presidency had so far 'been a relatively color-blind time'. The President replied that the focus on his race 'lasted about a day'. That was not quite true. President Obama got caught up in several 'race politics' controversies within months of his election triumph.

Race controversies in President Obama's first year

The first controversy over race during Obama's presidency concerned a monkey cartoon in the *New York Post*, which had supported John McCain in November 2008. The new President immediately sought a large-scale injection of federal money into the economy, in the hope of revitalising it. He introduced a stimulus bill into Congress. On 18 February 2009, the *New York Post* ran a cartoon that

What reasons does Source F give for Obama's victory, and why does it see that victory as significant?

showed two policeman standing over the bullet-riddled body of a marauding monkey (a violent chimpanzee had been gunned down by police in Connecticut two days before). The *Post* cartoon caption said, 'They'll have to find someone else to write the next stimulus bill'. The *Post* said the cartoon was meant 'to mock the ineptly written federal stimulus bill' and not, as many people thought, to equate the President with a monkey (there is a long history of whites portraying blacks as primates). The *Post* owner, Rupert Murdoch, personally apologised for the cartoon, in response to widespread anger and an NAACP call to boycott the paper. The *Post* cartoonist responsible, Sean Delonas, has frequently been accused of bigotry, and is nicknamed 'the Picasso of prejudice'.

Race jokes

President Obama was well aware that racial jokes were a politically sensitive issue, but that much depended upon who made them. His May 2009 address at the annual White House correspondents' dinner included a joke about the permatanned Republican leader in the House of Representatives, John Boehner. 'We have a lot in common,' said the President. 'He is a person of color. Although not a color that appears in the natural world.'

The second race controversy concerned black Professor William Louis Gates' arrest by a policeman who thought he was trying to break into a house in a wealthy suburb (it was Gates' own house and he had mislaid his keys). Nearly three-quarters of the white population of the United States perceived President Obama to be taking the 'black' side, which damaged his poll ratings.

A third race controversy was the **birther controversy**. Under the American Constitution, the President must be born in the United States. Some right-wingers claimed that President Obama was not. The Republican governor of Hawaii and others felt it necessary to verify Barack Obama's birth certificate. A July 2009 poll revealed that over 28 per cent of Republicans believed Obama was not born in United States and 30 per cent were not sure. Eleven Republican congressman signed a 'birther bill', demanding a birth certificate for future presidents.

On the other hand, despite the controversies, President Obama's selection of a 'rainbow cabinet' did not elicit a divisive national debate, probably because President Bill Clinton had introduced the idea of a 'rainbow cabinet' that reflected the population composition of the United States. President Obama's 21 Cabinet appointees included seven women, four African Americans, three Asian Americans and two Hispanics. 'He has a majority-minority Cabinet', according to Paul Light, a New York University expert on presidential appointments. 'In terms of white males – they are in the minority now.' On the other hand, it could be argued that only Attorney General Eric Holder of the four African American appointees held a major Cabinet position.

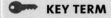 **KEY TERM**

Birther controversy Some right-wingers claim Obama was not born in the United States and therefore was not qualified to be President under the terms of the US Constitution.

The discussion of President Barack Obama's race suggested that the United States is a far from 'colour-blind' society. Some commentators said that President Obama's election saw the end of 'race politics', but that politics repeatedly raised its head on several occasions, perhaps most significantly in ex-President Jimmy Carter's September 2009 assertion that racism was behind the Republican opposition to Obama's healthcare proposals. In an act of unprecedented discourtesy, a South Carolina senator cried 'You lie!' when Obama addressed Congress on the healthcare issue, and Carter attributed this to the reluctance of some Americans to accept the legitimacy of an African American President. Not everyone agreed with Carter. Opposition to Obama could simply be due to partisanship, although Obama's own reaction to the Gates issue seemed to demonstrate his belief that 'race politics' and racial tensions did not end with his election.

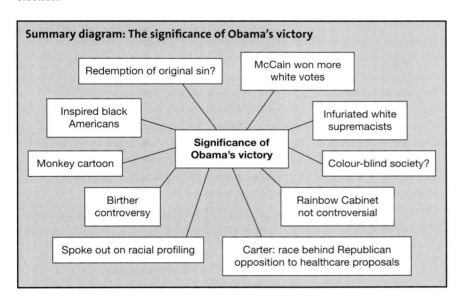

Summary diagram: The significance of Obama's victory

Chapter summary

Prior to the 1970s, there was a sustained black American exodus from the South, but then a slow black American drift back began. This was because the South had changed since the 1960s: it was a more racially tolerant and prosperous society, with a lower cost of living and a more clement climate than much of the United States.

In the late twentieth century, the economic, social, legal and political status of many black Americans improved, but problems remained. While the number of middle-class black Americans grew, and while they were increasingly well integrated into white American society, many black Americans remained impoverished and marginalised in the ghettos. Average black income and educational attainment remained far below those of white Americans, and *de facto* residential and educational segregation continued in many areas. The social and economic inferiority of black Americans was reflected in crime and imprisonment statistics. The number of elected black officials was not proportionate to the size of the black American population, but black political power and influence had markedly increased, as demonstrated by the political career of Barack Obama.

With a white mother, a Kenyan father, and a childhood spent in Hawaii and Indonesia, Barack Obama was not a typical black American. After an identity crisis, he aligned himself fully with black America. He worked as a community organiser in a Chicago ghetto, joined a black church, and married a more typical black American, Michelle Robinson.

Obama felt that black Americans had made great progress toward equality in his lifetime, but that more needed to be done, and after his election to the Illinois Senate and the US Senate, he focused upon black problems.

In 2008, Obama defeated Hillary Clinton for the Democrat presidential nomination. That victory owed much to his embodiment of the 'American dream', his emphasis upon hope and change, the mismanaged Clinton campaign, the primary calendar and Obama's outstanding fundraising abilities. Obama then defeated Republican presidential candidate John McCain. His victory owed much to the 'Bush effect', especially Bush's unpopular war in Iraq. It was also due to Obama's personality and rhetorical abilities, McCain's running mate Sarah Palin, Obama's new election strategies and superior fundraising and organisation, and his policies (especially on Iraq and healthcare). It also owed something to the minority vote.

Although it was highly significant for Americans to elect a black President, the election did not signify a post-racial or colour-blind society. Obama's race played a part in the election, appealing to some voters, alienating others. It continued to be a prominent issue in the first year of Obama's presidency, as seen in the birther controversy and in Obama's intervention in the Professor Gates racial profiling case.

Refresher questions

1 In what ways are autobiographies a problematic source?

2 To what extent had black Americans achieved economic, social, political and legal equality by the year 2000?

3 Why was Obama's speech at the 2004 Democrat National Convention significant?

4 Why were Obama's first two books important?

5 Why did Obama defeat Senator Hillary Clinton in the 2008 Democrat presidential nomination race?

6 Why did Obama defeat Senator John McCain in the 2008 presidential election?

7 What was the role of race in the 2008 presidential election?

8 To what extent did Obama's election victory suggest a post-racial society?

9 How significant was Obama's 'rainbow cabinet'?

10 Was the USA 'colour-blind' during the first year of Obama's presidency?

 Question practice

SOURCE ANALYSIS QUESTION

1 Assess the value of Source C (page 205) for revealing Barack Obama's appeal to voters and the nature of the relationship of white Americans with black Americans in the early twenty-first century. Explain your answer, using the source, the information given about its origin and your knowledge about the historical context.

ESSAY QUESTIONS

1 How far can the First World War be regarded as the key turning point in the changing geography of civil rights issues in the USA in the period 1850–2009?

2 'Barack Obama won the presidency in 2008 because he was black.' How far do you agree with this statement?

CHAPTER 10

Black Americans 1850–2009 – conclusions

The years 1850–2009 saw dramatic changes in the status of considerable numbers of black Americans, thanks to factors such as war, the federal government, white opinion, the media and black activism.

Aspects in depth – emancipation and moves towards greater equality

The five depth studies illustrate dramatic progress: the majority of black Americans were enslaved in 1850 (Chapter 1), but in 2008 a still majority-white America elected a black President (Chapter 9). However, that progress has not been uninterrupted and full racial equality has not been attained. As Barack Obama said in 1990, 'It's encouraging. But it is important that stories like mine aren't used to say that everything is okay for blacks.' As he added in 2006, 'Better isn't good enough.'

Although black Americans were 'free at last' after the Civil War (Chapter 2), and although their rights as free citizens and voters were supposedly guaranteed, there was a Southern white backlash against congressional Reconstruction. The reassertion of Southern white supremacy had the support of the federal government, particularly the Supreme Court, which repeatedly ruled in favour of the Jim Crow segregation laws (Chapter 3). The federal government was always the key to any black progress. This was illustrated again during the Roosevelt era (1933–45), in which black Americans received unprecedented economic aid, although they also suffered discrimination in the implementation of New Deal programmes (Chapter 5).

Although the mid-twentieth century is traditionally seen as the classic era of the civil rights movement, it can serve to distract from previous and sustained black efforts to attain equality, or at least a better life, whether through litigation (Chapter 3) or migration from the South (Chapters 4 and 6). However, there is no doubt that the civil rights movement was at its most effective in the years 1954–68, when federal government intervention, black protests and changing white opinion combined to ensure that *de jure* race segregation was ended and black Southerners were able to vote (Chapter 7).

The classic period of the civil rights movements and the affirmative action programmes that resulted from it helped to increase the number of middle-class black Americans, but even when coupled with the election of a black President

(Chapter 9), this could not disguise the fact that the social and economic status of many black Americans remained inferior, particularly in the ghettos of the North and West that developed as a result of black migration and the white response to it (Chapters 6 and 7).

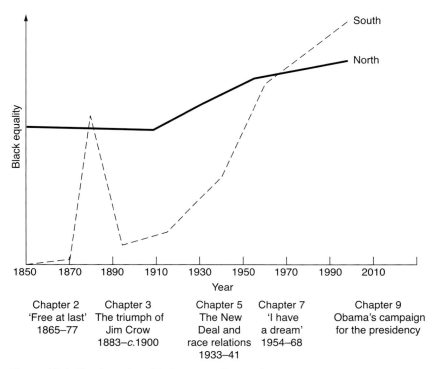

Figure 10.1 Graph to show black progress/regression.

Breadth study – the changing geography of civil rights issues

In the mid-nineteenth century, the 'black problem' was a primarily Southern one. Southern whites used slavery as a system of economic exploitation but also for race control. With the end of slavery, and the start of the slow drift North (Chapter 4), the black problem spread across the United States. Two world wars accelerated that drift into the 'Great Migration' (Chapters 4 and 6). While white Southerners relied upon *de jure* segregation, violence and intimidation to control the black population, white Northerners relied more upon *de facto* segregation and 'white flight', although they were not averse to violence and intimidation in order to maintain race control. The growth of the black ghettos of the North and West changed the geography of civil rights issues: although the 1960s saw improvements in the black situation in the South, central city areas with primarily black populations continued to deteriorate and the result was several 'long hot summers' of nationwide black ghetto riots.

Ironically, the story of black migration came full circle in the later twentieth century, when large numbers of black Americans migrated back to a 'New South' (Chapter 9), a narrative that, even more than the election of a black American President, illustrated the dramatic changes in civil rights and race relations in the United States by 2009.

Breadth study – changing portrayals of civil rights issues in fiction and film

Black progress – or the lack of it – was often traceable in literary and visual representations. The United States could never rid itself of racial antagonisms: throughout the period 1850–2009, there were demeaning depictions of black Americans, whether in minstrel shows in 1850 or in white supremacist caricatures of the black President in 2009. However, there were periods when literary and visual portrayals were more favourable.

Prior to emancipation, black Americans were not perceived as menacing, and abolitionist depictions were sympathetic, if occasionally somewhat patronising. The end of slavery and increased black assertiveness increased the demeaning visual representations, whether in cartoons or movies. However, as the twentieth century wore on, and particularly under pressure of war, visual and literary depictions of black Americans became increasingly sympathetic, although many black people still perceived some to be patronising. It could be argued that the much acclaimed television series *The Wire*, like the election of Barack Obama, indicated that the United States had developed into a post-racial society by the twenty-first century. However, *The Wire* avoided coverage of the racial tensions that undoubtedly existed in the great cities and, as one jaundiced History professor noted, what did Obama's election have to do with black ghetto problems?

While portrayals often reflected the changes in the black situation, it is difficult to decide when and if they shaped perceptions. Many people believe that they did, although it is difficult to find proof.

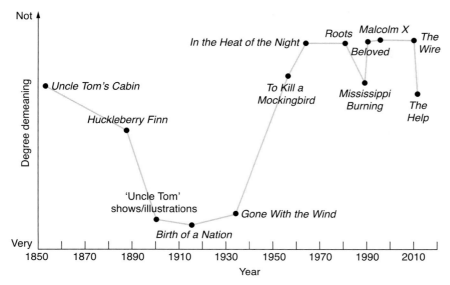

Figure 10.2 Changing portrayals of civil rights issues in fiction and film.

Edexcel A level History

Sources guidance

Edexcel's Paper 3, Option 39.1: Civil rights and race relations in the USA, 1850–2009 is assessed by an exam comprising three sections:

- Section A is a source analysis assessment. It tests your knowledge of one of the key topics in depth.
- Section B requires you to write one essay from a choice of two, again testing your knowledge of key topics in depth (see page 233 for guidance on this).
- Section C requires you to write one essay from a choice of two. Questions relate to themes in breadth and test your knowledge of change over a period of at least 100 years (see page 237 for guidance on this).

The sections of the exam relate to the sections of the paper in the following way:

Section A and Section B	Test your knowledge of the key topics in depth	Emancipation and moves toward greater equality: • 'Free at last', 1865–77 • The triumph of 'Jim Crow', 1883–c.1900 • The New Deal and race relations, 1933–41 • 'I have a dream', 1954–68 • Obama's campaign for the presidency, 2004–9
Section C	Tests your knowledge of the themes in breadth	Changing perceptions of race relations, 1850–2009: • The changing geography of civil rights issues • Changing portrayals of civil rights issues in fiction and film

The following advice relates to Paper 3, Section A. Paper 3 is only available at A level, therefore there is no AS level version of this paper.

Paper 3 Section A

Section A of Paper 3 comprises a single compulsory question which refers to one source.

The question

The Section A question will begin with the following stem: 'Assess the value of the source for revealing …'. For example:

> Assess the value of the source [Source 1, page 229] for revealing Martin Luther King Jr's opinion of the success of the civil rights movement and the relationship of black Americans with white Americans in the late 1960s.
>
> Explain your answer, using the source, the information given about its origin and your own knowledge about the historical context.

The source

The source will be a primary or contemporary source: it will have been written contemporary to 1850–2009, the period that you are studying. The source will be around 350 words long. It will be accompanied by a brief passage which will set out the essential provenance of the source. See Source 1 on page 229.

SOURCE I

From Martin Luther King Jr's 'Beyond Vietnam' speech at Riverside Church Meeting, New York, 4 April 1967. Quoted in Clayborne Carson *et al.*, editors, *Eyes on the Prize*, Penguin, 1991, pp. 387–93.

Over the past two years, as I have moved to break the betrayal of my own silences and to speak from the burnings of my own heart, as I have called for radical departures from the destruction of Vietnam, many persons have questioned me about the wisdom of my path… Why are you speaking about war, Dr. King? Why are you joining the voices of dissent? Peace and civil rights don't mix, they say. Aren't you hurting the cause of your people? they ask… I have several reasons for bringing Vietnam into the field of my moral vision… [First] A few years ago… it seemed as if there was a real promise of hope for the poor – both black and white – through the [Great Society] Poverty Program… Then came the build-up in Vietnam and I watched the program broken and eviscerated… and I knew that America would never invest the necessary funds or energies in rehabilitation of its poor so long as adventures like Vietnam continued to draw men and skills and money… So I was increasingly compelled to see the war as an enemy of the poor and to attack it as such.

[Second] We were taking the black young men who had been crippled by our own society and sending them eight thousand miles away to guarantee liberties in Southeast Asia which they had not found in Southwest Georgia and East Harlem. So we have been repeatedly faced with the cruel irony of watching Negro and white boys on TV screens as they kill and die together for a nation that has been unable to seat them together in the same schools. ..

My third reason… grows out of my experience in the ghettos of the North over the last three years… As I have walked among the desperate, rejected and angry young men I have told them that Molotov cocktails and rifles would not solve their problems. I have tried to offer them my deepest compassion while maintaining my convictions that social change comes most meaningfully through non-violent action. But they asked – and rightly so – what about Vietnam? … Their questions hit home, and I knew that I could never again raise my voice against the violence of the oppressed in the ghettos without having first spoken clearly to the greatest purveyor of violence in the world today – my own government.

Understanding the question

To answer the question successfully you must understand how the question works. The question is written precisely in order to make sure that you understand the task. Each part of the question has a specific meaning.

Assess the value of the source[1] for Martin Luther King Jr's opinion of the success of the civil rights movement[2], and the relationship of black Americans with white Americans in the late 1960s[3].

Explain your answer, using the source, the information given about its origin and your own knowledge about the historical context.

1   You must evaluate how useful the source could be to a historian. Evaluating the extent of usefulness involves considering its value and limitations in the light of your own knowledge about the source's historical context. Important information about the context of the source is included in the information given about the source.
2   The question focuses on two specific enquiries that the source might be useful for. The first is Martin Luther King Jr's opinion of the success of the civil rights movement.
3   The second enquiry is the relationship of black Americans with white Americans in the late 1960s.

In essence, you should use the source, the information about the source and your own knowledge of the historical context to make a judgement about how far the source is useful to a historian engaged in two specific enquiries. Crucially, you must consider both enquiries. An answer that only focuses on one of the enquiries is unlikely to do well.

Source skills

Section A of Paper 3 tests your ability to evaluate source material. Your job is to analyse the source by reading it in the context of the values and assumptions of the society and the period from which it came.

Examiners will mark your work by focusing on the extent to which you are able to do the following:

- Interpret and analyse source material:
  - At a basic level, this means you can understand the source and select, copy, paraphrase and summarise the source to help answer the question.
  - At a higher level, your interpretation of the source includes the ability to explain, analyse and make inferences based on the source.
  - At the highest levels, you will be expected to analyse the source in a sophisticated way. This includes the ability to distinguish between information, opinions and arguments contained in the source.
- Deploy knowledge of historical context in relation to the source:
  - At a basic level, this means the ability to link the source to your knowledge of the context in which the source was written, using this knowledge to expand or support the information contained in the source.
  - At a higher level, you will be able to use your contextual knowledge to make inferences, and to expand, support or challenge the details mentioned in the source.
  - At the highest levels, you will examine the value and limits of the material contained in the source by interpreting the source in the context of the values and assumptions of the society from which it is taken.

- Evaluate the usefulness and weight of the source material:
  - At a basic level, evaluation of the source will be based on simplistic criteria about reliability and bias.
  - At a higher level, evaluation of the source will be based on the nature and purpose of the source.
  - At the highest levels, evaluation of the source will be based on a valid criterion that is justified in the course of the essay. You will also be able to distinguish between the value of different aspects of the source.

Make sure your source evaluation is sophisticated. Avoid crude statements about bias, and avoid simplistic assumptions such as that a source written immediately after an event is reliable, whereas a source written years later is unreliable.

Try to see things through the eyes of the writer:

- How does the writer understand the world?
- What assumptions does the writer have?
- Who is the writer trying to influence?
- What views is the writer trying to challenge?

Basic skill: comprehension

The most basic source skill is comprehension: understanding what the source means. There are a variety of techniques that you can use to aid comprehension. For example, you could read the sources included in this book and in past papers. In this context you could:

- Read the sources out loud.
- Look up any words that you don't understand and make a glossary.
- Make flash cards containing brief biographies of the writers of the sources.

You can demonstrate comprehension by copying, paraphrasing and summarising the sources. However, keep this to the minimum as comprehension is a low-level skill and you need to leave room for higher-level skills.

Advanced skill: contextualising the sources

First, to analyse the sources correctly you need to understand them in the context in which they were written. Source 1 (page 229) reflects Martin Luther King Jr's opinions and preoccupation with ghetto problems in 1967. Your job is to understand the values and assumptions behind the source.

- One way of contextualising the source is to consider the nature, origins and purpose of the source. However, this can lead to a formulaic essay.
- An alternative is to consider two levels of context. First, you should establish the general context. In this case, Source 1 was written at a time when the Johnson administration was focused on dramatically escalating the war in Vietnam, where the number of American troops was approaching half a million. Second, you can look for specific references to contemporary events, people or debates in the sources. For example, when considering Martin Luther King Jr's opinion of the success of the civil rights movement the details in the source can be put in context in the following way:
    - 'Poverty Program' – President Johnson's promise of a Great Society in which poverty was eradicated had aroused the hopes of King and others that something would be done to help impoverished black Americans in the ghettos – an area in which the civil rights movement had been unsuccessful.
    - 'A nation that has been unable to seat them together in the same schools' – although the *Brown* ruling had declared segregated schools unconstitutional and the 1964 Civil Rights Act had further promoted school desegregation, white resistance had ensured that many schools remained segregated. After his Chicago campaign of 1966, King was very conscious that Chicago's schools remained *de facto* segregated, and that, because Mayor Daley was a political ally, President Johnson had not

pressed him to end it. There again, the civil rights movement seemed powerless – the civil rights movement had helped obtain the Civil Rights Act – but only some schools in the South had desegregated.
    - 'Desperate, rejected and angry young men' – younger ghetto residents felt the civil rights movement had done nothing for them and they were turning to Black Power radicalism, expressed in riots and sympathy for, or involvement in, the Black Panthers.

Use context to make judgements

- Start by establishing the general context of the source:
    - Ask yourself, what was going on at the time when the source was written, or the time of the events described in the source?
    - What are the key debates that the source might be contributing to?
- Next, look for key words and phrases that establish the specific context. Does the source refer to specific people, events or books that might be important?
- Make sure your contextualisation focuses on the question.
- Use the context when evaluating the usefulness and limitations of the source.

For example:

Source 1 is valuable to a historian investigating Martin Luther King Jr's opinion of the success of the civil rights movement because the reasons he gives for his opposition to the Vietnam War demonstrate his recognition that the civil rights movement had had little impact on the ghettos of the North. His first reason for opposition is that the war has diverted federal government money from the Great Society. He realises that the nation will 'never invest the necessary funds … in rehabilitation of its poor' so long as it engages in such foreign 'adventures'. King had seen the dire conditions in the Chicago ghetto where he had resided for several months during SCLC's

1966 Chicago campaign. Source 1 shows his realisation that ending ghetto poverty depended on federal government 'funds or energies' – and King clearly felt that the civil rights movement had failed to persuade the Johnson administration to invest sufficient 'funds or energies' to help black American ghetto residents. He does not mention the undoubted successes of the civil rights movement in the South in Source 1 – his preoccupation is the impact of the war on black Americans and he is addressing black New Yorkers preoccupied with the problems of Harlem. In many ways, Source 1 is only useful to the historian studying the ghettos.

King's second reason for opposing the war is that thousands of black soldiers are fighting 'to guarantee liberties' in Vietnam that they have 'not found' in the South or the North. Here he admits that, despite the Brown ruling and its supposed reinforcement by the 1964 Civil Rights Act, 'Negro and white boys' still do not sit together 'in the same schools' in some parts of the South ('Southwest Georgia') and in the North ('East Harlem'). There, in his recognition that de facto segregation continues across the nation, he sees that the achievements of the civil rights movement were limited even in the South. Of course, by 1967 he was increasingly depressed and disillusioned, so that Source 1 reflects the jaundiced opinions of his later years.

King's third reason for opposing the war is because it shows the government sees violence as the solution to problems – and radical young black ghetto males do too. King's strategy in the civil rights movement had been 'non-violent action', and here he recognises that Black Power advocates who are willing to use 'Molotov cocktails and rifles' have rejected his civil rights movement strategy. In that sense, again, his opinion seems to be that his civil rights movement has failed to convince young black males or the government of the value of 'non-violent action' to bring about change and improvement.

This passage makes inferences from details in the source to uncover a variety of ideas about the achievements of the civil rights movement, showing that the passage is of considerable use for this enquiry. Significantly, in order to do well it would also have to deal with the other enquiry: the extent of the source's usefulness for revealing the relationship of black Americans with white Americans in the late 1960s.

Essay guidance (1)

Paper 3

To get a high grade in Section B of Paper 3 your essay must contain four essential qualities:

- focused analysis
- relevant detail
- supported judgement
- organisation, coherence and clarity.

This section focuses on the following aspects of exam technique:

- The nature of the question.
- Planning your answer, including writing a focused introduction.
- Deploying relevant detail.
- Writing analytically.
- Reaching a supported judgement.

The nature of the question

Section B questions are designed to test the depth of your historical knowledge. Therefore, they can focus on relatively short periods, or single events. Moreover, they can focus on different historical processes or 'concepts'. These include:

- cause
- consequence
- change/continuity
- similarity/difference
- significance.

These different question focuses require slightly different approaches:

Cause	1	To what extent was President Johnson responsible for the passage of the 1964 Civil Rights Act and the 1965 Voting Rights Act?
Consequence	2	To what extent, in the years 1954–68, did the civil rights movement succeed in improving the status of black Americans?
Continuity and change	3	'Martin Luther King Jr demonstrated admirable leadership qualities in both the Selma campaign and the Chicago campaign.' How far do you agree with this statement?
Similarities and differences	4	'Public support for Martin Luther King Jr's campaigns in the South was more consistent and broadly based than public support for his Chicago campaign.' How far do you agree with this statement?
Significance	5	How significant was media coverage to the successes of the civil rights movement during the years 1956–68?

Some questions include a 'stated factor'. A common type of stated factor question would ask how far one factor caused something. For example, for question 1 in the table, 'To what extent was President Johnson responsible for the passage of the 1964 Civil Rights Act and the 1965 Voting Rights Act?', you would be expected to evaluate the importance of 'President Johnson' – the 'stated factor' – compared to other factors.

Planning your answer

It is crucial that you understand the focus of the question. Therefore, read the question carefully before you start planning. Check the following:

- The chronological focus: which years should your essay deal with?

- The topic focus: what aspect of your course does the question deal with?
- The conceptual focus: is this a causes, consequences, change/continuity, similarity/difference or significance question?

For example, for question 5 in the table on page 233 you could point these out as follows:

How significant[1] was media coverage[2] to the successes of the civil rights movement during the years 1956–1968[3]?

1 Conceptual focus: significance, specifically to the success of the civil rights movement.
2 Topic focus: media coverage
3 Chronological focus: 1956–68.

Your plan should reflect the task that you have been set. Section B asks you to write an analytical, coherent and well-structured essay from your own knowledge, which reaches a supported conclusion in around 40 minutes:

- To ensure that your essay is coherent and well structured, it should comprise a series of paragraphs, each focusing on a different point.
- Your paragraphs should come in a logical order. For example, you could write your paragraphs in order of importance, so you begin with the most important issues and end with the least important.
- In essays where there is a 'stated factor', it is a good idea to start with the stated factor before moving on to the other points.
- To make sure you keep to time, you should aim to write three or four paragraphs plus an introduction and a conclusion.

The opening paragraph

The opening paragraph should do four main things:

- answer the question directly
- set out your essential argument
- outline the factors or issues that you will discuss
- define key terms used in the question – where necessary.

Different questions require you to define different terms, for example:

How significant was media coverage to the successes of the civil rights movement during the years 1956–68?

You need to explain 'media coverage' (television, newspapers) and 'successes' (the desegregation of Montgomery buses, Southern lunch counters and interstate transport, along with the Civil Rights Act and the Voting Rights Act) to which the civil rights movement contributed.

'Public support for Martin Luther King Jr's campaigns in the South was more consistent and broadly based than public support for his Chicago campaign.' How far do you agree with this statement?

In this example, you need to take care to distinguish between the aims/achievements in the South, and those in the North. Along with differentiating between the situation in the South and North, you need to differentiate between the support of Northern whites, Southern whites, Northern blacks and Southern blacks.

Here is an example introduction in answer to question 1 in the table on page 233:

There has long been debate as to who or what deserves most credit for the passage of the 1964 Civil Rights Act, which ended de jure segregation, and the 1965 Voting Rights Act, which enfranchised black Southerners[1]. President Johnson said that 'the real hero' behind these changes was 'the American Negro', whose activism had drawn national attention to the abuses. However, Johnson was probably being too modest. He played an important role in the passage of the legislation, as did Congress, changing white opinion, and the media[2]. Overall though, black activism was surely the most important factor – without it, neither the federal government nor the media would have paid attention to the thorny issue of the South, segregation and states' rights[3].

1 The essay starts with a clear focus on the question.
2 This sentence introduces the other factors.
3 This sentence indicates what the essay's argument will be.

The opening paragraph: advice

- Don't write more than a couple of sentences on general background knowledge. This is unlikely to focus explicitly on the question.
- After defining key terms, refer back to these definitions when justifying your conclusion.
- The introduction should reflect the rest of the essay. Don't make one argument in your introduction and then make a different argument in the essay.

Deploying relevant detail

Paper 3 tests the depth of your historical knowledge. Therefore, you will need to deploy historical detail. In the main body of your essay your paragraphs should begin with a clear point, be full of relevant detail and end with explanation or evaluation. A detailed answer might include statistics, proper names, dates and technical terms. For example, if you are writing a paragraph about the role of the media, you might include the impact of the first on-the-spot television reporting at Little Rock, the newspaper coverage of the Greensboro sit-ins (there had been sit-ins a few years before but the media had not paid attention), and the television coverage of the brutality at Birmingham and on 'Bloody Sunday', which exposed Southern racism at its most brutal.

Writing analytically

The quality of your analysis is one of the key factors that determines the mark you achieve. Writing analytically means clearly showing the relationships between the ideas in your essay. Analysis includes two key skills: explanation and evaluation.

Explanation

Explanation means giving reasons. An explanatory sentence has three parts:

- a claim: a statement that something is true or false
- a reason: a statement that justifies the claim
- a relationship: a word or phrase that shows the relationship between the claim and the reason.

Imagine you are answering question 2 in the table on page 233:

> To what extent, in the years 1954–68, did the civil rights movement succeed in improving the status of black Americans?

Your paragraph on the political status of black Americans should start with a clear point, which would be supported by a series of examples. You would round off the paragraph with some explanation:

Clearly, the civil rights movement had played an important part in improving the political status of black Americans[1] *because*[2] *Selma and 'Bloody Sunday' finally forced Congress to pass Johnson's voting rights bill*[3].

1 Claim.
2 Relationship.
3 Reason.

Make sure of the following:

- The reason you give genuinely justifies the claim you have made.
- Your explanation is focused on the question.

Reaching a supported judgement

Your essay should reach a supported judgement. The obvious place to do this is in the conclusion of your essay. Even so, the judgement should reflect the findings of your essay. The conclusion should present:

- a clear judgement that answers the question
- an evaluation of the evidence that supports the judgement.

Finally, the evaluation should reflect valid criteria.

Evaluation and criteria

Evaluation means weighing up to reach a judgement. Therefore, evaluation requires you to:

- summarise both sides of the issue
- reach a conclusion that reflects the proper weight of both sides.

So, for question 3 in the table on page 233:

> 'Martin Luther King Jr demonstrated admirable leadership qualities in both the Selma campaign and the Chicago campaign.' How far do you agree with this statement?

the conclusion might look like this:

In conclusion, while King demonstrated outstanding leadership qualities in Selma, he was far less impressive in Chicago[1]. Clearly, as King himself recognised, it was far easier to lead effective protests against black disfranchisement than to persuade Americans to help the ghettos. Giving Southern black Americans the vote had no visible cost, but improving the ghettos would cost money[2]. In Selma, King managed to demonstrate the brutality of Southern segregationist law enforcement officials and gain sympathetic media coverage of non-violent protest, notably through 'Bloody Sunday'. The result was the Voting Rights Act. Chicago was a far more complex situation. While King successfully demonstrated the awful ghetto living conditions, he failed to win sympathy from the white press and public. Whites opposed black Americans marching into white residential areas to expose the fact that black Americans could not live there. Whites were convinced that black residents would affect property prices and the quality of schools. King achieved little in Chicago: as soon as he left, Mayor Daley reneged on his promise to combat de facto segregation[3]. While King deserved great credit for his leadership in Selma, Ella Baker criticised his 'top-down leadership' in Chicago. She said that he should have focused upon empowering the local community. However, while King got many things wrong in Chicago, it is doubtful that any leader could have persuaded white America to support changes to the ghetto that would have cost them money[4].

1 The conclusion starts with a clear judgement that answers the question.
2 This sentence begins the process of weighing up the different factors involved in King's achievement.
3 The conclusion summarises the relative effectiveness of the Selma and Chicago protests.
4 The essay ends with a final judgement that is supported by the evidence of the essay.

The judgement is supported in part by evaluating the evidence, and in part by linking it to valid criteria. In this case, the criterion is the distinction between winning productive support for black activism and disfranchisement in Selma, and failing to obtain support or meaningful action against *de facto* segregation in Chicago.

Essay guidance (2)

The following advice relates to Paper 3, Section C. Paper 3 is only available at A level, therefore there is no AS level version of this paper.

Essay skills

Section C is similar in many ways to Section B. Therefore, you need the same essential skills in order to get a high grade:

- focused analysis
- relevant detail
- supported judgement
- organisation, coherence and clarity.

Nonetheless, there are some differences in terms of the style of the question and the approach to the question in Sections B and C. Therefore, this section focuses on the following aspects of exam technique:

- Section C: the nature of the question
- Planning your answer.
- Advice for Section C.

Section C: the nature of the question

Section C questions focus on the two themes in breadth:

- The changing geography of civil rights issues, 1850–2009.
- The changing portrayal of civil rights issues in fiction and film, 1850–2009.

Questions can address either theme or both themes. There are two questions in Section C, of which you must answer one. However, you are not guaranteed a question on both themes, therefore you have to prepare for questions on both of the themes.

Section C questions are designed to test the breadth of your historical knowledge, and your ability to analyse change over time. Therefore, questions will focus on long periods, of no less than 100 years.

Section C questions have a variety of forms. Nonetheless, they have one of two essential foci. They will focus on either:

- the causes of change: for example, the factors, forces or individuals that led to change

or

- the nature of change: the ways in which things changed.

Significantly, the exam paper may contain two causes of change questions or two nature of change questions: you are not guaranteed one of each. Finally, questions can focus on different aspects of change over time:

- Comparative questions: ask you to assess the extent of change and continuity of an aspect of the period.
- Patterns of change questions: ask you to assess differences in terms of the rate, extent or significance of change at different points in the chronology.
- Turning point questions: ask you to assess which changes were more significant.

Comparative question	How far do you agree that film and television were more important than literature in shaping white attitudes to black Americans in the period 1900–2009?
Patterns of change question:	How accurate is it to say that literature reflected a continually improving perception of black Americans by the white majority in the period 1850–2009?
Turning point question:	How far do you agree that the First World War was the key turning point in the changing geography of civil rights issues in the USA in the period 1850–2009?

Planning your answer

It is crucial that you understand the focus of the question in order to make an effective plan. Therefore, read the question carefully before you start planning. Different questions require a different approach. Here are suggestions about how to tackle some of the common types of question:

Comparative question

How far do you agree that film and television were more important than literature in shaping white attitudes to black Americans in the period 1900–2009?

This is a comparative question which focuses on the causes of change. In this case you should examine the significance of 'film and television', the stated factor, and compare it to literature as a possible cause of change.

Patterns of change question

How accurate is it to say that literature reflected a continually improving perception of black Americans by the white majority in the period 1850–2009?

This is a patterns of change question which focuses on the nature of change. Here, you should examine the pattern of the depiction of black Americans in literature in the period 1850–2009. You should consider whether literary depictions became consistently more favourable, as opposed to an uneven trajectory of progress and regression.

Turning point question

How far do you agree that the First World War was the key turning point in the changing geography of civil rights issues in the USA in the period 1850–2009?

This is a turning point question which focuses on the nature of change. Therefore, you should examine the significance of the stated turning point, and compare it to two or three other turning points from the period 1850–2009. You should not just focus upon the First World War. You must consider other possible turning points. Additionally, when considering how far an event was a turning point you must consider both the changes it caused and the ways in which things stayed the same.

Advice for Section C

In many ways a Section C essay should display the same skills as a Section B essay (see page 233). However, Section C essays focus on a much longer period than Section B essays and this has an impact on how you approach them.

The most important difference concerns the chronology. In order to answer a Section C question properly, you must address the whole chronology, in this case the period 1850–2009. In practice, this means choosing examples from across the whole range of the period. Specifically, it is a good idea to have examples from the early part of the period, the middle of the period and the end of the period. For example, consider the following question:

How far do you agree that the First World War was the key turning point in the changing geography of civil rights issues in the USA in the period 1850–2009?

The question states a possible turning point – from the First World War – that is from the middle of the period. So, if you are considering other possible turning points you should choose one from the early part of the chronology (probably Reconstruction) and one from near the end (probably the Second World War or the legislative changes of 1964–5) in order to make sure you cover the whole period.

Equally, imagine you are dealing with the question:

How accurate is it to say that literature reflected a continuously improving perception of black Americans by the white majority in the period 1850–2009?

You would analyse examples of books that reflected changing perceptions throughout the whole period. These could include books such as:

- early: *Uncle Tom's Cabin*
- middle: *Gone With the Wind*
- late: *The Help.*

In so doing, you would be addressing the full chronological range of the question.

Timeline

1600s	White immigrants to North America imported and enslaved black Africans
1776	The Declaration of Independence
1787	Constitution of the new United States of America
1852	*Uncle Tom's Cabin* published
1861–5	Civil War between Southern slave states and Northern states
1862	**September:** Emancipation Proclamation announced
1863	**January:** Emancipation Proclamation issued
1864	**April:** Senate approved 13th Amendment (slavery unconstitutional) **November:** Lincoln re-elected
1865	**January:** House of Representatives approved 13th Amendment **April:** Civil War ended; President Lincoln assassinated **April–December:** Presidential Reconstruction/Reconstruction Confederate style **December:** New Congress blocked restoration of Confederate elite; 13th Amendment ratified
1866	**April:** Civil Rights Act Ku Klux Klan established
1867	Military Reconstruction Act: Congressional Reconstruction began
1868	Ratification of 14th Amendment (black Americans granted citizenship)
1870	Ratification of 15th Amendment (black American males enfranchised) Force Acts gave President Grant powers to crush the Klan

1872	Amnesty Act helped restore political power to ex-Confederates
1875	Civil Rights Act tried to prevent discrimination in public places
1877	Withdrawal of federal troops from the South ended Reconstruction
1879	20,000 black 'Exodusters' migrated to Kansas
1883	Civil Rights cases
1885	*Adventures of Huckleberry Finn* published
1887	Florida rail travel change
1890	Mississippi introduced income and literacy qualifications to stop black voting
1892	Anti-lynching campaigner Ida B. Wells fled the South
1895	Booker T. Washington's 'Atlanta Compromise' speech
1896	*Plessy v. Ferguson*
1898	*Williams v. Mississippi* Louisiana's grandfather clause
1899	*Cumming v. Board of Education*
1900	Serious race riots in New York City
1905	Mass migration into Harlem started
1908	Serious race riot in Springfield, Illinois
1909	NAACP established
1914–18	First World War labour shortage triggered Great Migration
1915	Box-office triumph of *Birth of a Nation*
1919	Race riots in Chicago and 24 other American cities
1920s	Harlem Renaissance
1920	Cotton prices slumped

1921	Black community destroyed in Tulsa, Oklahoma
1925	A. Philip Randolph established labour union for railroad porters UNIA membership peaked
1929	Wall Street crash triggered the Great Depression
1933	**March:** Roosevelt became President and initiated New Deal programmes; Civilian Conservation Corps (CCC) established **May:** Agricultural Adjustment Administration (AAA), Federal Emergency Relief Administration (FERA) and Tennessee Valley Authority (TVA) established **June:** National Recovery Administration (NRA) and Public Works Administration (PWA) established
1934	**June:** Federal Housing Administration (FHA) established
1935	**March:** Great race riot in Harlem **April:** Works Progress Administration (WPA) established **May:** Resettlement Administration (RA) established **July:** Wagner Act **August:** Social Security Act
1936	*Gone With the Wind* published (filmed 1939)
1937	**July:** Farm Security Administration (FSA) established **September:** Wagner–Steagall National Housing Act
1938	**June:** Fair Labor Standards Act
1941–5	US involvement in Second World War triggered large-scale black migration

1941	**June:** Roosevelt established the Fair Employment Practices Commission **December:** Japanese attacked Pearl Harbor, USA entered Second World War
1943	Notable race riots in Detroit and Harlem
1947	Construction of first Levittown began
1948	Supreme Court ruling against restrictive covenants generally ignored
1949	Congressional urban renewal programme
1951	Housing riots in Cicero, Chicago.
1954	Supreme Court's *Brown* ruling
1956	Montgomery bus boycott
1957	King established SCLC *Island in the Sun*
1961	Freedom Rides *To Kill a Mockingbird* published (filmed 1962)
1963	**Summer:** SCLC's Birmingham campaign; March on Washington; Kennedy promoted civil rights bill **November:** Johnson became president
1964	SNCC's 'Mississippi Freedom Summer'
1964–8	Annual ghetto riots
1964	Civil Rights Act
1965	**January–February:** King's Selma campaign **August:** Voting Rights Act; Watts riots
1966	King's Chicago campaign **July:** Meredith March CORE and SNCC increasingly advocated Black Power **October:** Black Panthers established

1967	**July:** Newark riots *Guess Who's Coming to Dinner; In the Heat of the Night*
1968	**April:** King assassinated; Fair Housing Act
1970s	Blaxploitation movies era Demographers noted black migration to the South Federal government promoted affirmative action
1977	*Roots* televised
1980s	School integration peaked
1987	*Beloved* published (filmed 1998)

1988	*Mississippi Burning*
1992	Rodney King scandal *Malcolm X*
2002–8	*The Wire*
2004	Barack Obama elected to the US Senate
2008	**June:** Obama defeated Hillary Clinton for the Democrat presidential nomination **November:** Obama defeated Republican John McCain in the presidential election
2009	*The Help* published (filmed 2011)

Glossary of terms

Abolitionists   Those who wanted to end slavery.

Accommodationists   Those who favoured initial black concentration upon economic improvement rather than upon social, political and legal equality.

Act   A bill passed by Congress and accepted by the President becomes an Act or law.

Administration   When Americans talk of a president's administration, they mean the government as led by that president.

Affirmative action   Help for those who have had a disadvantageous start in life, also known as 'positive discrimination'.

African American   A black American (in the past also called a 'Negro').

Agency   In this context, when black Americans took control of their own destiny, as opposed to having their fate determined by white Americans.

Agricultural Adjustment Administration (AAA) New Deal agency established in 1933 to aid farmers.

Alphabet agencies   Federal government bodies, established to combat the Great Depression, that became known by their initials. For example, the AAA.

Amendment   Under the Constitution, Congress could add 'amendments' (changes or new points) to the Constitution. Amendments needed ratification (approval) by 75 per cent of states.

Auntie   A common term used by white Southerners to refer to black women.

Bellhops   Porters.

Bill   If a member of Congress or the President wants a law to be made, he introduces a bill into Congress. If the bill is passed by Congress and accepted by the President, it becomes an Act or law.

Biracial   Black and white together.

Birther controversy   Some right-wingers claim Obama was not born in the United States and therefore was not qualified to be President under the terms of the US Constitution.

Black Codes   Laws passed by the Southern states in 1865–6 in order to control the freed slaves, especially economically.

Black nationalist   Favouring a separate black nation either within the USA or in Africa.

Black Power   A controversial term, with different meanings, such as black pride, black economic self-sufficiency, black violence, black separatism, black nationalism, black political power, black working-class revolution, black domination.

Black separatists   Black people who desired to live apart/away from whites.

Busing   Transporting white or black children to schools in an area other than that in which they live, to ensure integrated schools in that area.

Capitol   Building containing the Senate and the House of Representatives.

Cars   Carriages.

Civil rights   These include having the vote in free elections, equal treatment under the law, equal opportunities in areas such as in education and work, and freedom of speech, religion and movement.

Civilian Conservation Corps (CCC)   New Deal agency established in 1933 to offer employment through public works.

Confederacy   When the Southern states left the Union of the United States, they became the Confederate States of America, known as the Confederacy for short. Supporters of the Confederacy were called Confederates.

Congress   The American equivalent to Britain's parliament, consisting of the Senate and the House of Representatives. Voters in each American state elect two senators to sit in the Senate and several congressmen (the number depends on the size of the state's population) to sit in the House of Representatives.

Congressional Reconstruction   See 'Radical Reconstruction'.

Constitution   The rules and system by which a country's government works. The USA has a written constitution.

***De facto* segregation**   Separation of the races in fact if not in law.

De jure segregation   Separation of the races imposed and supported by law.

Debt peonage   White employers kept black farmers in virtual slavery by keeping them in debt, for example, by forcing them to pay inflated prices for materials such as seed.

Democrat   Member of the Democratic Party, which dominated American politics in the first half of the nineteenth century. It was pro-slavery and against a powerful central/federal government.

Depression   When a country's economy is nearly ruined. Prices and wages fall, and many people are unemployed, as in the USA after 1929.

Disfranchise   Deprive someone of their vote.

Draft   Compulsory government call-up into the armed forces, known as conscription in Britain.

Emancipation   In this context, freedom from slavery.

Executive powers   The Constitution gave the President 'Executive Power', a vague phrase that enabled successive presidents to act without Congress in certain areas.

Exodusters   Post-Reconstruction black migrants from the South to Kansas.

Fair Employment Practices Commission (FEPC) Federal agency set up by President Roosevelt in 1941 to promote racial equality in defence industries.

FBI   The Federal Bureau of Investigation was set up in 1924 to help deal with crime.

Federal Emergency Relief Administration (FERA) New Deal agency established in 1933 to help the unemployed through relief and job creation.

Federal government   The USA, as a federation of many separate states (such as South Carolina and New York), has a federal government. The federal government consists of the President, Congress and the Supreme Court.

Federal Housing Administration (FHA)   New Deal agency established in 1934 to help homeowners.

Filibuster   A procedure whereby the minority party in Congress can slow down proceedings so as to stop legislation being enacted.

First-come, first-served   Southern buses were divided into black and white sections. Sometimes black people would be standing while the white section was empty. They therefore sought seating on a first-come, first-served basis, under which black passengers would sit in the back rows of the white section, if the black section was full, but the bus would remain segregated.

Free blacks   In the North in particular, many blacks had been freed from slavery by their owners.

Freedom Summer   SNCC voter registration campaign in Mississippi in 1964.

Gestapo   Infamous Nazi secret police.

Ghettos   Areas inhabited mostly or solely by (usually poor) members of a particular ethnicity, nationality or religion.

Grandfather clause   Southern state laws allowed the illiterate to vote if they could prove an ancestor had voted before Reconstruction, which no African American could do.

Great Depression   Exceptionally severe economic depression that hit the United States after the Wall Street crash of October 1929, and also affected many other countries.

Great Migration   Between *c.*1910 and *c.*1970, over 6 million black Americans migrated from the South to the North or the West. Some historians subdivide this into two separate phases of migration.

Great Society   In 1965, President Johnson declared a 'war on poverty' and called for a revolutionary programme of social welfare legislation that involved unprecedented federal expenditure on education, medical care for the elderly, and an expanded Social Security Program.

Hispanics   Spanish-speaking people in the USA, usually of Latin American origin.

Howard   Prestigious black university in Washington DC.

Impeachment   Under the American Constitution, Congress has the power to bring an errant President to trial, to impeach him.

Integration   The social mixing of people of different colours and cultures.

Integrationist   Desirous to participate in the 'American dream' without separation of the races.

Jim Crow   An early 1830s' comic, black-faced, minstrel character developed by a white performing artist that proved to be very popular with white audiences. When, after Reconstruction, the Southern states introduced laws that legalised segregation, these were known as 'Jim Crow laws'.

Justice Department   Branch of the federal government in Washington DC with special responsibility for enforcing the law and administering justice.

Lithograph   A type of print.

Lynching   The unlawful killing of an individual by a mob.

Mammy   A black nursemaid or nanny in charge of white children.

Middle America   A term invented by the media to describe ordinary, patriotic, middle-income white Americans.

Military Reconstruction Act   The several Reconstruction Acts passed by Congress during 1867–8 are variously referred to as 'First Reconstruction Act', 'Second Reconstruction Act' and so on, or the Reconstruction Act(s) or the Military Reconstruction Acts.

Miscegenation   Sexual relationships between blacks and whites.

NAFTA   North American Free Trade Association, established during Bill Clinton's presidency to encourage trade between the United States, Mexico and Canada.

National Convention   Before the presidential election, the Republicans and Democrats hold conferences in which each party selects or confirms its candidate for the presidency.

National Guard   State-based US armed forces reserves.

National Recovery Administration (NRA)   New Deal agency established in 1933 to help business and manufacturing.

National Youth Administration (NYA)   New Deal agency established in 1935 to help the young unemployed.

New Deal   President Roosevelt's programme to bring the US out of the economic depression.

New South   Some people consider that the South was totally transformed after the Civil Rights Act of 1964 and the Voting Rights Act of 1965, legislation that helped bring about greater racial equality.

Passive resistance   Non-violent refusal to comply with a particular policy.

Platform   The policies of a political party during, for example, the presidential election.

Poll tax   Tax levied on would-be voters that made it harder for blacks (who were usually poor) to vote.

Post-racial society   One free of racism and discrimination.

Presidential Reconstruction   President Johnson's policies toward the South during 1865 allowed the Southern white Confederate elite to re-establish their power. This period is also known as Reconstruction Confederate style.

Primaries   Elections to choose a party's candidate for elective office.

Public Works Administration (PWA)   New Deal agency established in 1933 to offer employment through public works.

Push and pull   When people move to a different place, it is usually because there are attractions that pull them toward a new life, and factors that push them away from the old life.

Quakers   A Christian group notable for its pacifism and democratic religious meetings.

Quorum   In this context, the minimum number required for the House of Representatives to conduct business.

Racial profiling   The assumption by law enforcement officials that an individual who has the appearance of a particular minority race group is more likely to be guilty of a crime and should therefore be detained and investigated.

Radical Reconstruction   Also known as Congressional Reconstruction or Black Reconstruction. Post-Civil War policies imposed by Congress upon the South, which decreased the power of the old Confederate elite and increased the power of freed slaves.

Radical Republicans   Members of the Republican Party who were most enthusiastic about ending slavery.

Railroad   Railway.

Realtors   Estate agents who deal in real estate (property) sale and rental.

Reconstruction   The process of rebuilding and reforming the 11 ex-Confederate states and restoring them to the Union.

Reconstruction Confederate style   President Johnson's policies toward the South during 1865 allowed the Southern white Confederate elite to re-establish their power. This period is also known as Presidential Reconstruction.

Renaissance   A revival or exceptionally productive period for culture.

Reparations   Federal government payment of compensation for slavery to black Americans.

Republican Party   Emerged in the 1850s. It was against slavery.

Restrictive covenant   A clause in a property deed limiting certain uses.

Running mate   When a political party chooses a presidential candidate to represent that party, the candidate chooses someone to run with him, who would then become Vice President in the event of their electoral victory.

Secretary of State   Member of president's cabinet with special responsibility for foreign policy.

Segregation   The separation of people because of race (for example, separate housing, schools and transport).

Self-determination   The ability of black Americans to choose their own destiny.

Self-help   Booker T. Washington and Marcus Garvey emphasised black-owned businesses as typical of the self-help needed for black progress.

Separatism   Desire for black Americans to live separate but equal lives from whites, in all-black communities or even a black state or in Africa.

Sharecropper   A white landowner provided the land, seed, tools and orders, while a black worker (the sharecropper) provided the labour. The crop produced was usually divided between the two men.

Shock jocks   Right-wing radio commentators, such as Rush Limbaugh.

Social security   Welfare benefits for the needy, for example, the old, sick or unemployed.

Socialism   Political philosophy that society should be as equitable as possible in terms of economic and social standing.

Solid South   Prior to the 1960s, voters in the South invariably voted Democrat. The vast majority of those voters were white.

States' rights   Under the American Constitution, the states retained many rights (for example over voting and education) and resented federal government interference in their exercise of those rights.

Streetcar   Tram, bus.

Supreme Court   The judicial branch of the US federal government. The highest court in the land, it rules (adjuges) whether actions are in line with the American Constitution and the law.

Tennessee Valley Authority (TVA)   New Deal programme to revitalise the economy of several impoverished Southern states through the provision of flood control, electricity and employment.

Three-strikes law   After three convictions, for whatever minor offences, a person would be imprisoned for life.

Ticket   The platform (policies) of a party's presidential candidate and his running mate.

Union   The union of the United States, the secession of the South from which triggered the Civil War in which the North's forces were known as the Union forces.

United Nations   International organisation established after the Second World War to combat conflict, deprivation and discrimination.

Veto   The American Constitution gave the President the right to reject bills, but, with a sufficiently large number of votes, Congress can override the presidential veto.

Wall Street crash   Wall Street in New York was the financial capital of the United States, and when share prices crashed in October 1929, it helped trigger the Great Depression.

Wards   Urban electoral districts.

Welfare   Government payments to relieve poverty.

White trash   Poor white people, especially those living in the South.

Works Progress Administration (WPA)   New Deal agency established in 1935 to offer employment through public works.

Further reading

General texts

Jonathan Bean, editor, *Race & Liberty in America: The Essential Reader* (University Press of Kentucky, 2009)
Useful collection of source material, although geared to score political points at the end of the book

Adam Fairclough, *Better Day Coming: Blacks and Equality, 1890–2000* (Penguin, 2001)
Approaches changing race relations very much through an interesting, biographical approach to individuals

Vivienne Sanders, *Race Relations in the USA 1863–1980* (Hodder, 2006)
A popular A-level textbook, with balanced coverage of each decade

Stephen Tuck, *We Ain't What We Ought To Be: The Black Freedom Struggle From Emancipation to Obama* (Harvard University Press, 2010)
Lively account focusing on black victims and activists

Chapter 1

David Brown and Clive Webb, *Race in the American South: From Slavery to Civil Rights* (Edinburgh University Press, 2007)
Half of this book covers the period up to 1865. Valuable, detailed coverage of the years of slavery and historians' debates over it

J.M. McPherson, *Battle Cry of Freedom* (Penguin, 1988)
An excellent account of the causes and course of the American Civil War

Chapter 2

Eric Foner, *Reconstruction: America's Unfinished Revolution 1863–1877* (Harper & Row, 2015)
Much-acclaimed study of Reconstruction

Chapter 3

David Brown and Clive Webb, *Race in the American South: From Slavery to Civil Rights* (Edinburgh University Press, 2007)
Good coverage of the triumph of Jim Crow

Michael J. Klarman, *From Jim Crow to Civil Rights: The Supreme Court and the Struggle for Racial Equality* (Oxford University Press, 2004)
A fascinating study of Supreme Court justices and the reasons behind and results of their rulings. Argues with a seemingly irrefutable weight of evidence and repetition, that the justices reflect contemporary opinions in their rulings. Students planning to study law will find this a particularly stimulating book. It has an excellent section on the triumph of Jim Crow

Chapters 4 and 6

Jonathan Gill, *Harlem* (Grove Press, 2011)
An interesting and easy read

Michael J. Klarman, *From Jim Crow to Civil Rights: The Supreme Court and the Struggle for Racial Equality* (Oxford University Press, 2004)
An excellent contextual section on the impact of the Second World War. Indeed, all his contextual sections are outstanding

Isabel Wilkerson, *The Warmth of Other Suns: The Epic Story of America's Great Migration* (Random House, 2010)
A much-acclaimed book that humanises the migration and reads like a novel, but avoids analysis

Chapter 5

Anthony J. Badger, *The New Deal* (Hill & Wang, 1989)
Excellent overview of the New Deal, with some coverage of the impact on black Americans

David M. Kennedy, *Freedom From Fear: The American People in Depression and War, 1929–1945* (Oxford University Press, 1999)
A particularly good volume in the ever-reliable Oxford History of the United States

Chapter 7

Clayborne Carson *et al.*, editors, *The Eyes on the Prize Civil Rights Reader* (Penguin, 1991)
Classic collection of source material on the Black Freedom struggle

Robert Dallek, *Flawed Giant: Lyndon Johnson and his Times, 1961–1973* (Oxford University Press, 1998)
A detailed exploration of Johnson's career in these years that explores, amongst other things, his views and achievements with regard to race. Although not a great fan of LBJ, Dallek tries to present a balanced account

David Garrow, *Bearing the Cross: Martin Luther King, Jr., and the Southern Christian Leadership Conference* (William Morrow, 1999)
Sympathetic account of King. It includes many contemporary quotations, which give the reader a sense of immediacy

Michael J. Klarman, *From Jim Crow to Civil Rights: The Supreme Court and the Struggle for Racial Equality* (Oxford University Press, 2004)
Has interesting detail on how Warren and the Supreme Court arrived at the *Brown* ruling, although his argument that it reflected contemporary opinion is controversial

Manning Marable, *Malcolm X: A Life of Reinvention* (Penguin, 2011)
An outstanding biography that is firm but fair on Malcolm's ever-changing persona, and particularly valuable on sorting fact from fiction in Malcolm's autobiography

Chapter 8

Donald Bogle, *Toms, Coons, Mulattoes, Mammies, and Bucks: An Interpretive History of Blacks in American Films* (Bloomsbury, 2001)
A chatty, provocatively written account of years of stereotypical roles for black Americans in a Hollywood haltingly proceeding toward movie portrayals of Americans who just happen to be black

Richard Gray, *A History of American Literature* (Blackwell, 2012)
Sets the works of authors such as Harriet Beecher Stowe and Mark Twain in the context of other works of American literature

Mark Harris, *Pictures at Revolution: Five Movies in the Birth of the New Hollywood* (Penguin, 2008)
Fascinating and useful explorations of two groundbreaking movies on the subject of race, *Guess Who's Coming to Dinner* and *In the Heat of the Night*

Mary McDonagh Murphy, *Scout, Atticus and Boo: A Celebration of To Kill a Mockingbird* (Penguin, 2015)
A collection of essays by a variety of authors, all of whom attest to the ability of Harper Lee's novel to change lives

Mary Ann Watson, *Defining Visions: Television and the American Experience in the 20th Century* (Blackwell, 2008)
Invaluable, thorough account

Chapter 9

John Heilemann and Mark Halperin, *Game Change: Obama and the Clintons, McCain and Palin, and the Race of a Lifetime* (Harper Perennial, 2010)
Fascinating study of a fascinating presidential race

Barack Obama, *Dreams From My Father* (Random House, 2004) and *The Audacity of Hope: Thoughts on Reclaiming the American Dream* (Random House, 2006)
Interesting insights into the life and rhetorical powers of President Obama

Stephen Tuck, *We Ain't What We Ought To Be: The Black Freedom Struggle From Emancipation to Obama* (Harvard University Press, 2010)
Includes an interesting section on the significance of Barack Obama's career

Internet resources

Several interesting articles are to be found on the internet, amongst them:

William Frey, *The New Great Migration*, Brookings Institution, May 2004

Carmen Sisson, *Why African-Americans are moving back to the South*, *Christian Science Monitor*, 16 March 2014

Larry Hunt *et al.*, *Who is Headed South*? Social Forces 87, September 2008

Index